T0272404

FORTUNE'S FRENZY

A GOLD RUSH ODYSSEY

EILENE LYON

TWODOT®

ESSEX, CONNECTICUT
HELENA, MONTANA

A · T W O D O T® · B O O K
An imprint of Globe Pequot, the trade division of
The Rowman & Littlefield Publishing Group, Inc.
4501 Forbes Blvd., Ste. 200
Lanham, MD 20706
www.rowman.com

Distributed by NATIONAL BOOK NETWORK

British Library Cataloguing in Publication Information available

Library of Congress Cataloging-in-Publication Data
Names: Lyon, Eilene, author.
Title: Fortune's frenzy : a California Gold Rush odyssey / Eilene Lyon.
Other titles: California Gold Rush odyssey
Description: Essex, Connecticut : TwoDot, 2023. | Includes bibliographical references.
Identifiers: LCCN 2022058812 (print) | LCCN 2022058813 (ebook) | ISBN 9781493070060 (hardback) | ISBN 9781493070077 (epub)
Subjects: LCSH: California—Gold discoveries—Anecdotes. | Gold miners—California—Biography. | California—History—1846-1850—Biography. | Gold mines and mining—California—History—19th century—Anecdotes. | Blackford Mining Company. | Jenkins, Henry Zane, 1802-1882. | Makepeace, Allen, 1802-1871. | Pioneers—Indiana—Blackford County—Biography. | Frontier and pioneer life—Indiana—Blackford County. | Blackford County (Ind.)—Biography.
Classification: LCC F865 .L975 2023 (print) | LCC F865 (ebook) | DDC 979.4/04092 [B]–dc23/eng/20221228

Printed in India

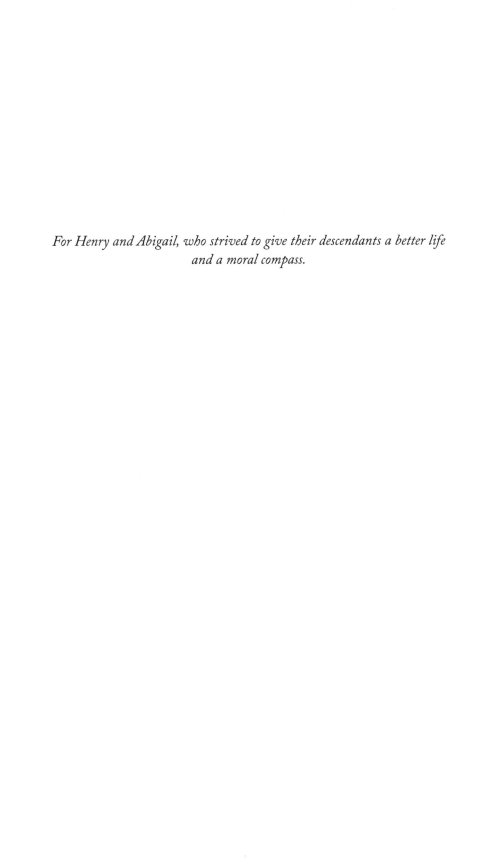

For Henry and Abigail, who strived to give their descendants a better life and a moral compass.

CONTENTS

CONTENTS

INTRODUCTION

Most nonfiction works on the California gold rush fall into two categories: first-hand accounts written in the nineteenth century, or examinations of the event as a whole. The latter draw from the stunning volume of letters, diaries, and memoirs left by the participants. Anecdotes provide a big picture but not a comprehensive narrative about any person or group. *Fortune's Frenzy* is more than a subjective eyewitness account and less than a scholarly tome. Combining a collection of first-hand reports with extensive genealogical and period research, it tells an engaging story about a company of gold-mining men from Indiana and the families and communities they left behind.

At first blush it might appear that poor people did not join the rush because it cost money to travel. The poverty-stricken had great motivation to participate, so they found creative ways to finance their journey. Many historians have noted they borrowed money at usurious rates but never mention the debts again, as if they played no further role in the argonauts' lives. As if they all became as wealthy as Jacob Astor. As if they had other funding options. As if the lenders forgave these obligations with great generosity of spirit. As if these crushing financial burdens did not consign them to a deeper penury than before they went to California. This is a significant untold story about the gold rush.

Andrew Jackson's populist administration dismantled Alexander Hamilton's US Bank in the 1820s, creating shortages of US currency by the mid-1800s. The US Bank was a publicly-owned institution—a bank of the people, by the people, for the people. Its destruction shifted the power to control money from the people's bank in Philadelphia to the money brokers on Wall Street, where it remains today.[1] State banks, approved by legislatures, filled the void.

In 1834, Indiana chartered a bank for a twenty-three-year period. Its directors had no notable banking experience. Apparently, this was a good thing because they ran a stellar enterprise that survived the Panic of 1837, an event that doomed many banks around the country. As a result, Indiana currency held its value well, unlike many other states' bank paper.[2] A banknote dollar did not equal a dollar in specie (gold or silver), so people relied on newspapers for the latest discount on various currencies. The State Bank of Indiana generated surpluses, which the directors channeled into a Sinking Fund and a School Fund. These reserves provided mortgages and business loans, promoting economic growth around the state.

Jay and Blackford Counties had no banks prior to the 1870s, most likely because these were agrarian counties. Farmers believed in hard currency and distrusted bankers, paper money, and credit. This attitude developed in the Revolutionary War era. The US government forced farmers to supply the Army's needs during the war and paid them in scrip. Whenever the feds needed more money, they printed it. As a result, the scrip eventually became worthless. And farmers held a lot of it.[3] Farmers, like elephants, did not forget.

The federal government also preferred hard currency. When the Land Act of 1820 passed, purchasers could no longer buy on terms but instead had to pay in specie, or paper backed by precious metals. Land speculators pouring into Indiana in the 1830s distressed and chafed their horses with the heavy bags of silver needed to buy patents. But coinage was scarce. Instead of currency, pioneers used ledgers.

People tracked what others owed them, not what they owed. Trading partners had their own ledgers or, more commonly, IOUs jotted on paper scraps. Typically, they settled accounts when someone died or left town. Beyond bartering, they traded in monetary terms but without cash. Again, they referred to newspapers for commodity values. Farmers knew the price of a bushel of corn, pound of pork, or hundred-weight of flour, based on the current market. They jotted those figures in their ledger, or received a signed promise to pay, when making a sale. Cash, the equivalent in goods, or labor at market rate would clear the books.

Farmers rarely relied on credit in the sense of borrowing and repaying principal and interest. Settlers had no surplus money to place on deposit, either. Therefore, bankers gravitated to communities where merchants and industrialists congregated. Businessmen used credit to build their establishments, unlike homesteaders.

Another under-examined aspect of the rush is the sea journey to California. The overland trail has long captured the American imagination, and in the first few years of the rush, perhaps half the American participants chose that route. But as more ships came into service in the Pacific, most traveled the route across the isthmus at Panama and Nicaragua. *Fortune's Frenzy* features several sea journeys, including one on a notorious death ship. Poor argonauts suffered more than just the usury of financiers. They also contended with barbarous ship captains who charged outrageous fares and filled their holds with gold-seekers, not food.

Henry Z. and Abigail Jenkins were born, reared, and educated in Philadelphia. Their family fortunes plummeted over the years as they moved westward. By 1849, they were struggling to survive in the swampy forests of eastern Indiana. Their urban background distinguished them from their often less-educated, rural-born neighbors. These hardworking settlers relied on connections to other families in the community—the Ransoms, Andersons, and Liestenfeltzes, among others—to manage from day-to-day and make modest lifestyle improvements.

The gold rush phenomenon upended America's Puritanical work ethic: a lifetime of labor for limited gains. For the first time, citizens beheld an opportunity to achieve rapid prosperity. Even the middle-aged fell victim to gold fever. Henry believed gold would solve his financial problems, so he decided to join a group of younger men forming the Blackford Mining Company. The prospective miners needed currency to go west, but thanks to Jacksonian monetary policy, they lived in a largely cashless economy. The company president, Sam Jones, devised a scheme to borrow from a wealthy merchant, Allen Makepeace.

Makepeace was the payday lender of his time—charging astronomical rates and ruthlessly collecting from his debtors. If the men survived the sea journey to California, they would have to find rich diggings, endure a lawless society, and resist their own baser temptations in order to repay Makepeace and return home to their families. Meanwhile, those families continued their hand-to-mouth existence without the help of the absent men. The women learned new roles as breadwinners and money managers—like it or not. They expanded their reliance on neighbors and friends beyond the norm, straining fragile ties within these newly settled villages. Even dismal reports from the mines did little to dissuade more men from following the Blackford Company to California, further depleting the local labor force.

The theme is age-old, yet still relevant today: desperate people falling for get-rich-quick schemes. They fail to consider the sacrifices they will make and the dismal odds of success. Many end up poorer than before. But some realize they already had what mattered most.

Fortune's Frenzy puts the experiences of the Jenkins, Ransom, Jones, Anderson, and Liestenfeltz families during the gold rush into context: their past; their community; their daily lives (and deaths) in rural Indiana, on the sea route to California, and in the mines. Many thousands of people experienced similar situations during the gold rush. This is history in starkly personal terms: the lives of ordinary people caught up in extraordinary events, and the impacts of those events on their futures. It is a story that evokes empathy and helps us understand our own part in the larger narrative of life's drama in any era.

A NOTE ON LANGUAGE

I have quoted from a variety of original sources. In many of them, spelling, capitalization, and punctuation are random or absent. To improve legibility, I have added minimal punctuation and capitalized the beginning of sentences. Otherwise, I have retained the spelling and capitalization as originally written. For clarity, I added some letters or words in brackets. Quotation marks and indentation denote material taken verbatim from sources. Some readers may be uncomfortable with certain terms, such as "slave" and "Negro." I have retained the language of the time for authenticity and do not intend any disrespect by the use of such words.

CHARACTERS

THE BLACKFORD MINING COMPANY
(AGE IN MARCH 1851)

Samuel "Sam" Jones, President (26)

Henry Z. Jenkins (49)

Humphrey Anderson (33)

John K. Anderson (29)

Jacob "Jake" Liestenfeltz (26)

Peter "Pete" N. Liestenfeltz (18)

John C. Teach (48)

Dennis Lowry (28)

(Asa) Harvey Hunt (33)

Preston "Pres" M. Gibson (24)

FAMILIES

The Jenkins Family

Ann W. (Zane) Jenkins, grandmother

Henry Zane Jenkins, father

Abigail G. Bedford, mother

[1]William Z.

Jane B.

[2]Ann Jane

(Thomas) Bedford

[3]Emma J.

Philadelphia

Mary

Barton B.

The Ransom Family

[4]James Ransom, father

[5]Elizabeth Anderson, mother

[2]William C.

[3]Robert

[1]Jane

Bazel

Samuel

CHARACTERS

The Anderson Family
William C. Anderson, father
Agness Grier, mother (deceased)
[5]Elizabeth
Asa

Bazel
Humphrey
William T.
John K.

The Jones Family
Thomas Jones, father
[4]Sarah Ransom, mother
Benjamin H. Jones

Samuel Jones
Rebecca Jones
William G. Jones

The Liestenfeltz Family
Conrad Liestenfeltz, father
Susan Bittman, mother
Jacob
Daniel
Peter N.
Conrad, Jr.

[1] Married in July 1850
[2] Married in February 1850
[3] Engaged to be married
[4] Siblings
[5] Same person

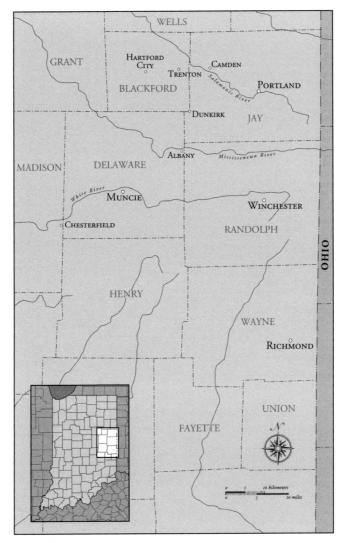

Figure Map of Indiana. East-central Indiana, home of the Blackford Mining Company and their communities.

If I had to battle against the world with the view of conquering, the first weapen I would choose would be a sack of gold dust.

—ELIAS D. PIERCE, *THE PIERCE CHRONICLE*

PART I
A GRAND SCHEME

CHAPTER 1

MIRED IN MISFORTUNE

*Well, I would not live there if they would give me the whole county;
one half of the land is under water and the other half is mud knee
deep.*
—ANONYMOUS OHIOAN, REFERRING TO JAY COUNTY, INDIANA,
REMINISCENCES OF ADAMS, JAY AND RANDOLPH COUNTIES

LATE FALL 1850—KNOX TOWNSHIP, JAY COUNTY, INDIANA
After a hard frost, the hog slaughter began. The swine—fattened on
woodland forage in spring and summer—had been sweetening on corn
in their pen while the Jenkins family harvested their leased land. But har-
vesting pork had to wait for colder weather to avoid maggots and spoil-
age. Henry Zane Jenkins breathed in the iron-tang as the long-legged
razorback bled out after he stunned and poked it. With help from his
sons, Bedford and Will Z., he hoisted the animal into a barrel of hot
water to scald for five minutes, to be followed by scraping. After the
bristles and scurf came off, Henry's pig carcass had a ghostly gleam. They
hung the meat to cool for a day before butchering it into hams, bellies,
lard, and other usable bits. Everything would be preserved.

Preparing for winter kept eastern Indiana pioneers fully occupied
in fall. The region, recently settled, had only small, isolated patches of
cleared land. The remainder still wore a dense cloak of native beech, walnut, hickory, sugar maple, and native fruits such as plums, blackberries,

paw-paws, and cranberries. If Henry had any surplus pork, he might have pooled it with his friend, Conrad Liestenfeltz, to be shipped to Richmond, in Wayne County, the nearest commercial market town, to acquire a little cash.

In their cramped cabin, Henry's wife, Abigail—or Abby, as everyone called her—layered shredded cabbage and salt into a crock. Her sauerkraut took weeks to ferment. Her family would devour it when the time came. Abby, a slight woman, wore a coarse dress of linsey-woolsey. The farm supplied flax and wool for fabric. Emma, age fifteen, wove the fibers into a warm but rough cloth. She also baked the breads and pies, using buckwheat and cornmeal—good wheat flour being beyond their means once their homegrown supply ran out. Family labor provided nearly all the food, clothing, and shelter required to survive in this virtual wilderness.

Henry and Abby hoped the food they put up would last the winter. They had no funds to fill any gaps. Rather, mounting debts threatened their fragile stability. Poverty, as a rule, defined the people of Jay County, and more so in neighboring Blackford County, but in a relative sense, the Jenkinses were among the most destitute. Despite that, their faith ran deep, and family bonds held strong.

More than food preoccupied the Jenkinses. The previous two winters produced waves of "plague," possibly typhoid fever; already, chills and ague began appearing in the neighborhood. Physicians abandoned treating the diseases with calomel—a mercury-based compound—because "when it was given, immediate death was the result."[1] Residents no doubt believed the stagnant water found extensively in Blackford County, and sporadically in Jay, contributed to the area's unhealthiness; it certainly provided a breeding ground for tempests of mosquitoes. At least cold weather would eliminate that particular pestilence.

Long before the gold rush disrupted their lives, the Jenkins family became mired in misfortune. Henry had his carpentry trade, but labor unrest in Philadelphia made his career there untenable in the late 1820s. New western towns needed men to build them, so early in their marriage, the Jenkinses moved to Ohio, taking a wagon across the mountains, then down the Ohio River from Pittsburgh.[2] After seven years, briefly in Cincinnati, then in Springboro, Henry and Abby continued west, pursuing new opportunities. Though they sold their lot in Springboro for enough to buy eighty acres from the government in Indiana, Henry chose not to embody Jefferson's yeoman ideal, plowing his way to independence. He wished to stand a rung higher, making his living as a merchant and tradesman.

Opening the first mercantile in Camden, Jay County, they found themselves in the role of local creditors, as people charged goods they intended to pay for after harvest. Having grown up in a large city where cash flourished, Henry and Abby may not have been savvy about the ledger system, leading to Henry's troubles with Goldsmith Chandlee.

Goldsmith Chandlee Jr. was the scion of a well-regarded family in Winchester, Virginia. Goldsmith Sr. had a successful business building tall-case clocks, as well as manufacturing surveying and medical equipment.[3] Goldsmith Jr. did not follow in his father's footsteps, leaving the clock dynasty to his brother. Instead, he forged his own path as a tanner and real estate investor. He relocated his family to southwestern Ohio, at Springboro, where he bought numerous town lots, selling one to Abby Jenkins's brother, Samuel Bedford.[4] The Jenkins family clearly knew the affluent Chandlees in Springboro.

Henry arrived in recently platted Camden, Indiana, roughly a hundred miles northwest of Springboro, in 1837. His wagonload of consigned goods jostled him mercilessly on the rough forest route, barely more than a footpath.[5] The town, just a dirt street and empty lots, situated in a meadow near the Salamonie River, embraced a man of ambition. He set up shop at Job Carr's home, west of town, and started building a store, helping construct the first homes in his spare time. His commission on the trade goods would fund his carpentry business. But he probably had not counted on selling his wares in a cash-poor place. Oh, he knew numbers and could keep the books. But people in desperate straits softened his resolve. Henry lived by the Biblical injunction to be his "brother's keeper." He simply could not harden his heart enough to be a successful businessman.

Abby tended to customers, efficient and polite, and educated children in her spare time.[6] Two years into this enterprise, competitors arrived, including Chandlee's son, John, and Anthony Pitman. Perhaps this spurred Henry in a different direction. Camden promoters published an advertisement seeking someone to build a steam sawmill and gristmill. "Persons of good, moral character, of business habits and sufficient capital will be preferred. A site for said mills will be given, adjoining Camden . . . where water privileges are not plenty," read the enticement.[7] He could supply a good, moral character. Capital might be a problem.

Henry proceeded to build the sawmill, which would provide him lumber to build homes and businesses. How this situation progressed is unknown, but Henry went into debt to Chandlee for $600, two years' average earnings in those times, and he acquired an eighty-acre parcel on the Salamonie River that likely had been earmarked for the mill site. The mill proved a dismal failure.[8] That mattered not to Chandlee. Chandlee demanded Henry make good on his note. Unlike Henry, Chandlee would not be put off by excuses and hard-luck stories.

Before new states established county governments, people found a neighbor to serve as a neutral arbiter in disputes. Once legal redress became available, though, settlers preferred the formality. Jay County got its first court in 1835. According to one county historian, "When a boy is possessed of a hatchet or a jack-knife, the temptation to use them becomes irresistible. . . . By the election of a Justice of the Peace, they obtained the facilities for going to law, and litigation commenced. Before this, all difficulties had been adjusted by third parties, without officers or fees, which generally resulted in the belligerent parties 'drinking friendship.'"[9]

Lawsuits between neighbors became a community mainstay, as settlers embraced their civic duties as justices of the peace (JPs) and jurors. Henry found himself facing Chandlee in court. Between the mill failure and local crop failures, he failed to repay his debt, so Chandlee pressed his claim in November 1840. Though the case continued to the May 1841 term, Henry surely knew he would lose.

On the final day of 1840, Henry and Abby Jenkins signed papers committing the Salamonie land as collateral for $300 from the State Bank Sinking Fund. (Job Carr had deeded the property to Henry just two days earlier.)[10] If Henry and Abby hoped the money would appease

Chandlee enough to drop the lawsuit and work out a payment plan for the balance, it was not to be.

When court resumed in May, Chandlee prevailed. Even after paying him the mortgage proceeds, Henry still owed about $350 less credit for "matters to be liquidated between" them.[11] This presumably meant the remaining consigned goods or items Henry used to construct the saw-mill. After Chandlee died suddenly in 1842, Henry attempted to assign his mortgaged land to the estate to get out from under the judgment.[12] This maneuver failed.

Henry also could not meet his mortgage payments, particularly after 1844 when the entire county, and especially his land along the river, flooded. No one could sow crops for the entire season, and no one would buy these properties. People fled to nearby towns.[13] The Jenkins family moved to Portland, the Jay County seat, for a couple years, where Henry did some work for the county. They then leased a portion of the school section (state land set aside to support education) in Knox Township, south of Camden and close to the Blackford County line. There, they made the required improvements, barely subsisting.

The state first advertised the Salamonie parcel for sale in 1845. Year after year, the balance grew, Henry defaulted, the state offered the land for sale, and no one bought it. Henry did not intend to reclaim that land. He just wanted his wife, mother, and children to live in some semblance of comfort. As his forty-ninth birthday drew nigh, the Sisyphean effort wearied him. There had to be an easier way to make money than by fell-ing trees and farming in Indiana. As the Jenkins family preserved food to see them through the winter of 1850–1851, a grim future loomed.

A few miles west of the Jenkins farm, across the county line in a com-munity called Trenton, lived the James and Elizabeth Ransom family. The Jenkins and Ransom families were close, despite their many dis-similarities. James Ransom and Elizabeth Anderson met and married in Belmont County, Ohio. James, a blacksmith, dealt in horses and other livestock. Likely, his desire for property, cheaper in Indiana than in Ohio, drove his decision to move west. After Elizabeth gave birth to their fifth child, in 1836, the family relocated.[14] Taking the National Road as far

Figure 1.1. James Ransom and Elizabeth Anderson Ransom, c. early 1860s. Credit: Courtesy of Mike Wickward.

as they could, they carved their way into the jungle that would become Blackford County, with not a neighbor within shouting distance, though Ohio friends and family soon joined them.

While building a house and planting their first crops, they lived in a half-faced camp, a rough shelter built against a felled tree, a fire kept burning at the entrance to discourage wolves and other varmints. Ransom acquired land at first by squatting and not buying, a common occurrence in that period. He added to his holdings and equity over the next fourteen years with the help of his many sons. The family grew, and their farm products were the envy of poor folk like the Jenkinses. Ransom also kept a store at the Trenton crossroads.[15]

James and Elizabeth's oldest son, William, handsome and outgoing, married Ann Jenkins, Henry and Abby's oldest daughter, in February 1850. Several months later, William's sister, Jane Ransom, married Will Z. Jenkins. Everyone anticipated a third marriage between the two families, when Emma Jenkins became old enough to wed Robert Ransom.

Will Jenkins lived with his parents while doing carpentry work nearby. His wife, Jane, lived with William and Ann Ransom, near James and Elizabeth's home. Jane Jenkins and Ann Ransom (having swapped last names upon marriage) shared their experiences of being newlywed and pregnant. The elder Ransoms and Jenkinses looked forward to the pending arrival of grandchildren. Becoming a grandmother may have seemed odd to Elizabeth Ransom, still bearing children herself. Henry's widowed mother, Ann W. Jenkins, would become a great-grandmother at age eighty, an incredible milestone in that time and place. She would delight in another generation to love and cherish.

For nearly two years, talk about California gold had infested every cranny of the country, including eastern Indiana. Possibly the first person from Jay County to reach the mines was a son of Joseph Wilson, a good friend of the Jenkins family. Wilson was one of the Quaker founding fathers who established Camden. Friend Sam Grisell platted the townsite, naming it first New Lisbon, then changing it to Camden (later Pennville).

Wilson bought adjacent land, divided some into lots, and sold it to new settlers. Wilson's wife died in 1837; he then married Grisell's daughter, Sabina, twenty-one years his junior. Wilson's oldest son from his first marriage, Willis, enlisted in the Army in St. Louis, Missouri, during the Mexican-American War. Upon his discharge in August 1848, Willis hightailed it to the west coast, along with many veterans, getting a full year's jump on the mass of forty-niners to come. He left it to his commanding officer to notify his father where he had gone.[16] Since then, no one had heard a peep from Willis Wilson; most figured he had perished. So many people died just trying to get to the mines, it was a reasonable assumption.

Other men from the community went west overland with the forty-niners. Among them was Elias D. (E.D.) Pierce, another Mexican War veteran, who lived on the James Ransom farm. It could be that the adventurous spirit that drove Pierce to Mexico had enabled him to join the wagon train to California. And whatever kept his Indiana friends from going to war also held them back from the gold rush—at least at first. Possibly an indentured childhood suited Pierce to Army life. Plus, with one notable exception, he lacked entanglements to keep him home. Pierce kept in touch with Ransom, who was like a father to him. His reports about California shimmered, but he planned to overwinter in Indiana. He wanted his friends, including the Ransoms, to join him on a second trip west.

All the chatter stirred something in Henry Jenkins. Gold. Perhaps his last chance to redeem himself from his failures. To get out of debt and furnish Abby with a comfortable old age. One major obstacle, though. It cost money—hard currency—to get to California. Henry owned neither horses nor oxen to pull a wagon.[17] It is doubtful he even had a wagon. Besides, the overland route was slow and dangerous. Going by sea made more sense, but he could not barter his way onto a steamship. It seemed a hopeless dream but one he could not dispel.

As a stark reminder of his precarious financial situation, the State Bank once again advertised "his" land near Camden for sale. It simply was not worth the current $450 asking price. Until he weighed that anchor, Henry had no hope of borrowing money to set sail. The answer to Henry's dilemma—how to get money to travel when he had no assets and many debts—came from an unexpected source.

CHAPTER 2

THE BLACKFORD MINING COMPANY

1849 TO EARLY 1851—TRENTON, BLACKFORD COUNTY, INDIANA
Two brothers from Belmont County, Ohio, Sam and Benjamin H. Jones, settled on a farm south of Trenton with their wives and children. Sam purchased the land from his uncle, James Ransom. They relocated in 1849 or early 1850. The Ransom and Jones families visited each other between Indiana and Ohio on occasion. The National Road, which passed through Belmont County and Richmond, Indiana, eased such movement in the days before railroad travel became ubiquitous. The Jones brothers farmed, but Benjamin was also a physician. His family later took up residence in Camden. He did not fall victim to gold fever, but younger brother Sam had a bad case.

When Ransom traveled to Belmont County early in 1849, perhaps to persuade his nephews to move, his tenant, E.D. Pierce, joined him. The tall, dark-haired, grey-eyed Virginia native was still skeletal from his bout with dysentery, acquired in Mexico. In Barnesville, Pierce met eighteen-year-old Rebecca, living with her parents, Thomas and Sarah (Ransom) Jones. Instantly smitten, Pierce proposed before heading to California. The young beauty accepted and promised to wait for him. He did not meet Rebecca's older brothers on that trip, however, and he left Indiana before they arrived in Trenton. But Pierce's letters to Ransom about his California adventures exhilarated young men like Sam Jones.

Trenton was more an idea than a reality. Boggy forests still dominated the landscape, though settlers cleared and drained more area every year. Robert H. Lanning, Bazel B. Anderson, Ezekiel Lanning, and William Cortright filed a survey plat with the county in 1847, attested by James Ransom, justice of the peace for Jackson Township, but little development occurred.[1] The men who laid out the town were all related to or associated with the Ransoms from their Ohio days. Pioneer settlements normally included such family groups, their interdependence key to persevering in difficult conditions.

Trenton needed businesses: tradesmen, a livery, and such. Schools and churches had yet to be built. Agriculture dominated, generating little cash flow for development. The gold rush changed everything. Suddenly, the locals needed currency to get to California, amass some gold, and return home to build the aspirational community. And there was none.

At twenty-six, Sam Jones was the father of three young children, including a baby boy. His wife, Eliza B. Zinn, was the younger sister of Benjamin Jones's wife, Mariah Zinn, making the two couples doubly close. The Jones's neighbors were their uncle's in-laws, the Andersons, people they knew from Ohio. Elizabeth Ransom was the second oldest of William C. Anderson's twelve children. Some of her brothers—Asa, Bazel, Humphrey, and William T.—were active in community service and politics. Bazel, the Trenton founder, died in 1849; his was one of the earliest burials in the Trenton Cemetery.

In May 1850, William T., Humphrey, and their father, along with Sam Jones, needed $150 in cash for some purpose. Creative financing arose from necessity, given the absence of banks. Sam discussed the problem with his brother. They decided to create a promissory note to sell. Sam and the Andersons' note said they would pay $200 to Benjamin H. Jones in nine months. Dr. Jones gave them nothing in return for the note—a fictional debt. His job: find a shaver to buy the note.[2]

Shavers, usually successful merchants (unlike Henry Jenkins), flourished in the banking vacuum. They bought promissory notes at steep discounts, earning enormous profits. One of these was a wealthy trader in Chesterfield, Madison County. "Allen Makepeace had the best store

Figure 2.1. 1850s daguerreotype believed to be Samuel Jones. Credit: Courtesy of Julie Work Beck.

and largest trade in the county, and generally was recognized as one of the best merchants in the country. A man of genial address, he never failed to attract people to his store."[3] He also had substantial real estate holdings, obtaining many parcels by foreclosure. He never hesitated to take someone to court.

Seeking a shaver, Dr. Jones rode the twenty-seven miles to Muncie. Though it was the Delaware County seat, a town of about 700 souls, "Muncie was a small place. You could stand by the court house and see all over the town."[4] Jones reined in at the hitching post in front of the offices of Swaar and Sample, Attorneys-at-law. The dirt street exhaled a pungent cloud of dust and dried manure. With the bogus contract from his brother in hand, he entered the office of James H. Swaar, Esquire.

Swaar had been admitted to the bar in 1842, at age twenty-three. He married in 1846 and, like Dr. Jones, had young daughters at home. Swaar and Jones may have barely known one another, or they might have been good friends. Possibly Swaar, used to handling various transactions for his clients, had suggested this type of note sale to Jones.

One of Swaar's patrons was Allen Makepeace. Having observed his client's financial success, Swaar decided to try his hand at shaving. To fund his experiment, he borrowed $500 from Makepeace. He and Jones agreed to a 25 percent discount. Jones endorsed the note over to the attorney and received $150 cash. Once Swaar collected the full $200 from Sam and the Andersons in nine months, his profit on the deal would be $50, a 33 percent return.

Sam Jones had to produce his $50 share by February 1851 to pay James Swaar. With any luck, he might be on his way to California by then. Sam may have preferred to go alone but probably saw it as foolhardy. Besides, plenty of gold bug-bit men in Blackford County itched to go. Some of the Anderson brothers expressed interest. Their friend Dennis Lowry was willing.

Dennis was a short, slender man with a high forehead who wore his facial hair in a mustache and goatee. He was the second youngest of eight children born to John and Nancy Ann Lowry. The Lowry family moved to Guernsey County, Ohio, when Dennis was young. By the early 1840s, all the Lowrys had relocated to Blackford, along with associated families such as the Andersons, Housers, and Duffys. Dennis married Mary Ann Houser in 1842 when he was nineteen and Mary Ann just thirteen. In 1844, their son, George Washington Lowry, was born. A daughter named Elizabeth came along in 1850.

Harvey Hunt, a newcomer to the county, also joined the company. Harvey, age thirty-four, was a native of upstate New York. He married Susan Trubey, of Pennsylvania, around 1836, and they settled in Ohio, where their first four children were born. They relocated to Indiana in 1847, settling first in Wells County, then in Blackford, just to the south. Harvey bought acreage in Blackford County prior to moving to Indiana. He also bought town lots in Camden. He had little connection to the community, having lived there only a short time and having no known extended family in the area. In the 1850 census, Harvey reported his real estate as being worth $350, but he was upside down financially. Like the others, he had no cash to finance a trip to California.

Sam and his mining partners would need to get a much larger loan. Most had farms. Unfortunately, Blackford County real estate was not a sought-after commodity. Obtaining mortgages would be unlikely. No one would give a small fortune to a group about to undertake a perilous journey, perhaps never to return.

A serious, hardworking man, Sam had aspirations beyond farming. Like his siblings, he had dark hair, light eyes, and cut a fine figure. He convinced others he had management skills and could obtain financing. Uncle James could introduce him to anyone in the area; he had been there since before the county's founding. Sam persuaded some older men in the community—men with property and standing, unlikely to go anywhere—to pledge their land as surety on a note. The Andersons soon signed on. At least two of the brothers planned to join the mining group, and it was a large family.

By January 1851, Sam had enough men to sign a $2,800 note, an amount he thought sufficient for himself and five or six others to get to California. The note simply stated that the signers would repay Dr. Jones in one year. As before, he gave nothing of value to the signers. Dr. Jones, who suffered from rheumatism, did not have the physical stamina to become a miner.[5] But he thought he could make some money by helping Sam finance his company. He agreed again to find a shaver and to doctor the men's families while they were gone, to be paid from their California gold.

Sam's Blackford Mining Company, over the winter of 1850–1851, created a detailed plan to get to the west coast post haste, acquire their kits, and skedaddle up to the mines to make their piles. They set March 10 as their departure date and put their affairs in order. The wives and children braced themselves, knowing the breadwinners were determined to travel thousands of miles for uncertain rewards. Though they certainly pleaded with their husbands to stay home, the women had no rights and little leverage. They pondered whether their menfolk had even a modicum of good sense left.

Dr. Jones returned to Muncie to look for a buyer. Volney Willson, the county treasurer, had money; he had lent some to gold-seekers before. He had been a bank director and owned extensive land and valuable livestock.[6] Willson looked over the note and asked Jones what he hoped to get. Jones said $2,500. Willson replied that was more than his piles; Jones would have to look elsewhere. Jones asked if Allen Makepeace might be interested and learned that Makepeace did not lend money but would buy good notes, backed by real estate.

Jones turned again to attorney James Swaar. Swaar let it be known that anyone wanting to sell a California note to Makepeace had to go through him. Swaar told him that Mr. Makepeace "had a good many thousand dollars and would let it go in that way."[7] Swaar was too busy to go to Chesterfield, thirteen miles west of Muncie in the next county, so he asked Levi Hunter to take the doctor and make the introduction. Jones mentioned to Makepeace he had been referred by Swaar and handed over the promissory note. Makepeace examined the slip of paper, his poker face betraying nothing.

I don't know these men—he pointed out to Jones—*or you, for that matter. Besides, if I was to buy a note, it would need to be done up properly.* Makepeace produced a pre-printed promissory note that included the phrase, "without benefit of the valuation or appraisement laws of the state," plus an annual interest rate.

If you want to sell a note, it will need to include these terms—Makepeace explained to the financially naïve young doctor—*I buy notes the way I would buy a horse. The interest rate is not important but whether it is sound. Understand my meaning, Doctor?*

He told Jones he would consider the matter, and if he decided to "let the money go," he would mail the doctor.[8] Two weeks later, Jones still had no word. During that time, Sam examined the pre-printed note. He may not have understood the phrase about valuation and appraisement laws, but the annual interest was clear enough. Makepeace would make his money by shaving the note 25 percent or more. Interest on the face value was just pure greed.

Makepeace also wanted a certificate from the Blackford County clerk showing how much property each man owned; land was as important to him as money, maybe more so. The original note signers refused to go along with the added terms. The Blackford Mining Company needed new silent partners. Sam drew up a revised note. Five men going to California were the principal debtors: Samuel Jones, Harvey Hunt, Humphrey Anderson, Dennis Lowry, and John K. Anderson. Eleven others offered their land for security but would stay home. Some were young, including Henry's son, Will Z. Jenkins (who had no land). Others were older men with established farms.

Henry asked Dr. Jones about getting funds to buy into the company. Thinking he would receive 75 cents on the dollar, he executed a promissory note, including Makepeace's stipulations, payable to Jones for $800. Henry may have considered using half his anticipated $600 proceeds to include his son-in-law, William Ransom, in the company. Henry asked his son, Bedford (a minor with no assets), and Joseph Wilson, his friend, to sign as surety. Henry was purchasing land but still owed Robert Hatten $96 to obtain clear title. He mortgaged his equity to Wilson so Wilson would have the means to pay Makepeace should anything happen to Henry.[9] Henry also promised Wilson that when he got to California, he would search for Willis, who had gone west after the war and had not been heard from since. Wilson no doubt missed the assistance of his adult son, having many young children at home to support.

Still, Dr. Jones received no word from Makepeace. Out of patience, Sam prodded his brother into action. Jones decided that Makepeace had implied he would buy a note with all his conditions met. He returned to Muncie in late February, where Swaar insisted on accompanying the doctor to make the deal.

Swaar and Jones mounted up and began the journey to Chesterfield, riding side-by-side up the frozen, hard-packed corduroy road. Nearing Chesterfield, they saw a horse-drawn buggy heading toward them. It was forty-nine-year-old Allen Makepeace himself. Makepeace was five-foot-eight and "of fair complexion, fine looking, and polished in his manners."[10] He explained to the men he needed to see about hiring a girl but would return soon. He and his wife had a toddler—their first child—and undoubtedly wanted a nanny for this late-in-life arrival. Swaar and Jones proceeded to town.

Chesterfield, on the eastern edge of Madison County, was a small but commercially important town, essentially created by and for the Makepeace family. The patriarch, Amasa, built the first house in what later became the town, and it was no mere log cabin. The two-story frame house had a large brick fireplace, whitewashed siding, and a grand front porch with a roof supported by four columns rising the full two stories. Allen, his oldest son, platted the town in 1830 on the small but vital Mill Creek, so named for the county's first gristmill situated on its bank, built in 1825 by Amasa, with the help of other early settlers.[11]

Amasa Makepeace ran several businesses and the post office in Chesterfield. His two oldest sons, Allen and Alfred, were also cut from an entrepreneurial cloth. The two boys, when still in their teens, started selling supplies from Ohio to the Indians and early settlers in Indiana. They grew their trade until they regularly hauled several wagonloads at a time from Cincinnati to Madison County.[12] Around 1850, Allen and another brother, George, erected fine brick residences on Chesterfield's main street. George's had an apothecary shop on the ground level with the family's living quarters upstairs.

After their brief encounter with Makepeace, Dr. Jones and Swaar rode into the village, past Amasa's place on their right, then past Allen's and George's brick buildings on their left. Across from George's store, they asked tavern-keeper Andrew Shafer to stable the horses and sat down to an early dinner to wait on Makepeace's return.

As they finished their midday meal, Makepeace returned to the livery. Jones handed the $2,800 note to Swaar and told him to make the deal. At the stable, Swaar vouched for the note signers and asserted Dr. Jones was good for it, urging Makepeace to buy. He said Jones wanted $2,400. Makepeace shook his head. They were too far apart to make a deal. Swaar wanted his $10 fee, so he proposed a counteroffer.

He said—*Look here, Mr. Makepeace. I have this 200-dollar note, made out by Sam Jones and the Andersons. I owe you 500, so why not take this as 200 toward my debt and you can return it to Dr. Jones, the original payee, and he can collect it. Offer him three for four, including the 200, like it was cash.*

Makepeace mulled it over and started toward his house, telling the attorney to meet him at George's store. Swaar returned to Jones on the tavern porch and relayed the conversation. The doctor resisted taking the earlier note as part of the proceeds.

They crossed the street and went up the steps into the apothecary. Jones, unhappy with the negotiations, paced the newly milled, aromatic flooring. He did not notice the local men warming by the crackling fire in a pot-bellied stove. Awaiting the financier, Swaar took in the scene: rows of earthenware canisters and glass jars with paper labels lining the shelves behind the clerk's counter, multi-drawered cabinets holding various medicinal herbs. George Makepeace stood behind the counter with his nephew, Alvin, observing the men.

Makepeace gathered sufficient bank notes to pay Jones, assuming they struck a bargain. This was hardly his first such deal. It was not even the first California note he had bought. Finally, after allowing the doctor to stew a while, he went to his brother's store. After haggling for an hour or two, they finally came to an agreement. Jones thought the amount too little to satisfy "those boys," as he thought of them (some were his age or older).

Unless I can come up with more from somewhere else, I don't think those boys will go for it—he told Makepeace—*What if they don't agree to it? Can I return it and pay you something for your trouble?*

They agreed Jones could return the money in two weeks and pay Makepeace $5, or the men would keep it and the deal would stand. Before heading home, Dr. Jones presented Makepeace with the $800

Jenkins note and asked if he would buy it, too. He was agreeable, and they made the trade.

Sam and his friends were mad as hornets when Dr. Jones gave them $1,667 and the $200 note. He explained the best Makepeace would do was two-thirds of the face value. Sam had counted on enough for himself and five others. Ruefully, they kept the money. They had little choice. It forced Sam to cut one man from his team. That was probably William T. Anderson, the sixth name on the note. In one year, Sam and the others would owe Makepeace $2,968. It amounted to an effective rate of 59 percent.

The next day, Henry paid Dr. Jones a visit in Camden. Jones handed him $533. Henry had anticipated getting enough for two shares in the mining company. Still, it was enough to pay some debts and have $300 to buy in. As had the others, he kept the money. He would just have to work that much harder to make the Sierra dirt pay.

A week later, Sam approached the doctor with yet another note. Two of the Liestenfeltz brothers, Jake and Pete, and a friend of theirs, John C. Teach, wanted to join the company. They heard Makepeace was paying two-thirds on the face value, so they produced a promissory note to Dr. Jones for $1,350, expecting to get $900 for the three men to buy in. Their father, Conrad Liestenfeltz, and several other men pledged security.

Conrad Liestenfeltz and his wife, Susan, were among the few immigrants in Blackford County. They left Germany in 1828 with their first two sons, Jacob and Daniel. They started from Baden to Paris, where the nearly penniless family had to remain while the boys were inoculated for smallpox. After the grueling Atlantic crossing, they landed in New York City and began looking for work and learning English, but no jobs came their way. They finally found employment on a farm in New Jersey owned by Peter Nevins. Susan gave birth to another boy, and they named him in honor of their benefactor.[13] When Pete was a toddler, the family moved to Warren County, Ohio. There they made the acquaintance of the Jenkins family.

About the time Henry Jenkins set up his store in Camden, Conrad Liestenfeltz purchased land on the eastern edge of Blackford County, moving his wife and children when the house was completed two years later. The family worked hard all year to make the farm productive. Pete helped his mother in the house while Jake and Daniel worked the fields with their father. The family income came from hogs. After butchering, Conrad took the meat to Richmond. By 1850, he had a respectable net worth. They were not rich by any means, but firmly in the local middle class. They were the first family in the neighborhood to obtain an iron cookstove. They also acquired the first buggy, which they graciously loaned to people for funerals and doctor visits. The Liestenfeltzes assimilated and made good on the heralded promise of their new country: anyone who worked hard had as much opportunity to succeed as the next person.

Pete began his schooling in Ohio and continued for a few years in Indiana when his parents could find teachers to hire, but he only made it to the fourth reader.[14] There may have been a lack of good teachers; certainly, this was a common complaint for Abby Jenkins, who ended up filling the gap at times. In the days before publicly funded schools, those with limited means struggled to impart the basics to their children. Conrad and Susan subscribed to English-language newspapers, and those, along with the Bible, had to suffice for any further education.

Though Lutherans back in the Old Country, the Liestenfeltzes gravitated to the Society of Friends in their new home. Susan, strict in her religious observance, made sure her sons toed the line. In all likelihood, the Liestenfeltzes believed their sons would do well out west. They had been taught good manners, strict morals, and a strong work ethic. It helped that their sons would not leave behind wives and children like the others—it would free them to focus their energy on success in the mines or at whatever opportunity came their way.

John Covest Teach had been a landless laborer much of his life and probably worked at times as a hired hand on the Liestenfeltz farm. Teach got his start in Pennsylvania and appears to have been orphaned by age twelve. He had some training from his older brother, a shoemaker, but made his living as a laborer with some subsistence farming. In 1830,

Teach married Ann Mustard in Ohio County, Virginia (the area around Wheeling, West Virginia, today). John and Ann Teach settled in eastern Ohio and had five children, two sons dying in infancy. Teach struggled against poverty, without much success. He moved his wife and three surviving children to Indiana. They settled in Harrison Township, north of Trenton.

John Teach had neither property nor cash to buy into the mining company. He wanted in on the California action, anyway. His son was an adult and could help Teach's wife, Ann, and two daughters in his absence. The Liestenfeltz note would cover Teach's share. Though payable to Dr. Jones like the others, Jones had tired of Sam's ruse. He assigned the note to "Samuel Jones" and told him to go to Muncie. Sam gave the Liestenfeltzes $900 for their note on March 6.

The financing done, the final tally was ten men who all borrowed $300 to join the mining company, with one possible exception, Pres Gibson.[15] (Gibson, John Teach's neighbor, probably obtained funding from his family.) Sam Jones served as company president, joined by two Anderson brothers (Humphrey and John), the Liestenfeltzes, Henry Jenkins, plus Gibson, Teach, Lowry, and Hunt. William Ransom, Henry's son-in-law and Sam's cousin, as eager to go as the others, had not been included. His plans were only temporarily thwarted.

The departure date, March 10, arrived. In smoky cabins on flat, wet farms scattered around Trenton, the miners-to-be readied for their journey while their families fretted about the hard times ahead. The cajoling, pleading, and tears were all but exhausted. Fathers tucked their children in the night before, hoping to be gone before they arose. Mothers knew they would be reliant on family, friends, and neighbors, well beyond the norm. Jake and Pete's mother, Susan Liestenfeltz, must have feared she would never see her sons again. The brothers packed their travel sacks with meager provisions and nary a single change of clothes.[16]

The likely scene at the Jenkins home can be imagined—a close family, loving and faithful: In the tiny cabin, Henry hugged Abby, clinging to her as to a floating log in the endless ocean. His aged mother, Ann, nearly blind and deaf, struggled to hold her emotions in check as she sat in the corner rocker, waiting her turn to say goodbye to the man she had reared. Ann's bond with Henry was spiritual as much as maternal.

Parting from his sons and daughters, though some were now grown, pained him equally. He knew that many people succumbed on the journey to California. He vowed to not be one of the casualties. Abby, resigned, prayed that this unwanted separation would somehow bring the prosperity her husband craved. The entire family gathered close, bowed their heads, and said a prayer to bless Henry's journey. He did his best to reassure Abby that this trip would change their luck and that the year would fly by, as they always seemed to at their age. Henry layered clothes and donned his warmest hat; he picked up his leather valise and rations. Then he strode out the door, not looking back, forsaking the warm bosom of his family, and began the four-mile walk to Sam Jones's farm.

As she closed the door against the frosty, early-morning air, Abby felt a portentous weight crumple her like an empty flour sack. She collapsed on a bench near the door. She knew that keeping busy would be her best defense against loneliness. Besides, who was she to complain? She had the comforts of home and family. It would be Henry who would suffer, sleeping on the ground, learning to find gold, and, oddly, taking care of his own domestic needs: cooking, washing, and mending clothes, caring for the sick—things she truly enjoyed doing. She did not sit for long; it gave her time to think, just what she did not want. She needed to comfort her mother-in-law and begin the day's chores. Abby crossed the cozy room to hug Ann. The children did not know how to react to this strange day.

The men milling about in Sam's main room had business to attend to before they set out for Richmond, a two-day walk.[17] The company needed an agreement detailing the rules they would be bound by as an organization. In this, they clearly heeded some uninformed, inexperienced advice.

The Articles of Agreement stated that the men would eschew gambling and alcohol. None would be deserted should they fall ill along the journey. Anyone who died would be entitled to a portion of the company earnings, depending on when the death occurred. If anyone left the company, they would pay an $800 fine to the remaining men. And if anyone broke the rules, the president would admonish him and expel him from the company. All earnings and expenses were to be shared equally.[18]

These farmers were used to cooperating with their neighbors. As a community, they built houses and barns, sheared sheep, and threshed grain. Their experiences had not prepared them for the vastly different undertaking of a mining company. They made erroneous assumptions that equal effort would produce roughly equal rewards. The presumption that all would contribute fairly to the work smelled of unsophistication.

While the agreement was heavy on moral obligation, it was light on practicalities. It lacked even a rudimentary outline for the division of labor. It did not address conflict resolution. While it gave the president a dictatorial enforcement authority, what if he broke the rules? Who would hold him accountable? Clearly, they did not understand the fundamentals of a joint business enterprise. Gold mining would be as different from farming as a long tom was from a plow.

Hoisting sacks of provisions and personal items, the Blackford bunch, wearing most of the clothes they owned, stepped out of the cabin onto a thin scrum of crunchy snow. Buoyantly, they followed their crystalline puffs of breath on their triumphant march southward.

CHAPTER 3
THE RIVER TRIP

He was bound for California to make his fortune, and visions of the riches soon to be his profoundly altered his estimate of himself and the world.

—OSCAR LEWIS, *SEA ROUTES TO THE GOLD FIELDS*

MARCH 1851—CINCINNATI, OHIO

After a butt-bruising twenty-hour stage ride from Richmond, the company arrived in Cincinnati at 11 p.m. on Wednesday, March 12.[1] They awoke Thursday morning to a whiff of approaching spring, promising a pleasant day ahead. But the morning's *Cincinnati Enquirer* held disturbing news that day for anyone planning a trip to the Sierras.

The Army clashed with Indians in Mariposa County. Scarce consumable goods commanded high prices. Letters from locals reported little success in the mines. None of this deterred the Indianans. For every realistic tale about miners averaging $2 a day, there were equally compelling counter-statistics. One steamship from Panama, headed to New York, carried a million dollars in gold freight, with another $300,000 amongst the passengers. Somebody was getting rich. Why not them? The company was eager to be off "to see the elephant," in the parlance of the day. They had shunned the slow route to California, overland, in favor of the fastest possible: by steamboat to New Orleans, then by sea, crossing the isthmus at Panama.

After securing passage on the aptly named *Indiana*, they spent the day exploring "Porkopolis," as Cincinnati was fondly called, due to its pork-packing industry. The clamor of the city coming to life assaulted their country ears, used to nothing louder than grinding millstones, clanging blacksmiths' hammers, or a rifle report heralding a meaty meal. Wheels and hooves of horse-drawn conveyances clattered on the brick streets. Teamsters created a din as they loaded and unloaded merchandise. The banshee screams of steam escaping from the riverboats' high-pressure boilers on the waterfront punctured the air, audible for miles.

Cincinnati had progressed since Henry had lived there two decades earlier. Swine were no longer the sanitation engineers, wandering the streets devouring all manner of refuse. But pig flesh was still the number-one commodity exported from the public landing, being shipped as far as Europe, the by-products put to good use by Proctor & Gamble as soap and candle wax. The city's odor had gone from barnyard offal to industrial waste, not necessarily an improvement, especially to a farmer. The hundreds of gas lights impressed them—what an improvement over the hickory-bark torches they used back home! Prowling the streets, the men saw an incredible variety of merchandise and craned their necks at the tall buildings crammed together in a solid mass—so different than log cabins and open spaces.

An 1851 Cincinnati directory lists nearly 400 occupations and the number of each, including, curiously, "Thieves......42." There were German sausage shops, confectionaries, bakeries, basketry, jewelry, tobacco shops, metal and glass wares, booksellers, milliners, musical instruments, daguerreotypes, guns, and an enormous variety of food available from over 500 grocers.[2] Butchers sold fresh meat at five large markets set in the middle of the broad avenues. Shoes and boots proliferated, given the ready availability of hides.

The men may have been tempted to purchase new, ready-made apparel, but they conserved the cash they had borrowed dearly to pay their way to California. Homespun, handmade duds would have to do. Though each contributed $300 to this venture, transportation prices were rising; they had no idea how much. They had never been in spitting distance of so much cash; it made them nervous about pickpockets in

Figure 3.1. Riverfront view of Cincinnati, Ohio, in 1848. Panel three of daguerreo-type panorama. Credit: From the Collection of Cincinnati & Hamilton County Public Library.

towns and on the river. They would have to get used to carrying their gold around, though. They were going to be rich men, after all.

The pump house for the city's massive water works stood at the river's edge at the end of Front Street, next to the new station for the Little Miami line, Cincinnati's only railroad service. They would have found the trains fascinating—iron horses did not come anywhere near Blackford County. Cincinnati's situation on the Ohio River was roughly halfway between Pittsburgh, the source, and Cairo, where it emptied into the Mississippi. It was the heyday of steamboats, with over 700 plying the western rivers, and Cincinnati was a shipping dynamo.[3] In mid-century, the city absorbed a large number of European immigrants, primarily German, who quickly assimilated, and secondarily the Irish. It was a cosmopolitan place, doing business around the world.

But the Indianans had not come to be dazzled by city life. It was a mere distraction on the way to their true destination, the place everyone was talking about, the land of gold—California! They were impatient to be on their way.

The canal packet *Indiana* arrived from New Orleans on Tuesday, March 11, pulling into the public landing alongside a dozen other steamboats.[4] Though scheduled to depart the next day, obtaining a suitable consignment of cargo took longer than expected. Finally, Thursday evening, the boat was ready for the downriver run.[5]

The company gathered on the landing. Henry likely twinged with guilt at the thought of his son-in-law, William, who had been left behind with his wife, Ann, and their new baby girl, Cordelia, Henry's first grandchild. Only a few days into this yearlong sojourn, he already missed Abby and their children. Before embarking, Henry mailed his first letter home describing their journey from Trenton to Cincinnati.[6] He would be a faithful correspondent, despite abandoning his duties at home.

The *Indiana*'s passengers included city residents, visitors, merchants, farmers with livestock and crops to move to markets, foreign tourists, and emigrants. There were four companies going to California: the ten farmers from Indiana, nine from Michigan, a trio, and a duo.[7] They made up just a small portion of travelers on board.

The "fancier" people booked staterooms in first class. They took their supper in the saloon running the length of the boiler deck (a misnomer—the boilers were below on the main deck). Sumptuous carpeting hushed the high-ceilinged room, except in the bar where men gathered and spat their tobacco juice, disregarding spittoons. The walls and ceilings sported gilded trim, reflecting light from cut-glass chandeliers. Doors decorated with landscape paintings led into the staterooms, so-called because each bore the name of a different state. For those wishing to play cards, euchre being popular, tables huddled in the center of the room. There was even a piano.[8] The crew included a steward and waiters. Chambermaids serviced the staterooms. The first-class passengers also had access to the hurricane deck above for promenading.

The Blackford men were not traveling in such lavish style, however. They rode on the main deck and brought their own food aboard. They bedded each night on whatever piece of cargo furnished the most comfort and protection from the elements. The "deckers" boarded just before departure since freight took higher priority. The farmers did not expect luxury. For a slight decrease in the already-low fare, they would be required to load cordwood when the boat stopped for fuel, even in the middle of the night.

As the sun set, the Blackford travelers picked up their packs—containing a few personal articles, tools, weapons, tobacco, and mementos of loved ones—and food intended to get them to New Orleans and beyond. Leather boots thudded on the boarding planks as they marched down to the boat and stepped onto the guards, the decking extending beyond the ship's hull, loaded floor to ceiling with wood. The boilers burned thirty cords a day, and the massive galley stove needed an additional cord. Barrels of pork, whiskey, flour, potatoes and lard, rolls of leather, crates of cotton yarn, and personal household goods, packed tightly by the Irish roustabouts, filled most of the remaining space.

The deck was clean for the moment, but human and animal waste, trash, and mud would change that soon enough. The high 'tween-decks space provided some ventilation—perhaps too much in winter. A long woodstove supplied a little heat and a place to cook, to be shared by all on the main deck. Crews treated deckers, more profit than liability, as inferior to livestock. Cabin customers, in contrast, paid a slightly higher fare and demanded lavish service, resulting in a loss.

The Blackford group made their acquaintance with the passengers, crew, and boat. This was the *Indiana*'s third voyage to New Orleans, having been launched in December from the Cincinnati boatyard. If she had a responsible crew, the most-feared calamity of steamboat travel could be avoided. By 1848, 185 boiler explosions had killed over 1,400 people on western rivers, and the carnage did not diminish.[9] These river tragedies did nothing to hamper business. Non-boiler-related fires occurred, too. People casually smoked near open cotton bales; kegs of gunpowder were treated the same as pork. Other risks abounded. Just two months earlier, the *John Adams* hit a snag on the Mississippi and went under so fast that nearly all the deckers drowned, unable to free themselves from the confining payload.[10] People tried not to think of it.

Figure 3.2. The *Ben Campbell* steamboat at landing, between 1852 and 1860, a boat similar to the *Indiana*. Credit: Library of Congress, Prints & Photographs Division, Daguerreotypes Collection.

The *Indiana* was 182 feet long, the maximum size to fit the Louisville canal locks because she had been built for the run between Cincinnati and New Orleans. Her two Martin Anschutz & Co. engines, plus a spare, drove the thirty-two-foot sidewheels, powered by four thirty-foot-long boilers.[11] The sidewheels operated independently, permitting tight turns. The pilot house perched at the highest point on the superstructure, above the hurricane deck and the officers' quarters (the "texas").

Departure time came well after sundown. The mate bellowed an alert—*All ashore what's not headin' downriver!!*

Guests of the first-class crowd, who had been admiring the upper decks and staterooms, scrambled to the landing, waving goodbye from shore. The captain yelled orders to the pilot to back out into the river. With sooty smoke blooming from the stacks signaling imminent departure, the bells clanged, and the pilot shouted down the speaking tube to the engineers below decks to run the wheels in reverse. The paddles churned the dark, shallow water, and the boat backed carefully into the icy, bracing grip of the mighty Ohio. A cannon boom startled everyone aboard but the crew.[12] Shouts and cheers arose from the passengers on deck. Henry, Sam, and the others delighted in being underway at last. Steamboats ran night and day as long as conditions allowed, usually laying to only for fog. Clear skies and a three-quarter moon beamed for navigating the eighty-eight miles to Madison, Indiana, where they would load additional goods and passengers.

Lanterns hung on the main deck, casting a dim light to help the men find their way among the barrels, kegs, and crates. Penned livestock gobbled and chewed their feed. In the close quarters, Henry and friends sought out the California-bound. They swapped stories they had heard and read, sharing plans for making their fortunes.

The temperature dropped noticeably after dark. Pete Liestenfeltz and others new to river travel reveled in the novelty, observing their passage. Propelled away from the Cincinnati lights, Henry and his companions watched the skeletal forms of winter-dormant trees drift past, bade goodbye to the city that had entertained them for the day, and continued their engrossing conversations with new friends. Eventually, they collected their bags and bedrolls and claimed a cubbyhole among the merchandise.

The entire boat shook with the vibration and thrum of the engines. The close air—redolent with burlap, wood, unwashed humans, and animal smells—oppressed anyone not used to camping in a barn with cattle. The men wrapped themselves in blankets, tucked their bags under their heads, and huddled together for warmth. Sleep, in this loud, crowded, unfamiliar place, was bound to be fitful. When they did manage to nod off, visions of gold nuggets glittered in their dreams.

In Madison, the roustabouts lashed a barge to the side of the *Indiana* and spent the day loading additional consignments. The shipmaster maximized profits for the boat's owners, disregarding the risk to cargo, passengers, and crew, even to the boat itself.[13] The average lifespan of a western riverboat was a mere three to four years, and the owners calculated precisely how to make a return on this short-term investment. They could buy a used steamboat for several thousand dollars and quickly realize a profit, unlike the hopeful passengers heading to California.[14] The flimsy boats were "built of wood, tin, shingles, canvas and twine, and look like a bride of Babylon."[15] A pioneering society, perceiving unlimited resources and potential, did not blink at the wastefulness of these short-lived crafts.

Henry remarked in his second letter home, "The barge and boat together have rising thirteen hundred tons besides a large number of passengers," an improbable volume for such a small boat.[16] The main deck under this full load sat so low that the amidships portion was nearly even with the water's surface, threatening to swamp the whole affair.

Henry was not the only one concerned for his family. Sam Jones, John and Humphrey Anderson, and Dennis Lowry had all added to their growing households the previous year. Childhood was a perilous time. Diphtheria and scarlet fever ravaged families in some years. Cholera outbreaks could decimate an entire community. Hundreds in Indiana died from the disease in 1849, brought in by riverboats from New Orleans, packed with sickly immigrants. With an outbreak in full throttle, houses filled with wailing at all hours, continuing as family members succumbed one after another, until a weary, resigned numbness took over. Then stone-faced men fashioned rudimentary coffins, collected the dead, and held funerals en mass.

Sam Jones knew the terror of scarlet fever epidemics. When he was six years old, three of his four brothers were taken within a few days, leaving just him, his older brother Benjamin—who apparently caught it and recovered—and their younger sister, Rebecca. All the Blackford men knew they might return home from California to find new graves and diminished households, despite the fact that Dr. Jones had promised to care for their families. How long would it take the news to reach them of any family tragedy . . . or joy?

The men re-boarded after supper, and at 10 p.m., the night run from Madison to Louisville began, which was just forty-six miles downstream. There was no urgency; they would have to wait until morning to enter the canal. The steamer ambled along past seemingly impenetrable forested hills, gliding over moonlit water, leaving behind only a pair of V-shaped wakes from its sidewheels.

As dawn arose Saturday morning, Henry ogled Louisville as the boat waited to enter the Louisville and Portland Canal. Since 1830, it allowed navigation past the Falls of the Ohio, the only natural barrier between Pittsburgh and New Orleans. The river fell twenty-four feet in this two-mile stretch. Prior to the canal's construction, goods and people had to be portaged around the Devonian-era fossil beds, driving the growth of Portland and Louisville. For years, teamsters fought the canal, which they assumed would decimate the need for their services. Eventually, the canal investors prevailed.

Colonel George Rogers Clark founded the city during the Revolution, naming it for King Louis XVI of France, who supported the Americans during the war. The 1850 census recorded over 43,000 inhabitants. The city boasted several universities and colleges, a substantial hospital and medical institute, and a thriving slave trade. Horse racing was a popular attraction, drawing immense crowds.[17] The South had few industrial cities like Louisville.

The *Indiana* entered the canal at about 9 a.m. It took four excruciating hours to traverse the man-made ditch. The boat's movement between the stone walls was barely perceptible. A series of locks finalized the passage at the Portland end. After clearing those, they docked for several hours.

Wandering through Portland, the passengers found a late dinner and bought newspapers, cheap novels, and other amusements from the hawkers on the waterfront. Unlike in Cincinnati, they saw Negroes loading freight onto steamboats. They wore only trousers and a burlap wrap to protect their shoulders, fastened with a nail at the neck.[18] The slaves doing this back-breaking labor were leased to boat owners when not needed on farms and plantations. Crew bosses yelled obscenities to hurry the barrels and bundles along and used an occasional whack with a stick for emphasis. The roustabouts eased the monotonous work by singing rhythmic rouster songs led by the coonjiner, also a Negro, standing on a capstan. Their coonjine "dance" bounced the gangplanks until the entire boat rocked and the mate ordered them to break step. British writer

Frances Trollope found the singing delightful. "We were much pleased by the chant with which the negro boatmen regulate and beguile their labour on the river; it consists but of very few notes, but they are sweetly harmonious, and the negro voice is almost always rich and powerful."[19]

> Love her in de sunshine,
> Love her in de rain!
> Treats her like a white gal,
> She give my neck a pain!
> De mo' I does for Sadie Lee
> De less dat woman thinks er me!
>
> Old roustabout aint got no home,
> Make his living on his shoulder bone![20]

Henry would have cringed at this ill use of the Negroes. But he likely enjoyed the two-toned moan of the steam whistles as boats arrived and departed, reminding him of his days as a city dweller. His downriver trip resumed in late afternoon and ran until a foggy shroud enveloped the boat, forcing the pilot to lay to at 1 a.m.

Sunday afternoon brought high winds, whipping a heavy froth on the river and hindering progress. For Henry, the Sabbath was holy, a day to convene in fellowship, to pray, and seek strength from the Lord. He lamented missing services. Most of the company was not particularly religious. The passengers, and more, the crew, prone to swearing and merriment, irked Henry to no small degree. "My dear and much loved wife . . . Often when surrounded on all sides with mirth and profanity do I think of our quiet peaceable home and wonder how you are getting along."[21] Peace and tranquility were far from his daily reality on this trip.

Henry served as the unofficial scribe for the company, though the others wrote home as well—all could read and write to some extent. His language contrasted sharply with the vernacular used by the other men, such as Pete Liestenfeltz and Dennis Lowry, evidence of the disparity in their educations. The elder Jenkinses had embalmed the linguistics of their Quaker forebears, giving them an antiquated air among their contemporaries. Henry was literate, verbose, and unabashedly old-fashioned. He kept a diary, recording events and noting expenses. He referred to it when writing lengthy epistles in his impeccable penmanship, ruler-neat rows perfectly spaced. All the letters would be shared with everyone at home. He repeated news several times to counter expected lost correspondence. Communication with Camden and Trenton, or rather the lack of it, would torment the company over the coming months.

By day, Henry marveled at the passing scenery. Each night, he curled up in his blankets, the sweaty scent of fellow passengers unnoticed as it merged with his own ripeness. Sounds of dancing feet and fiddle music in the cabin filtered down through the decking. The main deck had limited room for dancing, but singing and socializing filled the deckers' time. This may have been a classless country on paper, but not in reality. The difference was stark on steamboats. But even first-class passengers got their drinking and bathing water straight from the river. That, at least, was egalitarian.

Wind and rough water hampered the voyage over the next two days. At night, bone-chilling gusts penetrated the woodpiles, clenching jaws to stifle chattering teeth. In the daytime, the slanting rays of the late-winter sun did little to counter the cold. Humphrey Anderson remarked to John Teach that he felt some discomfort in his head; his face took on a ruddy color. Neither Humphrey nor Teach shared this information with the others.

Humphrey Anderson, his brother John, and their siblings were born in Ohio. Their mother died sometime prior to 1830, when both Humphrey and John were under age ten. The young brothers spent many days exploring the hilly Anderson property in western Belmont County. Their father owned a sizeable parcel, where he appears to have been an early tobacco producer. Coal seams lay below the Anderson land, and though coal was already being exported in the eastern part of the county, they apparently never exploited this resource. Mining the property must not have occurred to them, though Humphrey and John made the decision to try gold mining in California. Many years later, long after the Andersons had departed, industrial strip-mining companies plundered the coal and eventually reclaimed the surface, leaving just a shadow of its formerly buxom profile.

Their father, William C. Anderson, originally from eastern Maryland, returned there about 1834 and remarried the following year, most likely taking his younger children with him, including John and perhaps Humphrey. Humphrey was named for his uncle, also Humphrey Anderson. The elder Humphrey married Lavina Shannon, sister of a future Ohio governor. He took a job working on the National Road in the late 1820s.

This massive federal project became the first major interstate highway, a route that began in Cumberland, Maryland, and terminated in St. Louis, Missouri. In Ohio, it started on the river in eastern Belmont County opposite Wheeling, (West) Virginia, and continued through Columbus, and finally to the Indiana state line, just east of Richmond. The macadamized road, made with compacted layers of manually chipped and sorted stones, served as a vital trade route and gateway to westward migration, until supplanted by railroads. As Humphrey Anderson's work crew approached Zanesville in 1830, he fell ill with typhoid fever. A messenger hastened to Lavina to bring her to nurse him, but Humphrey succumbed before she arrived.[22] Instead of visiting his bedside, there was only his grave, a fresh mound alongside the gleaming white gravel roadway.

Humphrey, the younger, almost certainly knew the James Havens family in Ohio. After the two families arrived in Blackford County in 1837, Humphrey wed Harriet Havens in 1840, and they had five children over the following decade. Like virtually every other resident in the county, Humphrey farmed for a living. Even attorneys, doctors, and tradesmen had land under cultivation to feed their families and livestock. Compared to his brothers and many of his neighbors, Humphrey's farm prospered; he had thirty of his 120 acres north of Trenton cleared and improved and more valuable livestock than anyone else in Jackson Township.[23] Even so, the gold mines had unseated him from the source of his family's livelihood.

At last, the steamer reached the mouth of the Ohio at Cairo, Illinois, and entered the Mississippi. At the confluence, the Mississippi expands to several miles across, as the two rivers battle for dominance. Whereas the clear Ohio flows through a narrow valley, hemmed by hills and moving in gentle undulations, the muddy Mississippi drains a vast region and slinks like a coiling snake through alluvial sediments, forever changing course, forming and obliterating islands, its murky depths bearing away an eroded continent. It takes miles to blend the contrasting flows.

The Mississippi stood at flood stage. Only fools thought that men could ever boss this river around. They constructed levees and watched them crumble. Waterfront cities found themselves stranded inland after high water changed her course. Inland towns could just as easily become waterfront. The only question was how much mud people would shovel from buildings when the floodwaters receded. Sludge was a fact of life.

Going downstream, boats rode the center of the river, using the fastest water to make better time. The passengers and crew of the *Indiana* hailed the many rafts, flatboats, keelboats, and scows, sharing information about the river back and forth. In this colorful parade, the steamers stood out as the queens, always painted white, decorated with gingerbread scrollwork and gilding, with boat names painted large on their wheel housings in circus-style lettering. The Mississippi banks' unrelentingly flat scene exacerbated the boredom of travel. For men like Henry, used to a constant litany of chores, enforced idleness could be agony. When not pitching into the daily routine of cleaning up after the animals and loading wood, they sat around smoking, chewing, whittling, and most of all, speculating.

As they proceeded south, signs of spring began to appear. Henry noted the "peach trees in bloom and the trees beginning to look green." The warmer weather made Henry's rough woolen clothing intolerably hot and itchy. He wondered how bad it would be when they reached the tropics.[24]

They began passing plantations. Each had a white board posted at the landing with the name printed in large block letters—Vidalia, Morrissiana, Withlacoocheer, Ballamagan, Morganzia, Chatham, Golden Grove—some a play on the owners' names, others reflecting their country of origin. The *Indiana's* momentum ebbed as she made frequent stops to unload sacks of corn and hogsheads of bacon. As the boat approached from a mile upstream, the steam whistle and roiling inky smoke alerted the plantation crew long before she came into view. Landing involved running the long rake of the bow onshore and turning a paddle wheel to steady the boat while goods were transferred. The forecastle served as a dock.

Henry shared with Abby that, "The river is nearly as high as it generally gets. Very many of the plantations are entirely overflowed—others are kept dry by embankments or levys and some few are above high water. Some of the negro quarters look like villages and very neat laid off in strait rows and almost always whitewashed; some almost as large as Camden."[25] This was his first time in the South, and he was both curious and appalled by its peculiar institution. Slavery rankled his northern-born, Methodist sensibilities. A real man was the product of his own labor.

As the riverboat paddled through Louisiana, keeping to the river channel challenged the pilot. It could be difficult to distinguish from the flooded, treeless plantations, particularly at night. More than one steamboat had found itself at dawn surrounded by submerged sugarcane fields and unhappy overseers, far from the river proper. But for the *Indiana*, the remainder of the trip was uneventful. She pulled into New Orleans at 2 a.m. on Sunday, March 23.[26] At first light, the deck passengers hurriedly quit the boat and reclaimed their land-legs.

CHAPTER 4
ST. ANTHONY'S FIRE

New Orleans presented Sam's company with a spectacular scene. Though an American city, it felt foreign, given its Spanish and French pedigree. It was the country's fifth-largest city and one of its busiest ports. Immigrants from around the world poured in, using the network of western rivers to stake land claims on the continent's interior. Though southern, the city had a substantial population of free colored people in all shades: octoroons (one-eighth Negro), quadroons, black as midnight, with these last being descended from refugees of the 1804 Haitian slave rebellion.

The first order of business for the company: find reputable lodging. They selected "a good house at the rate of one dollar per day—we could get for 50 cts or 3.00 per week but think best to pay higher than run the risk of getting into some place where we might stand a chance of getting into low company and probably getting eased of part or all of our funds," Henry told Abby.[1] The "good house" was the Western Veranda Hotel at the corner of Julia and Tchoupitoulas Streets.[2] After the rough accommodations on the river, they welcomed a little comfort.

Henry admired the city's cleanliness but not the inhabitants' disregard for the holy day: "The Sabbath alas is almost totally neglected—stores, shops, and every kind of business is pursued with as much apparent eagerness as on any other day with a few honorable exceptions." With a new elderly friend from the steamboat, he spent the afternoon searching, almost in vain, for a church service, "when we heard singing

39

and following the sound found a negros meeting of Methodists—we went in and heard a good sermon and went away I trust much edified."

While Henry sought spiritual succor, Sam and the company explored the less pious parts of the city. They likely picked up a copy of *The Times-Picayune* because the front-page ads boasted no fewer than seventy-two seagoing vessels. Only a handful offered passage to the isthmus. They preferred a steamship for speed, and a US Mail packet would be leaving on Friday. Steerage cost $45. Lieutenant D.D. Porter of the US Navy, while on leave between wars, commanded the *Georgia*.[3] It would land at Havana, Cuba, where those bound for Chagres would transfer to her sister ship, the *Falcon*.[4] That matter settled, the men perused the city's offerings. They had five days to revel in their freedom.

New Orleans burst with color. Graceful palmettos set the backdrop for a dazzling kaleidoscope: bougainvillea, magnolias, dahlias, and climbing roses. Live oak trees sported Spanish moss beards. Markets overflowed with fresh fruit. Ladies, flaunting the latest Parisian fashions and parasols, contrasted with the women back home in their sturdy dresses and unflattering bonnets. The patois of French mixed with English added to the exoticism. The French Quarter's ornate iron balconies, hung with baskets of ferns, mimicked the Old World, the chief difference being that these straight streets all met at right angles. No self-respecting European village would have tolerated such an abomination. But none of them had ever been to Europe, except Jake Liestenfeltz, born in Germany. Having emigrated at age four, though, he could not recall much. They walked for miles, finally able to stretch their legs after the river trip. This lot was used to covering long distances on foot.

Visitors crowded the city, some on their way home from California with pockets bulging with gold, or so it appeared to the argonauts from Indiana. "We see persons daily from California mostly with plenty of gold and a good many going," Henry wrote. "The accounts are favorable in general." Certainly, those who had not been successful in the mines did not crow about it; more likely, they made their expeditious way home to fall into the embrace of their long-suffering families. The *Georgia* was quickly selling its berths to outgoing travelers and filling the steerage compartment; it would be snug by Friday's departure.

The waterfront offered an opportunity to examine ships up close. Steamships, schooners, and brigs crowded the dock area, the masts and chimneys clogging the skyline. Rigging clanged against the masts in the briny, humid air. Crews hustled cargo. Cylindrical cotton bales sat stacked everywhere, waiting to be loaded onto seagoing vessels. The lofty fiber floated about, alighting like snowflakes on every surface. "This was cotton season. Every thing was a rush. Negroes were hauling cotton. Their masters gave them so mutch if they hauled so mutch cotton. They hauled in one hourse carts. They went on the trot and back on the run," recalled Pete years later. "There was where I say [saw] my first chane gan[g]. They were negros that would not work and they were forsed to work."[5] He did not share his opinion of this labor, but Henry told Abby, "Thee recollects the market cleaning in Philadelphia by a man hired for that purpose— this morning I witnessed the operation performed by a gang of women— black of course. They were scrubbing under the directive of white <u>men</u>."

At the upriver end of the levee, deckhands loaded riverboats with sugar, molasses, and fruit. Screeching, squabbling gulls and silent pelicans circled overhead, diving for scraps thrown from ship galleys and fish-processing boats. As the heat became oppressive, the men in all likelihood sought refuge in one of the plentiful saloons. Inside, tobacco smoke hung thick in the air, motes drifting in sunbeams sneaking through louvered shades. They sampled the local cuisine. Fresh seafood included pompano, shrimp, and crawfish. They may have tried that peculiar sweet/spicy local dish, gumbo, and later wished they had stuck to familiar fare.

For the first time in their lives, they were free of women, children, and chores—bliss. Their ancestors had migrated from eastern seaboard states, where men who had once been self-directed tradesmen and merchants, with some leisure time, were becoming wage slaves to the industrial juggernaut, working long hours in manufactories, killing themselves in coal mines, and losing a sense for the true meaning of life. These things drove a great number to flee from the east coast to California. But the Blackford group had already headed west, taking up axes, saws, shovels, and plows, retaining their souls in the process. Did California offer them the ultimate in self-fulfilling freedom? How would their lives differ when they returned home with their own pockets full of gold?

They were having quite the party, all except Humphrey Anderson. As his health declined, the others realized that boarding the *Georgia* on Friday would be unlikely. Although their company Articles dictated no one would be left behind, the men, including Humphrey's brother John, agreed to press on to Panama. Henry, feeling a fatherly responsibility, offered to stay with Humphrey as he recuperated. In their altered plan, they would save a little of their meager funds, $20 each, by going on a sailing ship rather than the overcrowded steamer. The brig *Josephine* would depart on Saturday. Henry and Humphrey would catch a steamship the following week, probably arriving in Chagres about the same time as the *Josephine*.

Humphrey had concealed his condition to avoid hindering the expedition, hoping it would pass and he could continue on with the rest. By Friday, Henry insisted Humphrey needed to see a doctor, so the two made their way north to Charity Hospital. They entered the imposing three-story neoclassical building, its two wings stretching to cover 290 feet along Common Street. It featured high ceilings, wide halls, and

Figure 4.1 Charity Hospital, New Orleans, Louisiana. Wood engraving. Credit: Wellcome Collection. Public Domain Mark.

many large, multi-paned windows. It was a massive and impressive building, designed to move refreshing air through its roomy wards.[6]

Charity, the largest hospital in the world, primarily served the immigrants flooding the New Orleans port and indigent city residents. Its name was synonymous with its mission—providing medical care to the poor. It served as a teaching hospital for the nearby medical college and had four principal physicians, a resident surgeon, and a visiting physician. In 1851, there were 18,420 admissions and 1,871 deaths.[7] The 10 percent death rate is not a condemnation but a testament to the quality of care.

A doctor examined Humphrey's reddened, swollen face and diagnosed erysipelas, a bacterial infection also known as St. Anthony's fire. Outbreaks of the disease occurred with regularity in New Orleans, along with many other diseases brought ashore by immigrants, who frequently suffered poor conditions on long trans-Atlantic voyages. Due to the severity of his case, the hospital admitted Humphrey and placed him in a ward. Henry stayed a while, until Humphrey had been made as comfortable as possible.

Beginning in 1834, the hospital housed an order of nuns. Henry explained, "Speaking of charity reminds me of the Sisters of Charity . . ."

> There are some twenty or thirty in the Charity Hospital—and one—as soon as H was fixed in bed—tapt gently at the door of the room and was told by one of the doctors she might come in. She inquired verry particularly about him—his family, residence, destination, complaint etc, and finally if he belonged to any church . . . He replied—I have not religion but wished to have before he died . . . She is in manner a perfect lady—kind and tender as a sister—if she is a fair representation of the order doubtless they do much good—relieve much distress. They seem a sacrificing, self denying Christian order of women but as cold as if passions were not part of their nature. She says she has a patient who was worse than H of the same complaint who is now in a fair way of recovery and thinks we may hope for a favorable change.

On Saturday afternoon, Henry and two others went to the hospital. John Anderson declined, telling Henry—*I can't bear to watch my brother die and be buried.* Henry shuddered in disbelief. He would never leave a loved one in the sole care of strangers in their final hours! But he stifled his ire and told himself to see things from John's perspective. Less than two years had passed since John and Humphrey's brother, Bazel, had died, and perhaps the pain was too fresh. Everyone had their own way of dealing with death and loss. This was the first test of the company's Agreement, and they appeared to be failing miserably, especially John Anderson.

When the trio arrived at Charity, they found Humphrey much worse. The infection had deprived him of his sanity. He could not recognize his friends and had nothing to say about his home or family. He lay on the white sheets, damp with fever-sweat, eyes closed, near death. Henry committed to staying until the end, but the other two returned to the group, as the *Josephine* would depart at five o'clock. "No doubt you are somewhat alarmed at my separation from the ballance of the company and prolonged stay in this place," Henry wrote to Abby. "But be encouraged for I feel in the line of my duty and believe I shall be sustained in doing to others as I should wish them to do to me in similar circumstances."

Henry lingered by the bed until, at 4 p.m., Humphrey finally slipped away and found his peace. Dispirited, Henry said a final prayer for the dead man. He was just thirty-three years old. Like his namesake uncle, Humphrey breathed his last far from home and the embrace of his family. With weariness in his stride, Henry withdrew. Already mourning the loss of his friend, he shared his woe with Abby: "I engaged a person to shave and lay him out and bought muslin for a shroud and then returned to my lodgings. Thee may well suppose depressed in spirits and dejected but I have the consoling reflection of knowing I have tried to do all that was in my power for him while lieving and shall see him decently intered."

After engaging an undertaker, hiring a hearse and carriage, and arranging for a shallow grave to be dug in the Charity Hospital Cemetery, Henry went down to the dock, expecting to wave the rest of the company goodbye, but the *Josephine's* departure had been delayed until Monday morning. He related the sad news. A somber group returned to the Western Veranda for another two nights. Henry had not really prepared himself for tragic outcomes, especially so early in the trip. What might happen as they proceeded through the tropics, the Pacific Ocean, and on to the rough-and-tumble mining communities?

Settled in his room later that evening, Henry added to the lengthy letter that he had begun March 21 as they passed Vicksburg, Mississippi. He wrote, "We feel our loss but at the same time it seems to have a tendency to unite the rest of us more closely together as we see the necessity of standing by each other—particularly as it falls to my lot to write to his friends and I feel very inadequate to the task. Doubtless it will be heavy tidings to all and hard to bear up under." He set aside the letter to finish later. He then pulled a fresh piece of stationery from his satchel and stared at it. How on earth to begin telling Harriet Havens Anderson that her husband was gone, her five children now fatherless?

While Humphrey checked into Charity Hospital on Friday, the steamship *Georgia* left on schedule, sailing out of New Orleans to great fanfare with 197 passengers aboard.[8] Sam Jones's gang was not among them. They would be taking the slow boat to Chagres. Sunday, they followed the crow-black hearse from the hospital to the nearby cemetery that Charity's board of directors had established during the cholera epidemic of 1849.

The men hoisted the simple pine coffin from the carriage, carried it to the freshly dug grave, and laid it on the moist, alluvial loam. Charity was among the few cemeteries with underground burials in New Orleans. Henry stood looking down on the casket and read from his Bible as the others bowed their heads, removed their hats, and, contemplating death, wrestled with conflicting emotions. After a prayer, they buried the box, turned their backs on their fallen comrade, and shuffled back toward the river.

On Monday evening, March 31, they once again stood at the wharf, waiting to board the *Josephine*. Nearby vessels, finally cleared through health inspections, disgorged their exhausted migrants. Facial expressions revealed their confusion. Interpreters stood by to get them where they needed to go: customs, quarantine, or the hospital. Soon the Indianans, too, would be strangers in a strange land. New Orleans was exotic, but it was clearly in America. Between there and San Francisco would be foreign territory, Spanish-speaking, and their first experience in a truly tropical climate.

Henry worried about how Humphrey's widow would take the news. Though he might have used the death as an excuse to turn tail and go home, he did not waver. He had certainly assured the families that he would look out for their husbands and sons. With this first failure, he foresaw hard times ahead.

Time to board. Henry and his companions bade goodbye to solid ground once more. They found their space in steerage, stowed their belongings, and returned topside. They watched as daylight waned, turning the quayside buildings to amber. Well into the evening, the *Josephine*'s crew threw off her mooring lines, and she drifted into the current. The effluent of innumerable people flushed out to sea by the massive Mississippi was, in turn, pushed back upstream by the incoming tide. It would take more than a night and the next day to leave the city stench behind, traverse the Delta, and reach past the low islands and bars across the river's mouth to open water.

As *Josephine* set sail, guided by a local pilot, she attracted less fanfare than the *Georgia*, but still, people on shore waved her off. The men aboard, for it was nearly all men, were mostly jubilant. Some passengers stayed at the rail to watch the wake peel away from the ship and to jabber about the sights they might encounter on the way to the isthmus. Others settled into cramped bunks to get a feel for the unsteady sensation of being on the water.

Levees lined the route to the gulf to keep the river from inundating the lowland surrounding it. Beyond the artificial bank, Henry saw nothing prominent, save for the roofs of planters' villas and Negroes' huts. Sometimes they passed floating islands, composed of driftwood and entire leafy trees, felled by high waters eroding banks far upstream. Sugarcane fields went on seemingly forever. Cane then gave way to enormous bulrushes, harboring all manner of estuarine life, including crocodiles. Once the pilot maneuvered the sailing vessel over the bars, a boat took him to La Balize, the village of fishermen, pilots, and their families at the south end of the Delta.

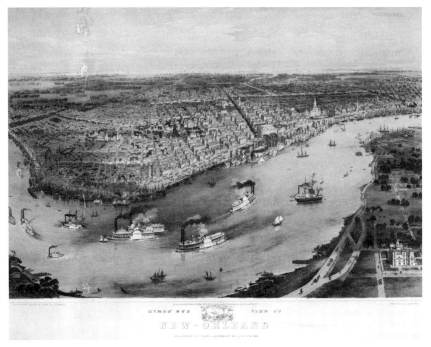

Figure 4.2. Bird's-eye view of New Orleans, 1851. Credit: The Miriam and Ira D. Wallach Division of Art, Prints and Photographs: Print Collection, The New York Public Library.

The river flowing into the gulf did not dissipate the bile thrust from the gut of the Mississippi Valley. It would be another day before they spied clear, blue water. But now, rather than the relatively smooth river current, the sea swelled beneath them. They had mostly fair weather, though clouds built up from time to time, casting their mottled deep-blue shadows on the water. They had chosen a good time to travel.

CHAPTER 5

CALIFORNIA, HO!

The *Josephine* was a three-masted brigantine, ironclad, and heavy in the water. Her mass of sailcloth required strong winds, but the gusts hit her head on, and she trudged through the Gulf. It took nearly two weeks to brush past Cuba's western edge. From there, doldrums hampered her progress. What should have been a ten-day trip took more than twice that.

Steerage was a step above steamboat deck passage. Class distinction disappeared. Attorneys and other professionals were as likely to be in steerage, on their way to pick rocks in California, as were the farmers, merchants, and blacksmiths. Rather than sleeping on cargo, they had bunks or hammocks. The crew provided food, though mealtimes could be akin to feeding at a trough. Men shoved their way to the buffet, grabbing what they could as quickly as possible, not wanting to be left hungry.

At first, most of the men, Henry excepted, spent hours at the rail, recycling their meals as fish food. Among the Blackford company, Jake, Pres, and Teach suffered the worst. "John Teach used to puke and insist on it he was not in the least sick," said Henry. "It was indeed laughable to hear him."[1]

Sam called a company meeting. They gathered in the shade of a sailcloth as the tropical sun hammered the deck and the ship rocked in calm waters, timbers creaking soothingly. Humphrey was on their minds. And money matters. Only four men (Sam, Harvey, John Anderson, and

Figure 5.1. The rush to dinner on board ship. Credit: *The Century Illustrated Monthly Magazine* V. 41 (1890–1891) "To California by Panama in '49."

Dennis) remained to cover the largest debt to Makepeace. Though the other five had their own liabilities, all nine agreed to share responsibility for Humphrey's portion. Some of it had gone to funeral expenses, but they would use the rest themselves. The logical arrangement relieved his widow of the burden.

When not moaning, leaning over the rails, or grabbing a bucket, the passengers sought entertainment to relieve the monotony. Drinking and gambling were favorite shipboard pursuits, but the Blackford men had sworn off these in their charter. Besides, they had no money to spare. Those who felt well enough to be on deck observed the sea life. They sometimes spotted porpoises diving through the waves off the bow. Flying fish might miscalculate and land, flopping, on the deck in front of a startled observer. Catching one could be a bit of sport.

Henry declined to participate in the frivolity; he had been a responsible, sober adult for so long that unwinding proved difficult. He worried that yielding even an inch to temptation would damn him. He did not trust his willpower and longed for a fellow Christian to bond with in solidarity. A Mr. Stephenson, who loaned Henry a theological tome, served this purpose. Henry spent as much time with him as he could without being rude. Stephenson's family was an exception to the testosterone-laden human cargo. He had spent enough time in California to know his future lay west. On this, his second trip, he brought his wife and four children. Henry clung to the family like a threadbare lifeline to his better self. He thanked the Lord for their company as the ship crawled its way through the Caribbean on a stingy breeze.

Henry was sociable, but most of the people on board were not the sort of company he preferred. His family became a principal preoccupation.

> I tried to look at my dear family . . . imagined you if in health enjoying your easter breakfast after family worship—which I feel assured is observed strictly and then class meeting and the converse of friends and above all the communion of the holy spirit . . . Perhaps thee would like to know how I spent the day— after thanks that I had been preserved through another night I arose (my only chance for prayers is in bed and even then amidst cursing, gambling and confusion) early as I mostly do—got my bible and Clarks Theology.

Reading was a favorite pastime for some, such as Henry. Journals became tedious and were set aside. Many spent time cleaning and re-cleaning their weaponry. Some, with foresight, brought board games such as checkers and backgammon. Some discovered their latent talents: artist, tailor, whittler, musician, storyteller, playwright. They put on skits, to the amusement of anyone whose ox was not being gored. Singing was popular, and the well-known "Oh, Susannah" became embellished with new lyrics pertaining to the California journey. The song prompted some to recoil in horror at the opening strains—*Gawd, if I hear that one more time!*

The seasonal shift in day length grew less pronounced, but the still-long hours gave the Blackford men an opportunity to reflect on why they were there, why they had left behind family and friends in search of metallic rewards. They could justify the adventure based on the value of hard currency, something not easy to obtain by farming in Indiana soil. It is safe to say they relished taking part in the Manifest Destiny that had the entire nation abuzz.

One day, Pete and others stood at the stern, watching a shark. "They would follow a ship 2 or 3 days to get food from the ship. I seen a small fish that thay called Pilot fish," he recalled. "They would swim in the sharks mouth and out off their gills."[2]

Henry also observed the large fish. "I have just been looking at a shark that is following us—he appears to me to be about 6 or 7 feet long but others say it is from ten to fifteen feet."

They had come equipped with guns and bowie knives—it would not do for a gold miner to wander around unarmed, naturally. One of the men drew his gun. *Pop!* went the first shot. The shark did not react. Another bullet blasted from the barrel. Still no reaction. After wasting a third round with no apparent ill effect on the carnivorous beast, the men got bored and wandered off to seek other amusements. On another occasion, "one of the passengers succeeded in shooting one of them in the head as he raised to the surface to take in a piece of meat tied to the end of a rope," Henry related. "The shot was fatal as he turned over like a log several times and then settled down head foremost and belly up settled out of sight accompanied by one of the others, if not all of them, as they were no more seen."

The wind finally turned in their favor. They arrived at the mouth of the Chagres River on April 23, and the *Josephine* dropped anchor. The passengers, ready to shed this iron cask bobbing in the waves, lined the rails, observing other ships at anchor loading people, freight, and mail headed from New Granada (as Panama was known then) to New York and other destinations.

Chagres's dirt streets had once been paved but had fallen to disrepair in the early 1800s. The village had little in the way of amenities other than transportation and two hotels, the Astor House and the Crescent City Hotel, the latter offering fine dining: stewed monkeys and iguana. Beef and pork were also available for the squeamish.[3]

San Lorenzo, a sixteenth-century Spanish fort, loomed above the north bank, its moss-covered gray stone sprouted like a natural outgrowth of the verdant cliffs below it. It had been reduced to ruins by the bucca-neer Henry Morgan. The sprawling edifice stood as a decaying testament to earlier invasions of gold snatchers and their impermanent existence.

Not many travelers over the isthmus in all those centuries gave a thought to their impact on the once-simple society there. The Spaniards had subjugated the Indians and converted them to Catholicism. They had also brought in African labor, and the three groups produced a rainbow of skin tones that Yankees seldom failed to remark on, including Henry, who said they were "of all shades from blackest to white, verry few of the latter excepting the transient visitors or travelers."[4] In the 1850s, it was the gold rushers' turn to transform Panamanian lives.

Below the fort, natives in dugouts and entrepreneurs with small steam-driven riverboats formed a mini-armada, all vying for lucrative dollars. Passage across the isthmus was in transition. Gold rush traffic fueled speculation for a railroad from the Caribbean to the Pacific coast, an idea that had been floating around for the past decade. Construc-tion began in 1850, but it would take several more years to complete. Until then, travelers crossed via boat up the Chagres River to Gorgona or Cruces, about forty miles, then by foot or mule to Panama, another twenty-six miles.

New Grenada had served as the crossroads of two continents and two oceans for centuries, and all the perils of each became concentrated on this narrow piece of land. Criminal behavior hindered some travelers. It had been a month since shocking murders occurred in Chagres. Two women, a child, and eight men, including John W. Steele of Indiana, had been brutally killed by robbers. The crime had been blamed on Carthag-inians (from Columbia), and at least a few had been caught and prose-cuted. Men returning from California could also be trouble because "the greater part were far poorer than when they first started to realise their golden dreams. And these . . . were as drunken and as reckless a set of villains as one could see anywhere. Stamped with vice and intemperance, without baggage or money, they were fit for robbery and murder to any extent; many of them I doubt not were used to it."[5]

Diseases stalked the migrants. Yellow fever became known as Pan-ama fever, Chagres fever, or jungle fever, brought in by foreigners and

53

spread by the local mosquitoes.[6] Insects swarmed in biting clouds, engulfing the travelers, crawling up their sleeves, flying into their eyes and hair, searching for a patch of bare skin, moisture, mining for salt and blood. Bonanzas of fresh flesh appeared on a daily basis. Malaria was the most often gifted disease. Even with its medical and criminal dangers, this shortcut held the advantage over the long, rough trip around the Horn of South America.

On shore, the Blackford company confronted the various options for getting upriver. At first, they planned to take a small steamboat for $8 apiece but then opted once again for frugality. In bungos, for the budget fare of $6, it would take them three days instead of one to reach Gorgona. Natives propelled the twenty-foot-long covered boats with oars and poles.

According to Pete, "They were large dark skin fellows with on only an apron tied around them." Before boarding a bungo with a few of his companions, Henry found an agent to get his latest letter onto the mail packet ship. The one-way conversation propelled his imagination. What was happening at home? How was Abby managing without him? Was Bedford following his instructions about the farm work to be done this month? He could ask all the questions in the world, but who knew if he would ever get answers.

They started upstream the same afternoon they arrived in port, managing the six miles to Gatun. Nothing like the gargantuan drainages that had taken them to New Orleans, the Chagres was only about 300 yards wide and hemmed in by monolithic jungle. Vines snaked around trees, binding them together into a solid mass of day-glow green, topping out above the canopy, and wearing blossoming bonnets of scarlet and magenta. In places, the draping branches of the understory dipped into the murky, olive-brown water, like the outstretched necks of watering horses. Colorful butterflies floated about, and exotic avian species splashed rainbow hues against the jade foliage. White-shouldered vultures lurked in the canopy, and herons waded in shallows near the banks. They camped at Gatun for the night, some onshore, and some at the bottom of the boats.

Figure 5.2. Gatun, the first stop on the Chagres River, showing a native bungo. Credit: *The Century Illustrated Monthly Magazine* V. 41.

Before daylight, "We were awoke by the howling of wild beasts on every side but what they were we could not find out as the men on the boat could not talk with us nor us to them. We thought some were wolves, they howled verry like them, another kind much louder we were informed were a small kind of lion and another kind large monkeys." Henry later observed primates, both large and small, multihued parrots, and a few alligators. The unsuspecting Panamanian fauna were frequent targets of bored Americans with guns and ammo to spare, much as the Caribbean sharks had been.

They started at first light and pulled into shore a couple hours later to make coffee and eat, doing the same at midday. Coffee could be had from the natives, but one traveler chose to go without when he discovered they had run out of sugar. Wondering what the serving girl would do about it, he followed her and watched as she got "a piece of sugar-cane, and commence[d] to chewing it, and occasionally she would eject the juice from her mouth into the coffee while it was being prepared outside the hut."[7] They stopped in the afternoon near a ranchito in time to cook supper before sudden darkness descended, there being no twilight in the tropics. Henry takes up the tale:

> Two New York steamers arriving at Chagres in the morning full of passengers, the foremost boats of them overtook us at this place and before ten at night there was twelve or fifteen boats crowded to overflowing and many of them highflyers or men of high life with their ladies intending a permanent residence. There were some naval and one or two land officers of high grade— judging from their actions they seemed to think they were cut loose from all restraint and as all had brought plenty of good drink there was little rest to be had midst the noise and revelry that was kept up most of the night. I kept watch on our boat until about three in the morning and then Teach watched while I slept till four when the moon arose and we started.

At times, the boatmen would forgo the poles, get into the water, and drag the bungos upriver. The hard work led them to take frequent breaks when they would disappear into the jungle and return with hearty servings of alcohol to fortify themselves for the next push upstream. Occasionally, they belted out phonetic versions of "Yankee Doodle" or the dreaded "Oh, Susannah" to the delight or dismay of the Americans. When his boat landed at noon, Henry stepped out onto the muddy bank and scrambled up. As he reached the top of the bank, where earlier arrivals were milling about, he heard a familiar voice.

It came as a shock to find someone he knew. But it was so. "I saw Harvy Brown of Portland [Indiana]. He informed me he started from home the same day we did and went to New York, took passage from there and arrived in Chagres the day after we did." Brown and his companions clearly opted for the speedier steam transport up the river.

From this point, the stream became harder to navigate with full loads, so some of the men, including Henry and Pete, opted to walk to Gorgona. Pete described arriving and heading overland to Panama. "We got to Gorgona. It was a[ll] bamboo huts. We stayed all night at an american who run a tavern. It was a nice frame house. We ate our supper and breakfast and paid 25 ¢ to get to sleep on the floor upstairs then the next morning we started for Panama and walked about 25 miles."

"I started nearly two hours after the rest of them," Henry explained, "staying to see the last of our baggage packed and on arriving close to Panama had to wait nearly half an hour for them to come up—on the road the train was scattered from three to four miles in length—seldom more than 3 or 4 together." Henry arranged for mules to carry their bags. The ill-treated animals, fed once a day on sugarcane tops, were one option for moving personal belongings between Gorgona and Panama. The locals would also carry up to 250 pounds on their backs, sometimes carrying people rather than luggage. Female travelers were taken aback at the skimpy attire worn by the porters; one remarked that "he who wore the least clothing was most in fashion."[8]

Henry and Pete did not report any threats from bandits, but the Indiana men did not make appetizing targets anyway. Luckily, they made the crossing before downpours became a daily occurrence. Even so, it was difficult ground to cover. Years of burro and mule trains, traveling more or less straight up and down the hills, had worn deep ruts on the slopes, exacerbated by heavy rains. In some places, the eight- to thirty-foot-high ruts were cave-like, darkened by a dense canopy of lianas and jungle trees. Before entering one of these narrow passages, riding travelers had to yell out "halloo" to warn people coming the other way—there was no room for passing. They slipped on paths of mucky red clay and sand slithering through a dense jungle. Manure spatters added another layer of ripe slime to slide through.

"When we got within six or seven miles of Panama we got on the old Spanish paved road and although done more than one hundred years ago it is almost as good as ever," Henry said. "Sometimes for a mile not a stone out of place and even the depressed places or crossways as perfect as ever."

Pete noted, "We walked from there on our road. We stopped at a Indian Tavern. He had cakes and soft drinks to sell. It was a dentz forest. There were no houses along the road. Then we came to a house, a palm leaf shac[k] where they sole whiskey. There was a pile of bottles about 3

Figure 5.3. Native hut between Gorgona and Panama. Credit: *The Century Illustrated Monthly Magazine* V. 41.

ft high outside the shed. We did not stop. We went on till we reached Panama."

Pete observed on approach, "There was this sid[e] of Panama about 50 acers that was cleared of[f] but it was not farmed. It had been farmed years ago. On this side of Panama we saw about 2 acers of bananows an[d] about 1 acer of watermelons." He had the impression of Panama being "a nice town. Panama laid out into the ocean. There was a wall around the town about 15 ft high. This wall was built about 300 years ago. All brick houses with tile roof . . . They had fine churches there."

Henry, being mature and with city experience, had a different take: "The town itself both within and out of the walls is most ruinous. The original buildings have been massive grand and large but they have mostly been suffered to run to ruin and those of a modern date are mostly poor and mean with the excepting a few within a year or two that are better. Take it altogether it is a distressful looking place and the inhabitants are in keeping with the place—worse if possible."

Dennis Lowry concurred with Henry: "The Natives of the Isthmus are ignorant indolent and filthy. They Live in miserable hovels coverd with grass, not as mutch Regulation about ther Buildings as their is among the Hottentots. Their is quite A number of them men wemen and children that goes Naked as they was Born. That Looks Ridiculous." Like Pete, he enjoyed eating watermelon in April.[9]

By evening, they saw the city's church towers and heard the incessant clamor of bells. Their triumphant march into Panama, through a dilapidated gate and archway, was tarnished by the poor condition of the bells. Many lacked clappers, being rung instead by boys holding stones, and most were cracked, issuing a sound like "a concert of tin pots and saucepans," according to one unappreciative audience member.[10]

Panama, established in the mid-seventeenth century, had about 8,000 residents, not counting transients. The houses, made of white-washed stone with red tile roofs, had roughly identical floor plans with wide verandas, interior courtyards, and window openings without glass. Originally quite grand and two stories high, they had fallen to disrepair, and all manner of semi-domestic animals and vermin swarmed nonchalantly through holes in the walls.

Figure 5.4. Panama City harbor in 1850. Credit: British Library, Public Domain via Wikimedia Commons.

Buzzards hunched on structures, competing with the dogs and rats for any scrap of food. "I seen on one building about 50 buzzards setting there. They were not allowed to be killed," according to Pete. Many cultures in the Americas and in Africa revered vultures as emissaries of the deities they worshiped. Natives of the isthmus may have had similar feelings about the birds.

The Blackford men knew they might be in the city a while and opted not to pay the going rate of $2 a day for lodging in town—assuming they could find space. A thousand people awaited passage to San Francisco. Instead, they chose a "very airy" place outside the walls, run by a Frenchman, that cost 30 cents a night. Pete thought the food tasty, but Henry's more refined palate was not satisfied. "We generally get a roll of bread sometimes two for ½ dime, coffee ½ dime per cup, dish of some kind of meat soup, potatoes, or rice, (I despise each) or a bottle of native beer very like ginger pop for ½ dime. We take what we like best and it generally costs from 2 to 3 dimes each per meal."

Henry completed his fourth letter to Abby, detailing their progress and plans for the last leg of their trip to California. He knew it would be months longer before he would hear from home, and it pained him. He told Abby he would not complain but complain he did. The men all around him behaved as if there were no reckoning. Vulgarity, drinking, and gambling were ceaseless. Even his companions had begun using foul language and drinking alcohol. He doubted his virtue could withstand it all. He closed his letter with as much optimism as he could muster, a blessing of low expectations:

> When we get to San Francisco I will write again and then let thee know where to direct to when thee writes—let me know how H. Havens takes the loss of her husband and everything that thee thinks will be of interest to any of us . . . With the exception of being tedious I have not found it near as unpleasant or hard to get along as I had anticipated. The weather is verry warm but quite bearable by being prudent and knowing. Love, farewell till thee hears from me again or till we meet in this or a better world . . . Tell the boys Wm and B to do all they can for

the comfort of the family and they shall not loose their reward. Tell the girls all to be of good cheer and mind their mother and I hope to be able to do something nice in a little way for them. Once more farewell.

HENRY Z. JENKINS

The next morning, they inquired about steamship passage. After the slow-going *Josephine*, Sam and company wisely determined that sailing to California would be folly. The steamer fares were comparable to the slow boats, and the journey would take roughly three weeks. When the company left home in March, the fare for steerage was $50 to $75. The US Mail Steamship Co. controlled the mail packet route on the Atlantic side of the isthmus, and the Pacific Mail Steamship Co. held the contract on the Pacific side. But that had not stopped them from running ships on each other's routes strictly for passengers. The two companies added steamers to their fleets for just the purpose, stimulating fare wars that led to steerage rates as low as $10—an unsustainable competition. As of April 1, Pacific had acquired the US Mail's Pacific fleet and vice versa, ending their rivalry. Given the demand for tickets, they could charge whatever the market would bear.[11] The current going rate was $150.

Sam, Henry, and company bristled at the elevated prices. No doubt checking here and there to see if there was a better alternative (there was not), they resigned themselves to using most of their remaining cash. The next departure, they were told, would be the small screw-driven *Columbus* on May 1. They handed over $1,350 for nine tickets. "We will have from 80 to 100 dollars each after arriving at San Francisco if nothing unfortunate intervenes and that will furnish us with tools, provisions to begin operations with," Henry said. It was a good thing they had been so frugal up to then. If the Indianans had had the luxury of foresight and the patience to stay in Panama for a few weeks, it would have been worth the wait. Eastern entrepreneurs aimed to get in on the lucrative market; new competition was on its way to Panama at that very moment. By mid-May, there were no fewer than six steamships in the harbor looking for passengers to California, and fares started dropping again.[12] The Blackford farmers landed on the peak of premium prices, the worst since 1849.

During the six-day layover in Panama, Pete and the others went to a river about a mile out of town to wash their clothes. They watched the locals, entirely naked, who performed the same function for hire, but again, these guys were on a budget.[13] So, they set to scrubbing their garments on the rocks with vigor, laying the damp clothes on hot stones to dry. It was a good idea to get in the habit because they could not count on finding anyone to do those domestic chores when they got to the mines.

The steamer *Columbus* was ready to embark, as scheduled. The men gathered at the beach, where the waves lapped limply in the tropical heat. Due to the height of the tides and shallow bay, ships anchored several miles out. Piloted by natives, small boats ferried passengers to the waiting seagoing vessels. As boarding time neared, Henry and his companions found themselves surrounded by boatmen vying for the chance to take their party—*Mistah, mistah! I got de best boats, de best price. You come see now!*

"Having concluded a bargain, they seized the passenger's belongings and made off for the beach, the owner following anxiously behind," recalled one migrant. "At the water's edge, the traveler climbed on the native's back, was carried through the surf, and was deposited in a bungo, which lay just beyond the breakers. This process was repeated until the frail craft was so loaded with men and goods that it seemed in imminent danger of swamping."[14]

Once again, the farmers felt their stomachs roil from the wave action, but the nausea soon passed. As they neared a floating flock of gulls, the birds rose like a cloud, then settled back in the sea at a safer distance, contributing to the vertigo. At last, the bungos reached the ship, which looked for all the world like the *Josephine*, with masts and rigging jutting from the main deck. The smokestack rising from the center, spewing the black plume characteristic of a coal-fired boiler, revealed the ship's true nature as a steamer. The skiff pilots pulled up alongside the hull and grabbed a line to steady the boat so the fifteen or twenty passengers could, one by one, clamber up the rope ladder to the deck above: a nerve-wracking transition for anyone, but particularly for those who could not swim.

If the *Josephine* had seemed crowded to Henry at the time, she now seemed, in retrospect, positively cavernous compared with the crush of flesh he had to endure on this last part of the journey. The *Columbus* carried a load of 220 passengers plus crew, including more women and children than had been on the New Orleans-to-Panama leg. Likely the close quarters with unhealthy people contributed to some minor illnesses among the Indiana company along the route. As usual, the men traded off keeping an eye on their baggage because larcenous types would rummage through bags and trunks hoping to find some squirreled-away treat: dried fruit, candy, a bit of liquor.

The California-bound travelers were grateful to not be at the mercy of the fickle winds, though a strong headwind did slow the ship to an extent. Sailing vessels, by contrast, had to venture far to the northwest, in the vicinity of Hawaii, in order to beat a path to San Francisco. The *Columbus* would head north, rarely, if ever, out of sight of land for the first part of the journey. Despite being close to shore, sometimes temptingly so—Pete remarked on seeing a man leading a train of mules that appeared the size of dogs from his vantage point—the ship stayed on course. The Pacific Ocean was yet another new experience for the men. The deep, cold water differed from the shallower, protected waters of the Gulf of Mexico and Caribbean Sea.

They stopped at only one port of call to replenish food and fuel: Acapulco. The *Columbus* took on "coal, watter and livestock—five beeves and several hogs and chickens out of number."[15] Loading the cattle proved quite the spectacle. After forcing them to swim to the ship, the crew roped them around the horns and hoisted them aboard, dangling with their entire weight on those lethal projections. Not surprisingly, they bellowed deafeningly, but the seamen, used to such complaints, ignored them. But they had to be wary of the flailing hooves as the animals were lowered to their pen in the hold. Some unlucky flunky then released the rope. This stop offered the only opportunity for passengers to disembark before reaching their final destination. Dennis Lowry recalled that "on the 15 of May the ship Landed at A small town in Mexico an took dinner with the Motley crowd."[16]

After passing Cabo San Lucas, the *Columbus*'s charted course carried the men beyond sight of land and into the sea's mercy. At night, sky and water merged, and only the million points of light above gave the passengers a clue to separate them. The moon provided solace that loved ones, no matter how distant, were viewing the same radiant orb. When fog bound them in its cool caress, they felt homesick as never before.

The variety of sea life added some interest to the journey. Pete said, "We saw many things. We saw sea turdles. Some weighed 500 lbs. Then we saw hair seals by the thousens. They are brown. They were about the size of a muskrat. When we reached lower California we seen all kinds of wild ducks by the thousand, all kinds."

The ship maintained a steady momentum northward, defying countercurrents and unfavorable winds. Being aboard was a tedious, unpleasant affair for the assembled horde. The same ennui, lack of exercise, and absence of privacy and personal space threatened nearly everyone's sanity. If the ship had landed anywhere south of San Francisco in California, many would have said to hell with it and hopped off, finding a way north by land. Passengers of Henry's nature found the company aboard a persecution. Hubert Bancroft, who did much to preserve the history of west coast development, described the feeling, "To the refined and sensitive, such an infliction, from which there was no escape for days and weeks, was torture. Of all the miseries I ever experienced on shipboard, sea-sickness, tempest, filth, and fever included, by far the worst has been the crowd, among whom there were always some supremely disgusting persons whose presence one could not escape . . ."[17]

Mining companies finalized plans for once they arrived—plans that would be jettisoned once the realities ashore became apparent. They fretted that the shipboard leisure had made them soft and they would not be able to compete with the hardy souls who had come by the overland route. Some sewed leather sacks called pokes to hold their anticipated gold. Others worked at transforming bolts of canvas into tents. Gambling and card playing continued apace. The food appeared to be palatable, or perhaps just unremarkable. It was the least they should have expected given the outrageous fares.[18] For the Blackford men, the voyage from Panama was largely uneventful. The men wrote letters, played games, or read. They stared at the wake. They slept. Henry studied his Bible and tried to block out the sounds of merriment from the other passengers. They all prayed for cooler weather. The engine droned ceaselessly, and its serenade accompanied the daily cycle of sleeping, eating, and daydreaming quite well.

Gradually, it turned a little cooler, to everyone's relief. Only minor illnesses bothered most on board. Just two deaths occurred during the passage: an infant, then later its mother.[19] Sam, Teach, and Harvey suffered minor bouts of fever and other ailments, but all felt well as the *Columbus* approached its destination. At last, the ship reached the Marin headlands. The Golden Gate lay before them. San Francisco was near at hand.

The strait received its apt name from explorer John C. Frémont a couple years before the discovery of gold at Coloma. He likened it to Chrysókeras, the "Golden Horn" harbor entrance to Byzantium. Likewise, he felt it would be a golden gate to trade with Asia. Early explorers may have either avoided the harbor entrance because of treacherous rocks or because they simply never saw it due to fog. The first European expedition to report it, in 1769, came overland. Sergeant José Francisco Ortega, the leader of a scouting party sent by Don Gaspar de Portolá to locate the Point Reyes headlands, reported back to Portolá that he could not reach Reyes because of the gaping channel. Juan de Ayala and the crew of the *San Carlos* became the first known Europeans to enter the bay in 1775.

The *Columbus* passed through the storied strait on the morning of May 23. What sighs of relief and subsequent jubilation for passengers weary of the long trip. But a quick landing was not in store. The tide was out, and the ship ran aground on Tonquin Shoal. And stuck there.[20] The city lay tantalizingly close. They had come over 7,000 miles. Now, here they were, in view of the land of gold, and they could do nothing but wait for the tide to turn. Oh, the frustration of it all. What agony! But they endured this as they had everything else, with resignation, though there may have been some underlying seething going on. At last, the sea swept back into the bay, and they floated once more. Soon enough, these neo-conquistadors would take their turn at pillaging the continent of its wealth.

CHAPTER 6
A TIME TO SOW

Uncouth men and women may become new settlers, but weak and cowardly men and women are not likely to brave the toils and dangers of pioneer life. Moreover, these toils and dangers invigorate the brain, and effectuate a strength of character which ease and luxury only hinder and prevent.

—R.S. Taylor, quoted in Montgomery's *History of Jay County Indiana*

Spring 1851—Blackford County, Indiana

After the miners left Trenton, their families settled back into daily routines. Despite the community being short ten able-bodied men, spring rituals began in earnest in March. The people of Blackford and Jay, like others in the west, relied on maple sugar for early spring calories and flavoring, so as the sap began rising, they tapped the trees, letting the sweet juice drip into buckets. They boiled it down for hours, wafting the woodsy sugar scent and setting mouths to watering. Then children and teens flocked for a taffy pull—just one of the many entertainments that doubled as work.

For several weeks, men cleared land. They felled and trimmed the trees, then took turns gathering at one another's property for a logrolling. On the appointed day, all the neighborhood men, carrying their log hooks, assembled for the heavy job of moving scattered boles into piles

Figure 6.1. A maple sugar scene. Credit: *The Farmer's Every-Day Book,* 1854.

to be burned. To make the process more fun, rival teams stacked their assigned tree trunks as fast as possible. Frequently, the teams were led by opposing candidates for local office. They also competed in various feats of strength, all for bragging rights. The women prepared a substantial meal while the men grunted and sweated through their woolen shirts. The dogs, being dogs, chased squirrels and followed toddlers around, hoping to snatch a snack from an unwary, pudgy hand. Laborers expected the property owner to provide whiskey to reward their efforts (though sometimes a devout temperance man got away with not providing libations). Whenever collective tasks could be turned into a party, the settlers took advantage.

As in other pioneer communities, the Indianans relied on each other in myriad ways. Rugged individualism is a persistent myth, belied by numerous firsthand accounts. This reliance was not always simple neighborliness. Favors—sharing the bounty of a hunt, giving some homemade product, or caring for the sick, for example—could be perceived as an obligation to respond in kind or to offer a form of payment.[1] In this area of Indiana, it appears a great deal of give-and-take without obligation occurred in the mid-century, likely because of the close kinship ties.

On the other hand, many tools were considered community property, expected to be loaned to whomever had need. When crowds gathered to perform a service such as barn-raising or logrolling, the recipient had a commitment to do the same for others. The county government also relied on labor as a form of taxation. Men had to devote a set number of days annually toward building roads. Anyone attempting to shirk these duties or trying to live as an outsider would suffer scorn. Some were willing to accept contempt to avoid unwelcome prying eyes and judgments. Rural life could oddly feel more oppressive than urban crowds.

Prospects for a good fall harvest looked promising. March saw sufficient moisture, most of it falling as rain. April started off with showers, though a hard frost hit mid-month.[2] Still, it seemed a major improvement over the bad years of the mid-1840s.

Bedford Jenkins's workday got off to an early start. Though his older brother, Will, was around, Will had his wife and coming baby to occupy his mind and energy. Thus, it fell to seventeen-year-old Bed to be the man of the house. His mother, grandmother, and sisters turned to him when they needed a masculine favor. Though his health could be touch and go, he shouldered the load admirably. He strode to the paddock, to the two horses kept there, where previously there had been none: Fan, who knew the plow, and an unbroken colt. Henry had purchased them from William Ransom before leaving, perhaps trying to make up for his absence from the family workforce. Bed would break the colt to the walking plow so he could turn over cover crops or loosen the soil in new fields to plant corn and wheat. Though the heaviest chores fell to him, the rest of the family had plenty of work.

For the Jenkinses, clearing land was just one of many spring activities. Their seven-year lease required them to plant orchard trees, which they had been doing for the past six years. Henry had also made most of the payments on eighty acres a mile east (the land he mortgaged to Joseph Wilson), where they would move the following spring when the county lease expired. They had much work to do there, as well.

While tending to their daily activities, Abby and Ann Jenkins, along with the families of the other miners, stifled their anxiety about the travelers while awaiting any correspondence from them. The nearest post office lay eight miles northeast in Camden, so anyone heading into town from the neighborhood picked up the mail for everyone. In March, Abby received Henry's first letter, mailed from Cincinnati, detailing their activities to that point. Receiving news so soon after the men left may have eased Abby's mind a little. Henry's correspondence would carry her along on the journey, if only in imagination.

By mid-April, the letters from New Orleans arrived. Abby unsealed hers to read descriptions about the places and things they saw along the Ohio and Mississippi Rivers: the Louisville canal, the slave quarters, the flooded city of Napoleon, Arkansas. Henry probably intended his words to comfort her, but instead, they revealed that he already had misgivings about leaving home. A fine time to think of it! Abby surely wished he had come to his senses before ever taking money from Makepeace. Henry also had a message for William Ransom, telling him to wait another year before following; the season was already getting late for travel through the tropics. Willing or not, William stayed put.

Reading on, she came to the first sign of trouble; Humphrey was ill, then so suddenly gone. The shocking news had an immediate impact but then subsided. Death so often came unexpectedly. Learning John Anderson had not stayed by his brother's side, though, was different. Hopefully, Henry had not told the Anderson family. But the letter Abby held would be shared with others. Abby excelled at grapevine communications and knew this would not remain a secret.

Thankfully, Henry and the others were still well. That one or more of the men would take ill and die on the journey could not have been a surprise, but the Andersons and Ransoms had not expected it quite so soon. They did not have a body to bury and mourn over, compounding their suffering. The oldest brother, Asa Anderson, now had a second estate to usher through probate. For their aging father, William C. Anderson, the situation looked dismal. His family legacy was crumbling with two adult sons gone. And it was possible that John might not return from this California humbug, either.

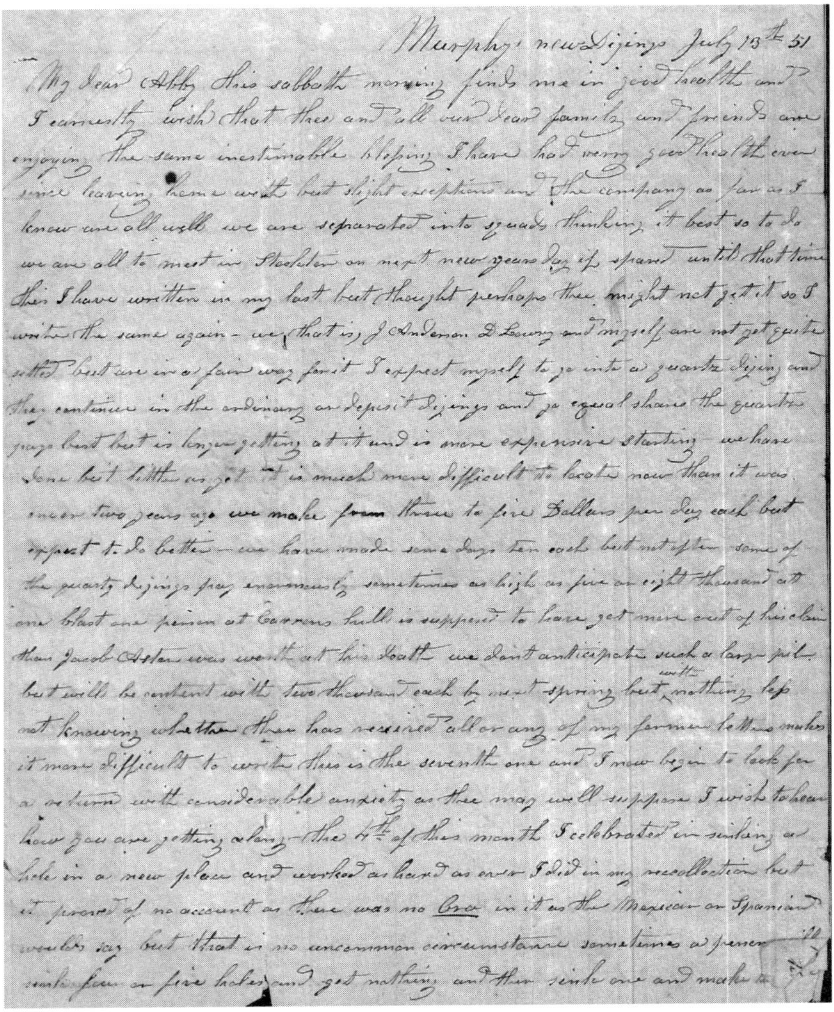

Murphys new Diggings July 13th 51
My Dear Abby this sabbath morning finds me in good health and
I earnestly wish that thee and all our dear family and friends are
enjoying the same inestimable blessing I have had very good health ever
since leaving home with but slight exceptions and the company as far as I
know are all well we are separated into squads thinking it best so to do
we are all to meet in Stockton on next new years day if spared until that time
this I have written in my last but thought perhaps thee might not get it so I
write the same again - we (that is, J Anderson D Lowry and myself are not yet quite
settled but are in a fair way for it I expect myself to go into a quartz digging and
they continue in the ordinary or deposit diggings and go equal shares the quartz
pays best but is longer getting at it and is more expensive starting - we have
done but little as yet it is much more difficult to locate now than it was
one or two years ago we make from three to five Dollars per day each but
expect to do better - we have made some days ten each but not often some of
the quartz diggings pay enormously sometimes as high as five or eight thousand at
one blast one person at Carsons hill is supposed to have got more out of his claim
than Jacob Astor was worth at his death we dont anticipate such a large pile
but will be content with two thousand each by next spring but with nothing left
not knowing whether thee has received all or any of my former letters makes
it more difficult to write this is the seventh one and I now begin to look for
a return with considerable anxiety as thee may well suppose I wish to hear
how you are getting along - the 4th of this month I celebrated in sinking a
hole in a new place and worked as hard as ever I did in my recollection but
it proved of no account as there was no Ore in it as the Mexican or Spaniard
would say but that is no uncommon circumstance sometimes a person will
sink four or five holes and get nothing and then sink one and make

Figure 6.2. Letter from Henry Z. Jenkins at Murphys to his wife Abby, dated July 13, 1851. Credit: The Huntington Library.

The extended family looked after Humphrey's widow, Harriet, and five children, but the reality of his eternal absence hit them hard. The littlest two would never remember their father. Being a "California widow," she might have accepted, but being a real widow shattered her. Surrounded by people who loved and cared for her, loneliness enshrouded her, and perhaps a sense of guilt. Had Humphrey been ill before he left home? Could she possibly have treated him and saved his life? Cures for erysipelas could be found in the newspapers—a sassafras and lye poultice and a bit of saltpeter in the drinking water were said to be effective cures for the disease if caught early on.[3]

Fresh as the pain in her heart was, practical matters intruded. Harriet would need to consider remarrying at some point. But maybe she could make it on her own. Her mother and older sister had also been recently widowed; they could help each other out. In fact, Harriet had virtually no control over her husband's estate. She could not even manage her own children's inheritance. They would be appointed a guardian for legal matters. Robert Ransom eventually took on this responsibility.

Harriet was one of five children born to James Havens and his second wife, Phebe. Harriet also had four older half-siblings. After their father's death in 1849, Harriet's brother, Sealy Havens, became the de facto head of the family. Sealy had signed as surety on the big note to Dr. Jones, enabling Humphrey to go west. Harriet could not hold that against him, though. Humphrey's brothers, Asa and William T., had also signed the note. They all hoped to cash in on the gold. As she mourned her husband, her fate and that of her children weighed on the young woman.

Ann Ransom's daughter, Cordelia, was born in January. In May, Jane Jenkins took her turn at motherhood. Elizabeth Ransom, having given birth eleven times herself and pregnant once again with what would be her last child, was well-equipped to help her daughter with the birth of the baby girl that Will and Jane named for her. Known to all as "Lizzy," the bundle of joy joined her cousin, Cordy, and the two girls became bosom buddies.

Having great-grandchildren helped Ann Jenkins stay light-hearted, though she pined for her son, Henry. The two infants spent many a day with their grandmama Abby, who took delight in watching them. It was such a shame Henry was not there to share the experience. The two women re-read his letters in lieu of his physical presence.

My dear and much loved wife . . . often do I think that it must be a large pile indeed to pay us for the sacrifice of the comforts of

home and all its endearing ties . . . Tell Bedford to try and do the
verry best he can in manageing and in makeing his mother and
family as comfortable as he well can . . . Several of the company
are writeing but as it was understood for each family on receipt
of letter to communicate to the others, please do so as far as
practicable and now in conclusion my best love and well wishes
to you all and in truth and sincerity I commend you to the care
and protection of our common Father until we meet again if not
in this I trust in a better world above.[4]

As she read, Abby contained her frustration that she would have to
wait until summer to know where to write so that Henry could receive
mail. She had plenty to say to him. It would simmer and fester in the
meantime.

As for news from California, E.D. Pierce wrote to the Ransoms
explaining why he had not returned that winter as he had promised:
too much snow. When Abby Jenkins read the letter, she had a different
take. "I rather guess from the tenor of his letter he has not been as successful as was intimated or he has spent more than he thought of."[5] If
a smart young man like Pierce, who had gone out with the first wave of
argonauts, could not make money, was there any hope for those going
out in 1851 or later? Surely, the gold would start to run out soon. Pierce
had begun running a pack train between Shasta City and Scott Bar in
northern Shasta County, where new discoveries drew miners from the
Southern Mines and from Oregon to the north. Abby knew Rebecca
Jones awaited his return. Perhaps Sam Jones, who had not met Pierce
during his visit to Barnesville, would meet up with his sister's fiancé out
in California. But surely, both would be back home by the following summer. Rebecca must have saintly patience to wait indefinitely for a man to
fulfill a promise of marriage.

Rebecca was not the only one waiting for a forty-niner to come
home. The Jenkins's friend, Joseph Wilson, still heard nothing from or
about his son, Willis. He did not want to believe the young man had met
his end. Willis had survived his stint in the Army during the late war
with Mexico. That itself was a feat. Wilson held out hope that Henry

would have luck finding news of the prodigal son, if not Willis himself. Given the rash of murders in the mines, anything could have happened to him.

The Indiana papers had reported the grisly murders at Chagres, committed by ruffians from Columbia. The news regularly had stories about "Judge Lynch" justice in California. It did not seem a fitting place for a sensitive, religious man such as Henry Jenkins. He could be tough, though. Pugnaciousness permeated rural culture, and Henry had gotten into his share of scrapes. While attempting to appeal his Chandlee judgment in 1844, he had assaulted the estate's attorney, Moses Jenkinson, and paid a fine of less than a dime.[6] But a fistfight paled in comparison to the knife and gun violence in the gold mining regions. How Henry would fare in that environment was anyone's guess.

PART II
A CONTINENT APART

Figure map of southern California. Map of San Francisco, Santa Clara, and the Southern mining region.

CHAPTER 7

GREENHORNS

It's a funny thing—I don't know any better lip-buttoner than what gold is; it will dry up a man that's ordinarily as gabby as a magpie . . .
—Robert Lewis Taylor, *The Travels of Jaimie McPheeters*

May 1851—California

San Francisco looked like none of the ports they had seen before. Cincinnati modeled Yankee efficiency; New Orleans, where the steamboats from the mighty Mississippi met their seagoing cousins, was a chaos of international commerce; overrun Chagres and Panama were dedicated to moving passengers across the isthmus. San Francisco, formerly Yerba Buena, the "sweet herb," was a supernova. Henry found it to "far surpass our expectation in point of size and appearance."[1]

Seamen had watched the tiny village turn into a thriving urban area in record time. So many ships came into the harbor, disgorging not only passengers but also captains and crews as well, that the abandoned vessels became an extension of the city. The packet-ship captains imposed strict disciplinary measures to ensure their deckhands did not join the argonauts. Still, the city harbor sprouted a forest of masts, liberally spattered with guano and acquiring a patina of algae and barnacles. One observer noted, "These ships had a very old, ruinous, antiquated appearance, and at first sight, gave me an impression, that this new-born city had been inhabited for ages, and was now going to ruin."[2]

The ships were steeped in the brine until the day some enterprising person gave them a new purpose, converting them into storehouses or hotels. Some had run aground, becoming immersed not in water, but mud, eventually fronting on the newest boulevard. Fill dirt gradually claimed many of the hulks. Some remain buried under the city. Though stone and brick buildings rose on many lots, the city was still susceptible to fire.

Saws grated and hammers pounded the ears of the passengers arriving on the *Columbus*. They poured onto the wharf and took in the sight of the burgeoning city, though a large section of the downtown area had been laid to waste just weeks earlier. The May 4 inferno devastated a large portion of the business district; damages were estimated at $12 million.[3] The residents began reconstruction as soon as the embers cooled enough to be cleared away.

The Blackford company disembarked, thankful to be back on terra firma. The dock, solidly in place, seemed to rock them as they regained their land legs, a sensation that would take days to fade. Henry wanted to explore the city, not in a rush to get to the mines. First, he had a promise to keep. He located a city directory to look up Willis Wilson, perhaps even E.D. Pierce. Their names were not listed. The name Sam Brannan caught his eye. Sam Brannan was familiar to anyone who followed the news from California. The Mormon elder was one of California's earliest and wealthiest entrepreneurs, and he was well known as the man who publicized the gold find back in 1848.

Henry thought to call on him but had no time. His companions had no interest in tarrying. They had found a steamboat to carry them to Stockton. From there, they would be off to get their gold. The men's impatience had roared back to life, and they pressed Henry to hurry up and get out of the city. Without even leaving the wharf, they boarded the boat for $3 each. Evening dappled the sky as they pulled out into the bay. They cruised past Alcatraz Island, sporting a lone house on the rocky outcrop. For once, Henry and Pete agreed that the supper on board was fine, indeed. They paid another $1.50 each for the meal "but never set down to better in the States," Henry remarked.[4] They made the most of the dining experience, knowing their rations at the mines would be bland and monotonous by comparison. Plus, they would be cooking for themselves most of the time.

As night fell, the *Jenny Lind*, named for the popular singer then touring the country, chugged at a good clip up the San Joaquin River toward the busy jumping-off point for the Southern Mines. The decks bulged with goods headed for the makeshift towns dotting the foothills. The passengers included miners heading back to their claims, new arrivals, merchants, and gamblers. Amid the crowd, the Blackford men enjoyed their last night of leisure and planned for a bustling day at the break of dawn.

Another fortune seeker heading to Calaveras County took the same journey and described the scene:

> When daylight again appeared we were in the San Joaquin River which is a River to be remembered when once seen. The country as far as the eye could reach was low level & mostly covered with water in which was growing long grass so thick you could not see into it 10 steps no more [than] 3 feet in many places & in many places were large ponds on the waters of which were sporting & feeding thousands of water fowl of all descriptions. Through this Italy of Lagunes & Grass wound the Rio San Joaquin a narrow verry croked and deep & muddy stream . . .[5]

The Calaveras River, flowing out of the Sierra Nevada, watered the land around Stockton. In the valley, it branched out to form several sloughs, rich with tule rush and abundant fauna. The sloughs were marshy from spring runoff until early summer and were dry the remainder of the year. The Northern Valley Yokuts, the native tribe of the area, used the tule to build their dwellings and kayak-like boats. They harvested the grasshoppers, plentiful in the reeds and grasses, as a protein-rich food source. The San Joaquin River teemed with salmon, trout, and sturgeon. Larger game foraged on vegetation that could grow tall enough to obscure even the most impressive elk or wild horse.

Jenny Lind traveled through the night, depositing her load of people and merchandise at Stockton. Henry expected to see another boomtown filled with hotels, saloons, liveries, shops, and blacksmiths; instead, his eyes beheld a sea of tents. Around the time of the conflagration in San Francisco, Stockton had also been leveled by fire. "Doubtless they were both the work of Incinilators," he said. People were prone to blame city fires on arsonists, but given the rowdy society and lack of safety measures, most probably began accidentally. From the ashes arose a canvas phoenix, populated by merchants eager to supply the new arrivals with their kits. "They are building again as fast as they can. Carpenters wages in Francisco is from 8 to twelve dollars per day and in this place 12 is the common price so that if we cant make anything in the mines I at least will not starve by turning to my trade, but the accounts from the mines is more and more encouraging the nigher we get to them."[6]

Though Henry had gradually exchanged his carpentry for farming when he moved to Indiana, he still enjoyed his first trade. There is something particularly satisfying about watching the framing of a new building taking shape. The smell of sawdust from mitered trim. The warmth in the now-dead yet somehow still-vibrant wood. The beauty of the grain, whether pine, oak, walnut, or hickory. Midwestern pioneer communities had previously held promise; it was now California's turn to grow and thrive—an exciting prospect for Henry. But he opted not to make Stockton his final destination.

Like Sacramento, which evolved from Sutter's Fort, a European immigrant, Charles M. Weber, founded Stockton. Unlike self-proclaimed "Captain" John Sutter, Weber earned his Captain title fighting against Mexico, first with Sam Houston's Texan army, later as part of the California contingent in the Mexican-American War. Weber wished to establish a cattle ranch in the San Joaquin Valley. In 1843, before he had established Mexican citizenship, he persuaded a partner to petition the Mexican government for a land grant in the valley. The grant—over 48,000 acres—encompassed what was then known as French Camp, for the Hudson's Bay Company fur traders.

Where the San Joaquin River met a Calaveras slough, Captain Weber established his ranch. When he heard, in March 1848, of the gold strike on the American River, Weber formed his own company to prospect the nearby foothills. The company included John Murphy and

Henry P. Angell, who would go on to establish their own mining camps after Weber disbanded the company in September. Sensing the oncoming rush, Weber capitalized on his advantageous location and set about turning his ranch into a supply hub. He laid out a town grid and started building. Some called it "Weber's settlement" or continued using French Camp, but the founder knew it needed a proper name. His inclination leaned toward Tuleburg or Castoria (in honor of the beaver). Instead, he settled on Stockton because Commodore Robert F. Stockton had made promises to him at the close of the war, promises the Commodore never kept. Weber later expressed regret for not sticking with Castoria. As of 1850, French Camp officially acquired its new moniker.[7]

As commerce and mining moved in, the need for agricultural land became evident. The exploding population could not feed itself on imports alone. The San Joaquin Valley began developing into expansive farms and ranches, draining the wetlands in the process. Even so, Henry would have heard the cacophony of egrets, ibis, ducks, and other waterfowl. Looking to the east, he saw the land rise gradually, sparse of trees, redolent in grass. These foothills had been grazed by the Californios' cattle for many decades. Beyond the low hills, far in the distance, the peaks of the Sierras wore their white cloaks year-round.

Miners and settlers roamed Stockton's wide dirt streets. Sam and company looked around, choosing their supplies. They would rely on staple foods such as flour, sugar, and preserved meat. If they did not inspect their purchases carefully, they could be in for nasty surprises. In Stockton, though, the men had time to be selective. Miners were not easily taken advantage of as a rule. They knew useful goods from those which were a waste of money. This group was particularly savvy; at a time when most sea-faring argonauts expected to spend $600 to $1,000 to get to the mines, the Indianans managed the feat for a mere $250 each, leaving them with enough to survive on as they got their bearings in the gold diggings.

Sam completed their purchases and arranged for a pack train to haul the food and other supplies. Henry, meanwhile, found a convenient perch from which he could comfortably write a letter. He instructed Abby to send mail to them at Stockton.

"My Dear Abby—Knowing thee would be anxious to hear from me I embrace the first opportunity of informing thee of our whereabouts. We arrived at this place about ½ past eight this morning, all in excellent health and in good spirits at the prospect of shortly being settled down to work." Though intended to be shared with friends, he did not hesitate to include personal messages and instructions to the family. He also had questions to ask, knowing well that a timely answer was impossible. "I wish particularly to know whether you kept the horses I bought of Wm R and whether he got started for California as he intended . . . before you get this you will know how the wheat crop turns out and recollect it is to be sown again this fall if possible . . . tell Bedford again to put on the man continually and I will not forget him."[8]

Henry clearly had mixed feelings about his son-in-law following in his wake to California. His and Abby's letters reveal their concern about the wanderlust in William's heart. Would he decide to come out west, leaving Henry's daughter and granddaughter, just as Henry and his companions had done? Or maybe worse, would he bring Ann and Cordelia with him? At least Henry and Abby's sons, Will and Bedford, seemed content to remain at home. He asked Abby to "remember me to mother, Wm Jenkins, Wm Ransom & Ann & Jane and kiss the little wean if it has come to town—tell E[mma] she must not get married before Pap comes home." He knew Will and Jane's baby had probably arrived by then. In reference to his companions, Henry dropped the first hint that this trip might last longer than they had said it would. "If our present anticipations are realised the most if not all of us will return this coming winter—but if not some will stay another season."

As the packer loaded the gear, they took their midday meal in town and then were ready to set off. Henry hustled to finish his letter. He mentioned the two mining camps they were considering: Murphys New Diggings or Mariposa. Just before sealing and mailing the letter, folded to be its own envelope, he scribbled, "Mira posa is our destination." But the company did not go to Mariposa. Nor did they march to Murphys. Something was amiss with the decision-making process in the group.

Nine opinions had to be taken into consideration, based on sketchy information, on the fly, in a place none of them had ever been to before.

Most likely, if the men were still getting along, Sam, as president, would have had the final say in the initial destination. The location could affect the financial outcome of their venture. But obtaining accurate assessments of each mining region was difficult. Successful miners had learned to keep secrets, unlike the early days when there seemed to be room and gold enough for everyone. For Pete and some of the others, the destination probably was not as important as just getting somewhere, soon. Two and a half months of close contact had fractured the group along personality fault lines. For now, though, they stuck together on this, their second day in California.

As the sun set behind the massif known as Mount Diablo, the golden rays washed across the distant foothills and turned the snowy Sierra peaks a bright salmon hue. The mule driver hauled their outfit, and the group began the long trek across the San Joaquin Valley. They felt the dying warmth of the sun on their backs as they followed their lengthening shadows into the dusk.

Approaching the mining region from the southwest, they saw the gradually ascending hills of Calaveras County, dotted with the spreading, evergreen limbs of live oak trees, appearing like a well-tended, albeit steep, orchard. Further east and upward, the manzanita tangled with other shrubs, punctuated by tall pines—emerald lords surrounded by minions. To John Anderson, familiar with eastern Ohio hills, the terrain felt a bit like home, but to Pete, used to Indiana flatland, standing in the narrow valleys and looking up was like being a gopher peering from its hole. They arrived at the Mokelumne River, where supposedly the bars—rocky islands in the river channel—paid well.

The Mokelumne flowed westward down a rugged ravine. While the river flowed green, its banks flowed crimson. Mobs worked the shoreline, dressed in the standard mining outfit: red shirts, dungarees, boots, and slouch hats. The river had been mined from the earliest days of the rush. But when Henry and company arrived, it was "the most unfavorable time for mining that can be—the river being too high to work the bars to advantage and there is no water in the gulches or dry digings, but the rivers will be down in 3 or 4 weeks and then we hope times will be better."[9] Even if conditions had been favorable, their chosen destination had been picked-over well before their arrival.

An estimated 80,000 miners, ten times the 1850 population of Indianapolis, were combing the Southern Mines and getting tight-lipped.[10] As Henry put it, "there are new digings found almost every week—some verry rich and yet it is no easy matter to find a proffitable place for the simple reason that there are so many on the look out and they are all verry sly and close mouthed and a new comer has but a small chance."[11]

To the groaning terrain, they added yet another burden of hopefuls seeking pay dirt. "We find every kind of people here that have ever been seen in any place almost—there are French, Spanish, English, Irish, Scotch, Dutch, Swiss, Chinese, Native Indians, Mexicans, Negroes, Portugeese, Italians, Genoese, Islanders of the Pacific and representatives from every state in the union in abundance, Russians, Poles and many others," he told his family.[12] Anglo miners were interspersed with abundant Hispanic groups and some native Miwok encampments here and there.

The area south of the American River, drained by the San Joaquin, became known as the Southern Mines and had extreme cultural diversity. The Northern mines, extending up the American, Feather, and Yuba Rivers, contained the first discovery site and the earliest mines but fewer ethnic groups. After 1850, mining regions opened in the far northern part of the state in Trinity, Shasta, and Siskiyou Counties, an area predominantly populated by Anglos and local tribes.

Many Americans did not know that the earliest migrants to arrive in the rush had more than a time advantage. The first to hear of the gold came from parts of mainland Mexico, Chile, and China. These were not random travelers. A combination of political circumstances at home, and their skill set, drew them to the gold fields. These men had mining experience. They knew their rocks and how to find what they were after.

Some Chileans brought peones—virtual slaves—to work their claims. American Southerners brought slaves as well, disregarding the state's prohibition. How could the Blackford group compete with such labor forces? Like sea lions attacking a ball of bait fish, there were more and more "predators" devouring a shrinking supply of gold.

For years, newcomers had arrived at the river and gazed at the glitter resting on the dark, sandy bed, their hearts pounding with the thrill of discovery. Experienced miners nearby chuckled at their naivete—*That there's fool's gold, you fools: pyrite. Real gold is heavy and sinks away. It never sparkles.* The newbies had a lot to learn.

If the Blackford men were lucky, they found someone like Jacob Crum to explain the basics:

> Gold is found in the ravines, gullies, and in the beds of streams. . . . We generally have to dig from one to five feet to find it. There are places where they dig from forty to eighty feet, and if they are lucky to strike it, they take out from $1,000 to $20,000 of the finest gold. . . . Gold is generally found deposited on the rock or on a hard blue clay ; it being heavy it sinks down on to some substance that will retain it. . . . All diggings have their own peculiar shaped gold ; nearly all of them differ as to shape and color. . . . Gold partakes more or less of the earth in which it is found as to color, (but it all seems to be tinctured a little with *yellow*.)[13]

As Crum pointed out, the gold was not pure; it consorted with all sorts of mineral ne'er-do-wells, most often quartz, but also silver and a variety of other metals and stone. Placer mining can be a solitary activity. Iconic images of the miner—with his pie-plate pan, crouched by a rocky stream, unshaven, haggard, clothes in shreds, focused and driven by obsession—perpetuate this idea. But more advanced mining methods required cooperation. Nine miners working a placer claim was too many, given the crude instruments at the beginning of the rush. Later methods required larger groups.

One or two men could work a simple cradle, three or four a long tom. Either method employed a wooden box with a hopper and strainer at one end to sift out larger material and riffles along the bottom to catch the heavy gold particles. Water flushed out the whole muddy mess. As the rush progressed, multi-part sluice boxes, stretching thirty feet or more,

Figure 7.1. Miners working with a sluice at Sutter Creek, California. Credit: Photo is used with permission from Wells Fargo Corporate Archives.

came into play because they could be run continuously and cleaned of their gleanings less often.

Men working individual claims seldom made more than ordinary wages: six to eight dollars a day at best. Buying and selling claims could generate larger sums, similar to playing the stock market. The holder hoped for the value to rise but did little to create wealth by working it. When a miner uncovered a rich strike, he likely did not grandstand about it. If he was trying to sell a claim, he exaggerated how much it paid daily. They might "salt" a claim: planting gold to make it look deceptively prosperous. Because miners had wised up to such schemes, some sellers resorted to shooting gold into the sides of a hole, making the tampering less obvious. The Blackford men sometimes bought claims; whether they fell for any such ruse is unknown.

The most sought-after claims gave a miner easy access to a bedrock ledge. The richest pay dirt settled in the first few feet above the ledge, or in streams, under the rocky rubble lying on the bedrock. This placer gold was the earliest exploited and fastest depleted. By 1851, digging on hillsides and beside gullies was the norm. Some had begun hard-rock mining in quartz seams, requiring much more capital to purchase blasting supplies and to develop equipment to crush the ore and extract its wealth. Henry described the diggings: "What is called a hole or claim varys in different places from fifteen to thirty feet square—if it is shallow diging they throw all the top off, but if deep they dig a hole just like a well down until the dirt will pay and then drift under the full size of the claim."[14]

Miners pulled off the grass and forbs, regarding the topsoil as worthless. Then the digging began, as deep as sixty feet. If they found no pay dirt, off the miners would go to prospect elsewhere, leaving the gaping shaft. More than one miner lost his life to collapsing dirt walls; others met their end by stumbling into abandoned diggings in the dark. The Blackford men escaped such calamities, though they might not have been innocent of creating them.

Now these Indiana farmers needed to learn what this gold mining business entailed. What did they know about rocks? At best, a building material. At worst, a major obstacle to sowing crops. Not that these men were afraid of hard work. Quite the opposite, in fact. To them, getting to California, sticking a pan or shovel into some river bottom, and fishing out the yellow nuggets and grains seemed easy compared to what they faced at home. They actually had an advantage over the doctors, lawyers, and shopkeepers who had come from eastern cities—men who soon found the work too intense. "The first kind of business I engaged in was mining. But the labor was too hard. I soon got sick. I was told I went at it too hard at first," reported one erstwhile physician-cum-miner to his friends back home.[15]

They probably watched other miners' efforts, perhaps pitching in on occasion, to learn the methods of washing dirt and extracting the gold. Soon, they put their own tools to the test. After getting the basics down, they prospected unclaimed territory. They moved away the larger rocks, dug into the gravel, and looked for the finer sediments on the riverbed.

They swirled it in their pans to find the color. If it looked promising, they staked a claim, ten-by-ten feet in the busiest areas, and began shoveling more dirt into their cradle or long tom, rocking it like a mesmerizing metronome.

In the excitement of prospecting, Henry momentarily forgot how much he missed home. "It seems like a long time to still be here until next new years day but time flies swiftly by and when gone we wonder what has become of it—no doubt it seems long to you at home but keep up your spirits as well as you can and it will apparently pass by the sooner."[16] The daily drudgery would catch up to him, however.

Wet-footed, grimy, and discouraged at the minuscule rewards for their efforts, the company gathered in the evenings to prepare supper. It had not been at all like they expected. Hard work should result in some suitable reward, but gold mining was chancy. At least the warm, dry weather made for comfortable living conditions. They needed no shelter. The men rolled their blankets out on whatever piece of soft ground was at hand, bodies too exhausted to notice the indifferent stars looking down on them. They fell into their slumber, serenaded by barking dogs, yelping coyotes, and howling wolves, and they rose in the morning to repeat the process.

"We went from Stocton to Clumbia bar on the Macalama [Mokelumne] river," Pete recalled. "We stayed there about 3 or 4 days, then we went to Sandy Bar. There we worked and made about $3 a day."[17] At Columbia Bar, they found a place to stash their food and belongings. Theft was infrequent. Everyone needed to trust that no one would pilfer, so miners punished thieves harshly. Lashings, branding, and banishment were common. Therefore, the Blackford men did not need to be overly concerned about their containers of food and satchels being disturbed, except possibly by free-range dogs. They could buy food at a store nearby, not cheap, but more budget-friendly than prepared meals for a minimum of a dollar apiece. Still, they had a dismal diet: beans, preserved pork, pickles, dried apples, cheese, and potatoes. Fresh beef could be had, but that was pretty much the gamut. If they wanted a covered place to sleep, they could pay 25 cents to roll out their blankets in a shared tent.

At the end of each day, Henry pulled out his compact black, leather-bound memo book and jotted a few brief notes on the day's events. He would refer back to it whenever he had the time and materials to compose a letter.

He reported the disappointing first efforts:

> We left . . . for Columbia Bar on the Moquolomne River (pronounced McColomy) but found it not to answer our expectations . . . we came to the conclusion after mature deliberation to separate into smaller companys, thinking it will result to our mutual benefit. Teach and the two Leistenfelts boys returned to Columbian Bar—Hunt, Gibsen and Jones remained at Sandy Bar—Anderson and Lowry stay there at present and I came down to Stockton to try and get work at carpentering but cannot succeed . . . we feel somewhat disheartened at the present aspect of things but hope times will mend. The most experienced with but few exceptions are barely paying their way. They work but little knowing there is better times close. None of us have made over 4 or 5 dollars per day as yet and not always that much. When all together we cooked our own victual and can live tolerably well at from 80 cents to 1 dollar per day.

They had discounted the myriad reports about miners struggling to produce $2 a day. That was hardly more than they could make at home. At that rate, they would barely maintain themselves. It would not cover the debt to Makepeace, let alone to others such as Dr. Jones and those who would help provide for their wives and children while they were gone. Bills were mounting. The single Liestenfeltz brothers, who had the backing of their semi-prosperous father, had the least of all to worry about. They also seemed the least likely to indulge in the self-destructive behaviors so prevalent in the mining region and beyond, given their Germanic heritage and religious upbringing.

The first few weeks in California disillusioned most miners. The scales fell from their eyes, and harsh realities overwhelmed them. That process had doomed many a mining company. Sam, Henry, Pete, and the others had stronger bonds than most. Their family ties, friendships, and trust had been tested on the outward journey and held. Realizing the difficulties of working as a group, they had split up. They would work independently, pool their earnings, meet in Stockton on January 1 to set aside a portion for Humphrey's estate, then prepare to head home. At least, that was the plan.

In Pete's succinct recollection of events many years later, "We were all going to work to geather but we could not agree so we went to working for our selves."[18] Though he made it sound as if they set out individually, that was not the case. As Henry put it, they worked in smaller groups, which fluctuated as to membership, but all nine gathered regularly and kept tabs on each group's whereabouts. To Abby, he confided, "dont be alarmed about our separation for it was thought to be for the best and was done for the best." They had personality conflicts, but the Blackford men remained surprisingly cohesive compared to other outfits. As they sought out pay dirt in the ravines and valleys between the Mokelumne River to the north and Murphys New Diggings to the south, they shared domestic duties and awaited word from their families.

The Indiana miners' daily lives mirrored those of others working in the area. They spent six days a week in a monotonous routine. Breakfast. Mining. Dinner. Mining. Supper. Sleeping. They prospected for possible claims, worked a claim (generally, they could only own one at a time), or tried to sell a claim. On Sundays, they did laundry, mending, and shopping for supplies. The terrain was so choked with dense shrubs in places that the miners' clothes were constantly being torn to rags. Standing in water disintegrated their boots. Just keeping clothed and shod was a challenge and cost money.

Even with such exposure to the elements, illness did not seem as much a problem as it had been back home. "The climate appears healthy—I never saw or heard of less sickness in any place," Henry said. Belying that statement, though, he feared the worst with regards to the young man he had been tasked to find once he reached the mines. "I have not yet learned anything of Willis Wilson and hardly expect to. Most likely he is dead."

CHAPTER 8

DISSENSION

Being the odd man out when the company split into pairs, Henry looked for work in Stockton, without success. Given that San Joaquin County boasted over 200 carpenters, it should not have surprised him that a disgruntled miner need not apply. If he had foregone the mines when he first arrived, he might have done well with his trade. He looked into the church situation: "There are two Methodist societys in this place—one M.E. and the other M.E. South, but as this is Wednesday and I leave tomorrow I shall hear no preaching as there will be none until Sunday next." He wrote a letter to Abby and informed her that "we can hear nothing of Pierce but we are in quite different parts of the digings, but rather expect he has returned—let us know when you write whether he has or not."[1] Pierce, by that time, had settled in the far north of Shasta County. Henry himself decided on a change of scene. He returned to the Mokelumne River to report back to his Blackford comrades—no news from home. Then he left for Murphys in southern Calaveras County.

Henry found the Calaveras hills made for difficult walking. Some trails and a road or two had been cut across the slopes and wound through the narrow canyon bottoms. Other roads were being developed between supply points and boarding houses, but diggings occurred any-where and everywhere the miners could find bedrock. John M. Murphy established Murphys Camp in the fall of 1848, after the Weber company disbanded, on a wooded plain in the foothills. Murphy hired Indians to do the backbreaking labor of digging, providing them with food, clothing, and other supplies in exchange. After a good, wet winter in 1849, Murphy reportedly left the mines with between one and two million dollars—and an Indian wife.[2]

Around the time Henry arrived, Murphys consisted of a single street lined with tent houses and the occasional wooden one. Angels Creek, thoroughly dug up by miners, ran through the middle of the flat. Gambling was rampant, and shootings were near-nightly events. In Murphys, Henry Jenkins met Henry P. Angell. At the start of the rush, Angell, who had been at Sutter's Fort in February 1848 and later part of Weber's group, established a claim in Calaveras County along the creek that became known by his name, about ten miles west of Murphys. His successful diggings netted him enough to build a commercial center known then—and today—as Angels Camp, much as his former colleague had developed Murphys. Angell lived in California for some years prior to 1848; he hobnobbed with prominent citizens in Monterey before the Mexican War. Angell sold out and went home to Rhode Island early in 1849, but the lure of western-style freedom (and more gold) drew him back permanently.[3] Later, Henry Jenkins would capitalize on this connection.

As Henry moved through the Calaveras camps, he encountered almost no women—at least not white ones. The few there tended to be wives of tavern keepers and merchants. A woman's arrival in camp drew men from miles around just to gawk. Because the stable society such women promoted (as opposed to prostitutes) was sorely lacking in the mines, vice ran rampant. The absence of women and children meant the absence of schools, churches, and other facets of family life. Men had ample opportunities to wager away their piles of gold or drink it to nothing. Serious and frugal miners were the exception, not the rule. Miners frequently traded partners, seeking a complementary personality, work ethic, or special skills. The Blackford group, for much of the time they lived in Calaveras County, worked with each other, sometimes trading partners, but within the company unit, making them unusual. Though Henry

Figure 8.1. Henry P. Angell was living in California at the time of the gold discovery in 1848. He joined Captain Weber's party that summer and later established his own mine at what is now called Angels Creek and the town of Angels Camp. Credit: P77-2255 Western Americana Collection, Holt-Atherton Special Collections, University of the Pacific Library.

complained about the others falling into bad habits, they seem to have been hardworking men.

Henry realized he should have stayed home but would make the best of the situation. He bemoaned to Abby about their separation: "But on my part has been gone into voluntarily . . . Thy case is different—submission has been thy part for I must and do believe that nothing this side of heaven could have induced thee to have left me and our dear children as I have done."[4] In another letter, he wrote, "what privileges have I thrown away and for what, but it is too late now to lament but I will strive with all my power to regain them as soon as possible."[5] The inability to have a two-way conversation with his wife created a psychological strain he had not prepared for, especially with no church services to shore up his sagging spiritual strength. He worried this lack of religious fellowship would cause his downfall. He pleaded for the prayers of his friends and family at home. He had not been to a service since his time aboard the steamship *Columbus*. Sundays, in fact, were far from days of worship in the mines.

According to Henry, "there is but verry little working on the sabbath day but at the same time it is the general day for business and trading."[6] Another miner noted that there was "more intoxication, more fighting and more disturbance on the Sabbath than any other day in the week."[7] A visiting diplomat said of San Francisco, "All work and every amusement goes here as freely on Sunday as any other day, except perchance it be that which is under the control of some rare person whose respect for religion equals his love of gold—by the by, rather an unusual occurrence in California. No one puts any guard upon his tongue, for there is not delicate ear to be shocked by profanity or vulgarity."[8] He could have been describing Henry—seeking more to find God than gold, and with a delicate ear, besides.

He further observed, "where a great superabundancy of the male population existed over the female, . . . the social condition of the place was inferior, and I have now had an opportunity of proving the truth of this remark. There are [a] hundred males here to one female, and children and youth are not to be met with at all. All the restrictive influence of fair women is here lost, and the ungoverned tempers of men run wild."[9]

As the city had more women than the mining regions, the latter were several degrees worse.

Henry did not dislike California, but he found its inhabitants unpleasant. The Blackford miners were not exceptions to the general rudeness. As he put it, "for my comrades most of them seem to have given themselves up to vulgarity and prophanity which was verry annoying."[10] As each man delved into the argonaut lifestyle, he ablated his eastern identity like a snake sheds its skin. The early gold rush years were characterized by a lack of civility and coarse behavior. The murder rate was astronomical. It reflected the extreme social imbalance—too many young men, very few women. And the men relished a previously unknown level of freedom—freedom to be as base and undisciplined as their fellows would permit, and permission was readily granted and reciprocated.

"It is a verry poor place for a young man to come to and a married one has no business to come at all," wrote Henry, indicting both his mining partners and himself.[11] Henry faulted his behavior, but reserved more energy for criticizing others. No doubt his sanctimonious attitude, as the other men shipwrecked their morals in the god-forsaken, free-for-all California mines, had created a gulf between them. It was true, though, that most of the Blackford Mining Company men had left behind not only wives, but many children, and even aging parents, to seek an improbable fortune.

Part of Henry's troubles stemmed from the fact that he had tethered himself to younger men. The youthful sowed wild oats: drinking, gambling, swearing, and fighting. (There was probably little fornication going on, given the male-female ratio at that time; they would have to travel to the larger towns like Stockton or Sacramento to find prostitutes, though there were a busy few in the mines.)

Henry attempted to inspire his companions. "I tried for some time to have prayers in the evening and they would conform for the moment but go immediately to their vulgarity again so it seemed so much like mocking that I thought it best to desist."[12] In fact, he was probably the butt of some amusement. Though not a Quaker, his mother and wife had been until 1842, when they joined Henry in the Methodist congregation, and thus he had a very Quaker-like temperament.

The others most likely hid their vices from him whenever possible. Having the company of "those from home . . . has a tendency to keep [the miner] steady, for nothing is more dreaded by a young man than to have a report go back to his early friends and childhood home that he has gone to the bad."[13] Henry reported to friends and family on a regular basis, and he did not pull punches on his partners.

"I must not (nor do I intend to complain)" was among the smallest of lies Henry told himself as he picked his way through the California rubble.[14] The biggest lie was that any day now would be his turn to strike it rich, the delusion of all lottery players. For some, such as Sam Jones and Harvey Hunt, the trip to California was a deadly earnest treasure hunt. Sam's idea of success was money, lots of it. Harvey, hounded by creditors, needed to strike it big. For some, though, the trip was more about a grand adventure, gold or no gold.

Though work made time pass quickly, it did not take their minds off their families and farms back east. Everyone anxiously awaited mail. One San Francisco arrival remarked, "The first building I entered in California was the Post Office, and to that sacred spot (the most sacred in California) I directed my steps immediately upon landing."[15] When Henry headed to Stockton, he had no real expectation there would be any mail for the men. And there was not. It disheartened him further. He despaired of seeing his mother again. Though he wrote directly to her, he usually closed out his letters to Abby by expressing concern for Ann: "Tell Mother I dont forget her and wish verry much to see her once more this side of Heaven. If it should be otherwise ordered I have a strong and confident hope we will there meet to part no more."[16]

Henry related to his family and others back home the current status of the company men in early July while he dug holes around Murphys. "Jones and myself are in this place—he is now by my side writeing—Lowry and Anderson are 12 miles from here on McKinnys Creek—Hunt and Gibsen on the same creek 3 miles further and when last we heard from them, Teach and Jacob and P.N. Leistenfelts were on the Moquolomne river from 30 to 35 miles from here—all well and doing tolerably well." Knowing that future waves of gold seekers from home would be following, he requested, "when thee writes be particular to let me know if Wm Ransom succeeded in getting off to the mines and what part he started for." And he kept up with news of the region, reporting that "San Francisco has again been visited with a distressing fire burning a large proportion of the place and it is said the citizens caught several of the incendiarys and lynched them on the spot—some by pushing into the fire of their own kindling and some they shot down on the spot."[17] It was the only time he alluded to the violence that permeated his temporary home state.

Around the middle of July, the company gathered and worked all together again. They had procured a tent for storing their personal belongings by this time. They probably divided some domestic duties, trading off

Figure 8.2. Photograph from Elizabeth Lowry Bender's album believed to be her father, Dennis Lowry. Credit: Courtesy of James W. Baker.

who would be responsible for cooking for a day or week. Henry boasted that he could now bake bread as well as his daughter, Emma.

A late July day found Dennis Lowry alone in camp. Summers in the Calaveras foothills are dry, and temperatures routinely reach over a hundred, but fire was a necessity for preparing meals. Perhaps that fateful day a hot wind blew through the camp and an ember landed, unnoticed, on the canvas tent or dry grass nearby while Dennis was occupied by other tasks (or napping). The fabric erupted in flames while the hapless cook frantically grabbed whatever he could and threw it outside. The heat and acrid smoke soon overpowered him, and he could do nothing but stand there—coughing and listening to the crackling blaze—and watch it burn to the ground.

Henry, who seemed not to blame Dennis, said "he managed to save some few articles and but few—my valise was saved and my blankets I had with me. Both my coats, best pants, one shirt etc. were burnt. Anderson, Lowry and Jones lost almost everything. It is a serious loss to all."[18] Indeed, the devastation scattered the men once more, at least until mid-August, when all except Pete reunited in Murphys.

After the tent's destruction, Henry lived alone, but being surrounded by Germans with whom he could not communicate made him terribly lonely. Giving up on solitude, he partnered with Lowry, Jones, and Anderson in a quartz mine in the Murphys area, but the heavy labor and low pay discouraged the men. Small companies had minuscule chances with quartz mines. Insufficient extraction methods left most of the gold locked in the ore. Eventually, crushing mills and smelting operations would rectify this, and quartz mining surged for a time, though not supplanting placer mining. In certain circumstances, the payoff from quartz could be large but infrequent. As Henry put it, "Some of the quartz digings pay enormously—sometimes as high as five or eight thousand at one blast."[19] The work was difficult, dangerous, and expensive. The other three men quickly tired of it, and Henry ended up with the entire claim.

"I bought Jones share at cost and the other two getting out of heart with theirs they gave me their share, but no thanks are due them as they . . . failed to share with me their proffits elsewhere as was our agreement," he groused to Abby.[20] He told her that the other men were earning money on the side, but with two claims to work, he had no chance to do likewise, and he would soon have to sell one. The company's profit-sharing arrangement was doomed to fail. Most of them made barely enough to feed themselves. They likely had debts to boarding houses for meals and to others for claims they purchased.

Most depressing of all, the men had been gone from home for five and a half months, and not one had received a single letter.

In August, the Blackford men resumed working in pairs in the McKinneys Creek area—with one notable exception. As the calendar turned to September, Sam Jones abruptly left the company, going back to the Mokelumne River, where they had begun in May. Conditions there had improved, and he made a reported $6 to $8 per day, a notch above average wages in the $3 to $5 range in Calaveras County at the time. Even at that rate, paying $450 plus interest to Allen Makepeace would be difficult for any of them, let alone saving enough to get home and have a surplus.

Sam likely justified setting out on his own as being better for everyone. He would be Makepeace's principal target if the debt went unpaid, and he probably did not see Hunt, Anderson, and Lowry working as hard as he expected. Without responsibility for running the ragtag company, something he seemed to lack the skill for, he could focus on making money and getting home to his family. Whatever kind of success he found at the Mokelumne, he kept quiet about it. He was a shrewd man and had seen what California made of careless and lazy miners. Many had gone from riches to rags, or worse. He had no intention of going from rags to rags.

Though they had agreed to work individually, Henry resented Sam's defection. "S Jones is not with us nor have we seen him for three or four weeks but hear he is on the Moquolome River 19 miles from here and doing verry well . . . I think I may safely say he will hold onto what he gets get it as he may."[21] Henry felt that Sam had not only abandoned them but was also hoarding his gains. It left a chink in the group's collective armor, and Henry felt the jab in particular. Would the others abandon him, too?

99

CHAPTER 9

COMMUNICATION

Man rarely places a proper valuation upon his womankind, at least not until deprived of them
—Jack London, *The Son of the Wolf*

SUMMER 1851—INDIANA

By mid-June, Abby Jenkins had a routine that did not include Henry. Henry's mother now shared her bed instead. Abby's parents were gone, but she had brothers and sisters, most living in Ohio. Abby corresponded with her Bedford siblings, encouraging them to visit Indiana. They would promise, then she waited in vain for them to appear. Abby arose daily and shared morning prayers with her family. Sunday services were held at individual homes; the area had few churches or school buildings. Lacking transportation, Abby and Ann relied on good weather and a ride from friends or William Ransom to get to services, which did not always work out. When necessary, Abby conducted a Bible study at home.

That month, Abby received two letters from Henry. As she unfolded the first letter, sent from Chagres, Ann and the children gathered close. *What's it say? Where are they? Did Pap mention me?* The questions came from all sides. None of them had ever been to sea. Henry's descriptions of the Caribbean marine life intrigued them but did not convey enough detail to form accurate images in their minds. "We have seen many porpoises, skip jacks, and one dolphin and some other smaller fish, amongst which is flying fish in abundance."[1] Fish that fly! What a wondrous thing that must have been to behold.

Abby quelled any disappointment about the letter's brevity, concluded in haste as the men arrived at the isthmus. It seemed the tedium of riding a sailing ship in the windless sea had robbed her husband of all imagination. Surely there had been some activities aboard the ship to describe. He said they had good and plentiful food but wrote nothing about what they actually ate. Aside from mentioning the seasickness most had suffered, Henry said nothing about his comrades. Their families would be dismayed when the letter made the rounds. Hopefully, they had received letters, too. The men had plenty of time to write on that slow journey to Chagres. Perhaps just mulling over Humphrey's death made it difficult for them to put pen to paper and convey optimistic words to their families.

Henry poured his sufferings on Abby: "Spiritually I feel the great need I have of the prayers of my friends, of watchfulness and prayerfulness myself, and then the great need of sustaining grace of my heavenly father—surrounded as I am on every side at all times by profanity and wickedness of the grossest kind."[2] Was he suggesting his companions suffered likewise, or was he complaining about their behavior? It must have given Abby pause to wonder.

Tucking the letter away until she could hand it over to another family, she donned her bonnet and stepped into the dooryard to tend the kitchen garden. The rich soil nourished healthy vegetables, but rodents, particularly squirrels, presented an ongoing threat to all their crops. The spring rains gave them a strong start. Abby checked the pea and bean trellises, collecting any ripe vegetables for their supper and inspecting the plants for pests. The sun kept her warm, radiant energy permeating her homespun dress, a rather shapeless garment that did nothing to flatter her figure. Humidity added a haze to the air. Even the cats and dogs sought out cool shade as Abby continued with her daily labors. If anyone came down the Hartford-Portland Pike past the farm, they stopped to talk with her, passing along any relevant news. No local papers existed, as none were needed.

The chores and chats pushed her concerns about Henry's well-being to the recesses of her mind. All the children, young and grown alike, had the business of their daily lives to distract them: milking the cow, feeding chickens, baking and sewing, visiting with friends, and inventing games. Ann Jenkins, too, enjoyed visits from her many friends; she rarely left the property. She struggled to get around and was developing a cough—probably a cold coming on. She felt gratitude for the long life her Creator had blessed her with, despite the hardships. In the evenings, she sat in her corner chair where she could hear the buzz of conversation but not pick out the words—she had a loquacious family—and worked on her knitting, sure that her feeble eyes caused her to drop a stitch every now and then. She figured this pair of socks for Henry would be her last. The Lord would bring him home to wear them, she prayed.

The second letter that month came from Panama, bringing tales of tropical fauna—as unimaginable as the porpoise and flying fish. What an exciting adventure dear Pap was having. Abby and Ann knew the perils of the isthmus crossing, chiefly diseases. Reading about Henry's encounter with Harvy Brown perhaps reaped a good chuckle. How on earth had the Blackford group not known there were men from Jay County making the trip at the same time? But maybe Harvy had joined up with some of his friends from Ohio.

She would have to wait for one more letter, this time from far-off California (how could it be even more remote than Panama?), before she could share all her own news, troubles, and concerns with her errant spouse. Though the men missed the ship they had planned to take, and paid a high price when they did find tickets, Henry seemed much more upbeat than in his previous note. He only mentioned his two older sons by name, though. Abby would remind him to mention all their children when he wrote, so none would feel slighted.

Emotions swirling, Abby refolded the message from the tropics and arranged for it to be passed to her married children in Trenton. From there, it would make the rounds in Blackford County before returning to Abby for safekeeping.

Figure 9.1. Photo believed to be Ann Widdifield (Zane) Jenkins. Tintype, probably a copy of an earlier daguerreotype c. 1850s. Credit: Author's collection.

Another month passed, as summer days filled to overflowing. Abby attended quilting bees, where she caught up on local gossip. House- and barn-raisings brought all the neighborhood together. Men maintained the county roads and built new ones. At last, the long-awaited letter from

California arrived, the one from Stockton. Finally, they could begin a true correspondence. Again, it was brief, giving slight details about their Pacific journey. They had scant time in San Francisco. But Henry had found a local business directory (that seemed downright cosmopolitan), saw the name Sam Brannan, and thought to mention it to Abby, thinking he might be an old friend of hers.

The name Brannan did resonate with Abby, taking her back to Evesham, New Jersey, in the 1820s. She and her older sister, Philadelphia Bedford, had been in their twenties then. Their mother likely wanted to marry them off to members of the Society of Friends. They moved from Monthly Meeting to Monthly Meeting in the greater Philadelphia region. The three women probably earned their room and board as domestic help, while the rest of the family remained at home in the city. Certainly, the country air lacked the city's miasma and promoted better health.

Abigail Bedford considered herself a woman of good humor. She grew up in a house full of younger brothers, on whom she doted. She felt comfortable socializing in any gathering, and she had been educated, something of which many working-class women could not boast. It was part of her religious heritage. Quakers treated girls as equal to, though not the same as, boys. That included teaching them to read and write, at a minimum. She would make an excellent helpmate to whomever won her heart.

In Evesham, they met members of the large Branin family. Abigail and Charles Branin joined the Upper Evesham meeting in 1822. On March 30, 1826, Abigail and Charles requested permission from the Philadelphia congregation to marry. Charles's mother (his father was dead) and both of Abigail's parents attended to give their consent. Quakers commonly married in their mid- to late twenties. Charles was twenty-four and Abigail twenty-five. The meeting assigned two women to ascertain Abigail had no other commitments and to report back the following month. They approved the marriage in Philadelphia on April 27.[3]

Abigail no doubt looked forward to the next stage in life: marriage and children. As they made their matrimonial preparations, Charles came down with a fever. Soon, he took to his bed, quivering with chills. Efforts to break the fever and usher him to recovery failed; his condition grew dire. On May 9, he succumbed to the sudden illness.[4] Instead of a joyful spring wedding, Abigail dressed in mourning and buried poor, dear Charlie Branin. Having invested years in developing a relationship, only to have it end so tragically, left Abigail contemplating her probable future as a spinster. Rather than a family of her own, she would support her aging parents and be an auntie to her younger siblings' children.

Then God saw fit to bring Henry Z. Jenkins into her life, and they were able to forge a true partnership. Henry knew about her association with the Branin family and clearly harbored no jealousy about her earlier near-marriage. Though Samuel Brannan was unknown to her, it was sweet of Henry to think of her old friends when he saw Brannan's name in the directory.

With instructions on where to send mail, Ann and Abby both wrote letters to Henry on July 21.[5] They undoubtedly would have written weekly, but it was not economically feasible, given the cost of paper and postage. The miners also had to pay for the letters they received, usually a dollar or two for a courier to bring them from the nearest post office, in this case, Stockton. But at last, a two-way conversation could begin, or so it seemed. Abby asked Henry to describe the countryside where he lived. She did not hesitate to say the family struggled without him. They had no money to buy things, like coffee, that they could not produce themselves.

By mid-August, Abby received one or two more letters from Henry, but he still had no word from home: "Not knowing whether thee has received all or any of my former letters makes it more difficult to write . . . and I now begin to look for a return with considerable anxiety." He found a list of unclaimed letters in a July newspaper that named a Henry Jenkins, "but it lacks the Z and I dont know whether it is for me or not."[6] (It probably had been, but he apparently decided otherwise.) Henry wrote these letters in June and July. He enclosed a small amount of gold in the July letter. Unaware of its presence, Abby may have spilled it as she unfolded the paper. She would be cautious when opening her mail in the future. Henry sent very little, due to its weight. Someone might suspect its presence and lighten the postman's load.

Henry inquired about the harvest and instructed "Bedford to not fail in sowing that same field down in wheat and if possible in good time."[7] Henry always attempted to direct the activities back on the farm—plow this field, plant that crop, pay that bill, and so on. Physical absence was no excuse to neglect his duty to tell everyone what to do. But, of course, his words reached Indiana too late to be of use. The home team knew what to do; they had been doing it for years. At least he shared more news than his previous two reports. It did not sound encouraging, though. The men had not made much money and had split into smaller groups. And it seemed they spent as much, or more, than they were making. That left nothing to help out at home, much less accumulate anything toward paying off the mounting debts.

On August 20, Abby again laid down a sheet of paper and ink pot and took up the pen to begin her third or fourth letter. They must have seemed like instruments of torture. On the one hand, composing a letter to Henry instantly focused her mind on how far away he was. "My dear Henry," she began. "Again do I attempt to address thee but the thought of the distance between us almost unnerves me."[8] On the other hand, Henry suffered a worse torment. Abby received every letter he wrote, and each made clear he had received none from her, nor from anyone at all. What mental anguish it must be to not know the fate of those back home—if they were getting along well without him (was he unneeded?) or were the crops failing (yet again), and creditors bedeviling them (still?). She worried about his lack of spiritual companionship in that wicked place and strove to provide him with uplifting messages of encouragement.

"Oh what a comfort it is to think we have an ever present friend who hears our mutual prayer though so far separated," she cheered him but followed with, "Oh my love let us be faithful to grace already given us that if we meet not here we may meet to part no more in never ending bliss."

On the surface, life proceeded much as usual. Everything cycled with the seasons. She dutifully repeated the important events she had covered several times already, knowing Henry was still ignorant of them. Maybe some of her letters would never reach him at all. Then she turned to current affairs, no matter how mundane.

"Mother is picking beans, Bedford is working at Places whenever he can leave home." In order to earn a little extra, Bedford helped out at the neighboring farms, particularly at William Place's close by. Place and his wife, Esther, hailed from Rhode Island. Esther brought three daughters by her first husband to the marriage, and they had four young children together. But they did not have any sons old enough to help with farm work. Henry would be forever grateful to his neighbor: "Place has my warmest thanks for his friendly bearing to my family for that is indeed a true saying (a friend in need is a friend indeed) may he get his reward here and a hundredfold hereafter."[9]

Abby reported on who was ill and who had been borne along to the grave, but assured Henry that his kin were all well. As the weather warmed, insects swarmed. Their role in carrying disease was unknown at that time, but the fevers that had abated over early spring revived in abundance. The pestilences spared no age group. Though the settlers seemingly dealt with the horror in a matter-of-fact manner, the toll had to be depressing.

She shared news about their children. Will was working in the cranberry marsh for a couple months. The boggy land lay about eight miles north of Trenton. Wading through the calf-deep water to pick berries left him chilled in his wet clothes. A bushel of cranberries might net him a dollar. Will's wife, Jane, stayed with her parents, along with baby Lizzy. Speaking of their granddaughters: "Will J has a little girl they call Elizabeth Ann, a fine child but not as pretty as Cordelia E—she is a fat saucy little pet almost ready to run." This would be welcome news to Henry, knowing the babies were doing well. They were the most vulnerable to health issues.

Bedford had put up one wheat crop and industriously sowed the orchard and west field. He worked as hard as any teenager ever did, and Abby felt tremendous gratitude for having such a dedicated young man there for her in Henry's absence. Emma was at home, too, minding her father's admonition not to marry Robert Ransom before Pap came home.

She may have been young for marriage, but she was a sturdy girl and as hardworking as her brothers. Among her siblings, she enjoyed good health overall. Bedford and Ann seemed more prone to catch every disease that crossed over the stile.

One thing topmost on Abby's mind, though, was her flighty son-in-law, William Ransom. That man was a pie-in-the-sky dreamer and a vagabond at heart. Tiny Trenton would never hold him, she could see. He talked of following Pierce and the Blackford Company to California one way or another. What about the sacrifices his wife and baby girl would make if he left? Could he not see what Abby and the other wives were dealing with? Here she had endured Henry's absence for six months, and it seemed an eternity. William and Robert had bought land from their uncle, Asa Anderson, which she sincerely hoped meant William would settle down and stick with his lot in life. He had a talent for dealing with horses, even if he was not much of a scholar. He had also taken an interest in medicine after nursing his friend, E.D. Pierce, back to health after his return from Mexico. He had borrowed some medical texts to study. Maybe he would make something of himself someday.

Abby thought her girls might remain close to home, but circumstances could change so quickly. At least her son, Will, seemed to be working toward making Indiana his permanent home. He hoped to buy some school land with the proceeds of his cranberry harvest. Then he would build a cabin for his family.

Abby had worked so hard to raise these industrious, loving, devoted children (with Henry's and Mother's help, naturally). And the Lord had always provided, no matter how hard times had gotten. They were not starving (though sometimes the larder seemed rather bare). The land provided a bounty if one had the gumption to endure thorns and muck to procure it. Living off the land offered beauty and hardship in measure, quite unlike their old city life. As for the crops, the corn had never been better—Henry should have been here to stuff himself. The cabbage was coming along well. Abby looked forward to making kraut. Would her love be home to indulge in that family favorite? No, impossible. She knew next summer would be the earliest he would return.

At least she occasionally got to see her older children and grand-daughters in Blackford County when they sent a horse around for her, but she worried about Ann while she was gone. "Mother does not like me to leave home. She is failing. She is much deafer than when thee left and blinder and much more inquisitive of course but she gets along wonderfully." She leavened the news a bit so as not to worry Henry too much on Ann's account.

She told Henry about her brothers, Joe and William Bedford, in Ohio. The Bedfords were more family to Henry than his own kin back in Pennsylvania. Overall, it seemed his family was getting along fine; they had enough to eat and enjoyed generally good health. If Henry started finding success in the mines, as he expected, then maybe they could look forward to 1852 being a good year. Some of Henry's friends considered going to California and pestered Abby for information, wanting to know Henry's take on the prospects. Re-reading his letters, Abby could see Henry convincing himself he would strike it rich, eventually:

Men often times work here for weeks, months and sometimes almost years barely paying their way and then in three or four days or weeks make their pile and then leave . . . one person at Carsons Hill is supposed to have got more out of his claim than Jacob Astor was worth at his death. We dont anticipate such a large pile but will be content with two thousand each by next spring, but with nothing less . . . I celebrated in sinking a hole in a new place and worked as hard as ever I did in my recollection but it proved of no account as there was no bra in it as the Mexican or Spaniard would say, but that is no uncommon circumstance. Sometimes a person will sink four or five holes and get nothing and then sink one and make his pile out of it.[10]

Such talk seemed rather dubious. Next, she shared more local gossip, particularly about people related to Henry's mining partners.

"I was at Asa Andersons at a quilting when I saw Harriet Anderson [Humphrey's widow]. She seems lonely and sad more so I think than she did. [Sam Jones's] wife and child were there well or rather better—the child looks delicate." Eliza Jones's baby, Edwin, was just about nine months old. Her two daughters were toddlers and perhaps under the care of her sister, Mariah Jones, Dr. Jones's wife. Probably, Rebecca Jones came to help her sister-in-law while Sam was in California. Rebecca had little reason to remain in Ohio. All her nieces and nephews were in Indiana, and her beau was in California. Her younger siblings could help their parents back in Barnesville.[11]

Abby paused to dip her pen in the ink pot before resuming her litany: "Before I came home I heard she [Eliza] had got a letter which still speaks of not much success." There, she came right out with it. What she probably feared all along. This misguided adventure would leave them worse off than before. How could she convince Henry he should pack his valise and come home? "Don't talk of years, months seem too bad—it makes gloom pass over our sweet little home."

All this correspondence did nothing to bridge the yawning divide. Letters were a pallid substitute for face-to-face conversation. She could hardly imagine the men in California, fending for themselves as far as food, clothing, and healthcare needs. Did they not realize how much they needed the women in their lives? Not only for the domestic pleasantries but also as a civilizing force, to keep them from becoming just brutes. Did she envision Henry washing his garments in the creek? What a ludicrous sight it must be: men on their knees, in their undergarments, all up and down the banks on a Sunday—what should be a day of rest and worship—clutching handfuls of calico and flannel rather than shovels and gold pans.

Abby turned to church matters; speaking of civilizing, maybe not so much. "Brother Christopher Timberlake was turned out of meeting for telling a lie (is not our church pure)," she began in her ironic way. "Dr. Freeman sued him (and Chris) and accused him of being too intimate with M. Pitman and much like stuff . . . So they managed to turn out the best member they had. So much for Dicksonian government . . . no doubt he will be reinstated."

As for the future, Abby and the children would be going to a camp meeting in September. These popular revival-style events had been going strong for half a century. Even a month ahead of time, Bedford and William were preparing a campsite. Religious matters were a hot topic between Abby and Henry. Henry had persuaded both his mother and wife to join him in the Methodist congregation. But Abby clearly found Methodist politics no better than the Quakers'.

In closing, she wrote, "Now my love farewell. I know thee will not forget us, forget not thyself and may thee be supremely blessed is the prayer of thy faithful and affectionate wife. A G Jenkins." Then a post-script, "Thee must mention all the children when thee writes or they are jealous and think Pap forgets them. Write very often, all the consolation I have."

CHAPTER 10

EASTERN CURSES

FALL 1851—CALAVERAS COUNTY

After Sam's defection, Henry and the others quit the quartz mines in Murphys. They had heard that Pete Liestenfeltz was lucky in McKinneys Creek, where they had been in August. Pete's memoir explains, "Then we went up to McKinneys Creek. It was about 15 miles up in the mountains. This creek was fed by springs. There was where I made things pay. I made $80.00 a day for a while. I found one peace that made $26.51."[1] Pete was a small man with big hands and a big heart. He took the lessons from his parents seriously, though he liked to have fun, too. He and Jake, being the only single men in the Blackford Company, had as much reason as anyone to run wild, but they remained steadfast to their family ideals. Pete, unlike many miners, did not squander his earnings. Being a sociable guy, he must have been pleased when the others joined him.

The group collected their meager belongings and hiked the narrow trail that wound through the chaparral-covered hills. The heat had abated, but the dust-choked shrubs gasped tan clouds as they brushed by. They reached a small, open valley with a tiny creek that ran dry by midsummer. McKinneys had a dreadful appearance, much like other ephemeral mining camps. Shelters—cabins, tents, twig tepees—randomly littered the steep landscape, surrounded by tree stumps and excavated claims: heaps of dirt and rock surrounding deep holes. Discarded, worn-out clothing and other detritus lay strewn about, some of which might be collected by the Miwok who still roamed the area. The grasses had dried to a monotonous blond hue, alleviated only by the scattered evergreen of manzanita and perhaps a few remaining pines. A spectacular cave lay hidden in the vicinity. As for gold prospects, McKinneys quickly earned the sobriquet of "Humbug," which miners dubbed any touted rich region that turned out to be a dud. But, as Pete's experience showed, additional prospecting in the area produced a good yield.

As cooler weather and the hope for winter rains neared, the men eschewed sleeping out in the open or in tents and built cabins. These basic dwellings were eight feet by eleven feet, built of pine logs, with a canvas roof, a stone hearth, and a chimney. One miner described his cabin as being "divided into two parts, inside and out. Inside all one room, same outside. Rather than wood for floors which decay . . . have a slab from Mother Earth—durable and always in its place."[2]

Loneliness prompted Henry to share a cabin. Only John Teach was about his age and was apparently the only one who tolerated living and working with the dour Henry. McKinneys became the hub for the Blackford men for the duration of their time in California. They wandered, primarily through Calaveras County, but this ravine in the foothills was their "home away from home." With Sam gone on his own, the other eight paired off into their snug abodes with four men in the first (Hunt and Gibson; Anderson and Lowry); the Liestenfeltz brothers in one; and Henry and Teach in the last.

Teach proved to be an acceptable companion, perhaps even amiable. "Teach and myself appear to suit each other tolerably well in most things which was not the case with most of the others," Henry confided.[3] Teach was not only close to Henry in age but also in financial circumstances. When he left for California, the children at home were Bill, age twenty; Margaret, age seventeen; and Mary, age nine. He was especially close to his son and anticipated news from the family like the others. When Teach went searching for gold, he left his wife, Ann, as destitute as she had ever been. Thank goodness her son was an adult, perhaps more so than her partner. She could count on Margaret to take care of herself, which the young woman did by working as a live-in domestic for a family near Camden. One could hardly blame Ann if she did not write to her husband.

Though crude, the new accommodations were a step up. In August, Henry described retiring "to my lonely bed . . . some weeds strewn on the ground—my dirty clothes spread on them—then any old bags, on top of them a piece of muslin (left from my tent) the two small but tolerably good blankets and my valeese for a pillow."[4] In the cabin, he boasted an actual bunk, off the ground at last, and he and Teach had "made ourselves ticks and filled them with dry grass—two blankets each and intend getting each one another blanket—so thee may see we are trying to take care of our own precious selves be the situation of our family what it may."[5] He knew his family was harried at home, but if he allowed himself to get sick or die, they would fare even worse. Unfortunately, a good, warm bed at night did not insure against such a disaster.

Mines in McKinneys Creek were dry diggings. Teach and Henry worked side by side, throwing up dirt from their claims, awaiting rain to wash it in a long tom or rocker to collect the gold. They thought the dirt would pay at least 5 cents per bucket. "Teach says we have at least forty thousand buckets thrown up (rather doubtful)." But the dry weather persisted well into the fall. The two men contemplated an alternate plan. "If it should happen to be a dry winter we intend to purchase a donkey make a truck wheel cart and haul our dirt to watter."[6]

Though the drought continued, the Blackford group felt optimistic about returning home in the spring. They planned to leave about March 1 and go by sea via Nicaragua and New York City. The trip could be made in two months or less, buoying their spirits. When he heard the talk about going home, Henry had grave doubts about his own chances, having had less success than the others, likely due to his efforts in the quartz mine. Examining his current financial situation, he found himself fifty dollars poorer than when he had arrived in California. Not encouraging at all. He had plenty of company in such circumstances. As a correspondent in the Feather River mines put it, "You have no idea of the hand to mouth sort of style in which most men in this country are in the habit of living."[7] Henry hesitated to admit his lack of success to Abby but came (almost) clean about it in his September letter.

"And now my dearest what shall I say to thee—I repent sorely for leaving thee even for the hope of gold but I will make all the amends I can by returning as soon as possible. Gold or no gold, poverty with my family rather than separation."

In late September, Henry and Teach arranged to get their winter provisions as the costs "get verry high in winter in consequence of bad roads." They stocked up: 400 pounds of flour, 100 pounds of pickled pork, 13 pounds of onions (the only common vegetable besides potatoes), 30 pounds of sugar, five pounds of tea, 40 pounds of beans, 21 pounds of cheese, plus pickles and dried peaches, which totaled $110. They planned to buy 200 pounds of potatoes to round out their stores.[8]

All through the sweltering summer and into early October, the troupe waited in vain for mail from Stockton. They fretted at the lack of communication, or rather its one-way nature, not even certain their letters ever got to Indiana. But they saw others receiving mail, so the system must work. Not a single letter from home had arrived, and the disconnection weighed on them more than their failure to find a rich strike. Only Dennis Lowry had received a reply—from a friend—to their many outgoing missives. As they hit the seven-month mark since their departure from Trenton, the courier from Stockton arrived.

The word spread around the diggings "like wild fire, men came from the hills, ravines gulches, and out of the ground, made the very heavens ring with their shouts and cheers. The crowd waiting with inexpressable feelings and anxiety to hear their names called."[9] Again, nothing for Henry or the others. It was maddening! If there had been any inkling that the mail would be so slow and unreliable, maybe he would have stayed home. Ah, probably not, but still, how long could he endure the torture?

Soon he had a more serious problem. As a treat, Henry and Teach sampled the cheese they had purchased. Several days later, constipation and other gastric distresses alerted them something was terribly wrong. They felt weak and nauseous. Vomiting did nothing to alleviate their agony. They would not be going back to work any time soon, if ever. As their symptoms escalated, they suspected the cause, and dread sunk in. Milk sickness was highly lethal and endemic in their home state of Indiana and surrounding states but not west of the Mississippi. There was only one possible source—the cheese. It must have been made from tainted milk back in the Midwest. To test their theory, the afflicted men gave some to a dog and waited. Days later, the cur was as ill as Henry and Teach.

The irony could not have been lost on Henry. In his letters, he boasted about healthy California. Compared to swampy eastern Indiana, Calaveras County had remarkably little disease. Back home, his neighbors, maybe even his family, were dying of fevers, consumption, cholera—and possibly, milk sickness. Now, thousands of miles away, this scourge had followed him.

The early gold rush migrants suffered a curse. Poor quality and useless goods piled up on the waterfront in San Francisco, left to rot. But enterprising, unscrupulous opportunists packed some to the mining regions where scarce goods fetched high dollars. Aside from bad roads, a lack of competition worked against the miners. In 1851, much of the flour in California was imported; some spoiled in transit. Food items that would not pass muster in San Francisco or Sacramento—off to the mines with it! Miners had little choice but to buy whatever food became available. Sometimes their purchases turned out to be moldy, wormy flour or, worse, milk-sick cheese.

Henry and Teach knew the signs and prepared to face the end. They laid limp in their bunks, their bowels agonizingly constricted, the air in their tiny cabin reeking of the acetone they exhaled with every poisoned breath.[10] A year earlier, Henry had been surrounded by family, expecting the arrival of his first grandchildren. His debts and failures seemed then like insurmountable problems that only a gold rush could solve. Now there was a very real chance he might perish in his lonely self-exile so far from home.

Milk sickness first appeared in the early nineteenth century when settlers began crossing the Allegheny Mountains. Before they had cleared and fenced pastures, pioneers turned their livestock out to forage in the woodlands. Animals tended to avoid white snakeroot, but in late summer, forage became scarce, leaving them with little else to eat. The plant's toxin disrupts a metabolic process and leads to acidification of the body, much like diabetes. Chemical starvation and muscular weakness lead inexorably to coma and death. Poisoned cattle, horses, and sheep developed a facial tic, a condition called "The Trembles." They usually died within two weeks. Because of the delay in the onset of symptoms, people would consume the tainted milk, or they made it into cheese or butter, equally toxic. Dozens of people in a community could die within a short time.[11]

The Blackford miners did what little they could to comfort and nurse Henry and Teach as they lay spent on their bunks, barely able to move. They had no desire to eat; food would make them feel worse. They knew of no effective treatment. By sheer luck, they clung to life and gradually improved. Perhaps someone had thought to mix some saleratus (aka baking soda, a staple in a miner's larder) with water to soothe their digestive distress. Alkaline sodium bicarbonate could effectively counter some symptoms of the poison, but it was not known then as a remedy. Even the local native population, with their natural remedies, could not have helped, since the culprit plant did not grow in California.

The muscle weakness caused by the poisonous cheese left them feeble, a condition known as "The Slows." Recovery took a long time. Through the coming months, Henry and Teach monitored their diet and avoided strenuous activity. Exertion brought on bouts of retching, curtailing their ability to work. All through the winter of 1851–1852, the two men battled recurrences. For now, the Blackford crew had cheated death, but there were other perils to their health, which they declined to discuss with their families.

Even in California, death from a variety of causes happened as regularly as back home. Just getting to the state took a major toll. The overland travelers contended with cholera most of all, but scurvy was common on the trail. Those going by sea also had to take care to avoid scurvy. It could be found in the mines, too, because fresh vegetables, fruits, and meat were not regularly available. Fevers, measles, and malnourishment took many a miner's life, even young men who had been hale and hearty back east.

Until the rains began, the men had free time to amuse themselves. Calaveras County's novel landscape beckoned the Indianans to explore. Henry and his companions investigated the nearby cave after the worst of his illness had passed. A week later, the *Calaveras Chronicle* published a description: "bright crystals flashing in the light of torches, give the appearance of gorgeous chandeliers suspended from some richly finished dome to shed their lustre upon the magnificence that lies scattered around, while in some of the apartments floor, walls, and ceilings reflect back such a flood of light from innumerable stalactites as to be almost blinding."[12] Unfortunately, the miners who visited the cave were prone to break off formations and tote them away as souvenirs, forever marring these geologic time capsules.

On occasion, the men would claw their way through the dense mountain shrubs to the hilltops to take in the view. Henry described the surroundings to his family:

> In the mineing district as far at least as I have been there is seldom land level enough to be ploughed—and points or camps that may be but six or eight miles apart requires two or three that distance of travel to get from one to the other and verry often quite impassable for any wheel carriage of any kind. If you are in a valley where the sun strikes it is verry hot but on the contrary if the sun seldom shines in them, and there are many such, it is quite cool particularly mornings and evenings. If you think you will get onto some high hill nearby, you will find on makeing the trial valleys between, and on gaining the desired point, the view is indeed beautiful and grand but still the prospect is limited in a great measure by other still higher ranges and single peaks—some covered with a growth of stately pines—others by low shrubby bushes—others again entirely bare mostly of a red colour—but some again are nothing but huge piles of rock verry evidently of volcanic origin and gold in small quantities in almost any place but too little to pay for collecting while living is as high as it now is. No doubt gold will be sought and found long after our children have followed us to another world.[13]

Pete recalled making a visit to the Big Trees: "I went up on the table mountain. You could see all of the main rivers for miles around. That was the most prettyest sights that eyes could see. Those trees were 300 ft high . . . They were redwood. There was one bored down and a house built on the stump."[14] When miners first found and described the giant sequoias to their friends in the camps, they were met with skeptical derision. Later, though, enough had made the trek, fifteen miles east of Murphys, to see the wonder for themselves. Awed into silence, they stood apologetic and reverent.

They began to notice more wildlife around Calaveras, but the animals had learned to be wary of people. "There is beginning to be plenty of deer and some few grislys about but we have not killed any of either as yet but would like to right well." Henry said.[15] Fresh (and essentially free) meat would be a welcome change in their poor diet, even greasy bear seemed appetizing.

Grizzlies fascinated the immigrants from back east and inspired ferocious fear. Sometimes miners had terrifying, and occasionally fatal, encounters. Some hunted the mighty carnivores, bringing pelts and claws back to town as trophies. One killed by E.D. Pierce reportedly went on display in a Sacramento museum.[16] A few daring entrepreneurs trapped the bears and used them for blood sport. A good-sized grizzly in captivity was worth $1,500 or more. Speculators widely publicized their bear-and-bull fights, drawing throngs of spectators. Many gold-rush-era writers described them in detail. The fights were not just about killing animals; betting was featured prominently. Though the outcome was important to the gamblers, the spectacle needed to last long enough to be worth watching, too. If one of the animals died too quickly, a howl for refunds would arise.

It was a rare bull that came out on top. In some instances, the bear was handicapped by tying it to a stake. Sometimes there might be a little bonus entertainment. A visitor to Sacramento described a fight that drew as many as 3,000 fans.

A little before the fight was to commence a half drunk Spaniard fell over the pallisades into the arena. The spectators immediately raised the cry that the 'Bear is coming' and the poor fellow jumped up half frightened to death. He first attempted to climb up the posts, but from fear or intoxication he could not succeed.

He then ran around the ring, crying and begging to be taken out, but there was no door but the one the bear was to come in through and nobody would give him a rope. At length when the fellow was almost frightened out of his drunken fit, one of his friends hauled him through a small opening in the pallisades, which was as tight a squeeze as he had ever had, since the day he was born.[17]

All these entertainments paled next to the excitement of news from the states. The Blackford men's agony finally came to an end on October 24. Henry received three letters that day; he clutched this sustenance with a new bounce in his step, relief flooding his soul.

My Dear Abby—I feel encouraged to write again to thee as I now know my letters reach thee of which I had my doubts until the 24th of last month when I received one from Mother 7th Mo. 21st, one from thee of the same date and another of them dated 8th Mo. 20th. D Lowry also got one by the same

Figure 10.1. Bear-and-bull fight illustration by J.D. Borthwick. Legend has it that *New-York Tribune* founder Horace Greeley based Wall Street's bull and bear on this gold-rush-era sport. Credit: J.D. Borthwick, *Three Years in California.*

messenger, and thee may well rest assured it was the cause of much joy to all of us . . . we are now looking every week for letters as doubtless there are several on the way.[18]

His letter from Stockton had reached home in just under two months. The first letters from the family took three months to reach him. He read and re-read the letters until they were falling apart. Everyone in the company relished Abby and Ann's newsy dispatches. Henry felt relief that all his letters had gone through and that two-way communication had begun. His near-death experience had humbled him. The aches in his heart spilled from his pen, gushing his sorrows, frustrations, and failings, as a husband and as a man fallen from God's grace. He also heeded Abby's admonition to address each of his children by name, rather than his previous shortcuts, such as "Children one and all young or old—single or married."

> Truly I feel much in need of thy sympathy for on a close investigation I must acknowledge there is a sad lack of spiritual life— the sure reward of unfaithfulness—I will not try to extenuate or excuse myself further than to say this is indeed a hard place to live a Christian life and no one can succeed if not sustained by grace divine. I sit down to read a chapter—on all sides my ears are saluted with songs, jesting, swearing and every kind of annoyance—it is almost impossible to read with proffit but I mostly find in secret devotion—if I can get away from the noise and confusion—satisfaction and answers of peace and it is most consoleing to know that thee and all my kind friends are from time to time interceding at a throne of grace in my behalf.[19]

He did his best to stick to the narrow, righteous path he had carved for himself in his middle years, but in the end, Henry confessed to giving in to the negative influences surrounding him. It weighed heavily on his mind because, in his younger days, he had overindulged in alcohol.

> Thee may have some misgivings of my resisting an old besetment but I am truly glad to be able to say I think thee need have no

fears on that head for I do not (as formerly) feel any inclination to partake when it is circulating freely all around me, but rather disgust at and pity for the poor deluded victims of the fell monster Intemperance. I would not wish thee to think from what I have said that I never taste it, for in several instances when I thought I really needed something of a stimulating nature I have taken a small portion and believe I was benefitted thereby, but I do think nothing shall ever induce me to abuse myself and it by the too frequent use of it in any way shape or form.[20]

He was not repentant, and he assumed Abby's forgiveness would be forthcoming. "Thee has ever proved thyself faithful and constant in every trial I have had to pass through and I cant help but feel I have made thee but a poor return in leaving thee as I have. My only excuse (and it is a verry poor one) is I was blinded and led away by the hope of acquiring a little yellow dust and thereby makeing our old age more comfortable. If I fail I cant help it was done for the best."[21]

Henry's alcohol consumption was not the only disturbing news Abby received. All the men had deep concerns about repaying their loans from Makepeace. However, John Anderson was making trouble. "He is a most singular man; sometimes he talks as though he had plenty of money and that his dirt will realise him all that he cares about getting and at other times he has nothing and dont expect to get more than enough to take him home, if that much . . . The individual spoken of is so given to lieing that Teach, Jacob, Peter N. and myself dont pretend to believe anything he says."[22] Even worse, Anderson planned to send a letter to his brothers saying that he could not pay his note and they would be on the hook to pay Makepeace instead. No doubt, Anderson's behavior had contributed to Sam's decision to leave the group.

Henry explained to Abby, "Whatever may be his motive for so writeing I think it verry wrong as it is cause to create uneasiness in the minds of all our friends and those that are concerned in the notes . . . I will just say tell the Anderson boys not to be uneasy. Teach says he would like J. Walker and C. Leistenfeldts to see or be made acquainted with the facts above stated."[23] (James Walker and Conrad Liestenfeltz had signed as surety on the note that provided passage for John Teach and Conrad's two sons.) Indeed, such talk was bound to worry the already cash-strapped families in Indiana. Though most of the note signers had property, they had little cash and, in some cases, probably still owed on their land. Henry had reason to worry—his two older sons were signers. But then, the young men had no assets for Makepeace to seize, perhaps an intentional deception.

Two Anderson brothers were on the hook as well: William T. and Asa. The landholding signers could be certain that if the miners did not pay Makepeace, they would be paying lawyers' fees and battling in court for years, possibly losing it all in a sheriff's sale. The one person whose name appeared on all the notes, Dr. Benjamin Jones, had no fear of being liable. He was simply the intermediary and would come out smelling like a rose either way.

Henry and Teach waited for rain with nearly as much impatience as they had awaited mail from home. Dry digging was probably the safest gold mining method, but relying on precipitation made the payoff uncertain. Henry had begun to consider other options. "We hear of some men makeing large piles by deep or hill diging but that kind is so precarious that we have as yet not tried it, but if the rains keep off verry late we will most likely try it as we think we have found a good spot near our shanty."[24] Henry's decision not to try hill digging was probably wise. Miners dug these "coyote" tunnels to reach old riverbed gravels that had become buried over millennia. They could pay well, though they sometimes collapsed, punishing the miners for their hubris.

In October, they went to the dry Calaveras River to "see if we can get anything there by turning up the stones in the bed of the river . . . we will be 3 or 4 miles from our shanty but have a good tent and will return about once a week for provisions."[25] Still the sky did not provide. "We are waiting impatiently now for rain, as we have considerable of dirt thrown up ready for washing and dont care about throwing up any more and there is but little else that we can do."[26] And when it did, it just teased. "The night before last it commenced raining and continued with but little intermission until this morning but it is now clear. Still we have hope that the rains will now set in and give us a chance to wash our dirt and perhaps find something better as there is a better chance of prospecting when there is watter in the gulches."[27]

In need of funds, Henry found work in the El Dorado camp, a couple miles from McKinneys, earning $6 a day at a quartz-crushing mill. The early mills, driven by steam, crushed the ore using poles with round, rotating metal plates at the bottom. These noisy contraptions were only a slight improvement over the Spanish arrastres—heavy rocks pulled by mules. The pulse of the stamping mill echoed and magnified a hundredfold the pulse of Abby's butter churn, both producing their own versions of gold.

Quartz operations were being funded by urban capitalists, at terms detrimental to the miners. According to the *Calaveras Chronicle*, a San Francisco consortium fronted the money to put machinery on promising veins "on the conditions that the first nett proceeds shall pay for the mills, and one half of the subsequent proceeds shall go to the erectors." The editors railed at the arrangement. "The miner discovers the lead, perhaps having spent all the money he had saved from surface digging in a couple years, and when he has found a lead of gold-bearing quartz, which will, with proper machinery, yield fortunes to a large company, he must needs give the first proceeds to the capitalists, and then only remain equal partner with them after the mill has been paid for."[28]

In Henry's case, he simply provided day labor, having sold his quartz claims. This was not the work life he had envisioned when he left Philadelphia in his twenties. Like others in the western migration, he wanted to become self-sufficient, to be his own man. Industrialization in the eastern states reduced men (women and children, too) to cogs in a machine, working for wages, with very little say about the conditions of their labor. Now, industrialization had rapidly flown west, catching him up in the whirlwind of progress, dashing his dreams.

Along with a basic education, young Henry Zane Jenkins had to learn a trade. In the early nineteenth century, indentured service was the norm, though not always a pleasant situation for the child or teen involved. One did not get to choose one's master; personality clashes arose regularly.

The Jenkinses would have known many tradesmen from their daily encounters, church congregations, and the extended Zane, Widdifield, and Jenkins families. (These Jenkins people were on his maternal, not paternal, side of the family.) The fact that Henry named his first child William Zane Jenkins might offer a clue to his master. Whomever his mentor happened to be, he released Henry when he reached his majority of twenty-one years. That did not mean he had the freedom to become an independent craftsman, though.

Trade guilds controlled the industries in Philadelphia. Before attaining the status of Master, and thus his independence, Henry had to pay his dues as a journeyman carpenter, working on the whims of the masters. Henry's workday began at sunrise and ended at sunset. Not bad in the winter months but exhausting in summer. Ideally, the seasons balanced the workload throughout the year, but in reality, master craftsmen often laid off their crews in winter.

Journeymen, mindful of their country's recent struggle for independence, saw that the battle had been fought for the benefit of men of power and property in America, not the average citizen. In 1827, labor began organizing in Philadelphia, not in trade guilds run by masters, but instead across the construction industry for the benefit of laborers. In June of that year, Henry and the journeyman house carpenters went on strike, known then as a stand-out (the term "scab," though, was already in use). The painters, glaziers, and bricklayers joined the carpenters in their demand for a ten-hour workday: "From Six to Six" was their rallying cry, with an hour off for breakfast and an hour for dinner (lunch).[29]

The previous year, an umbrella organization called the Mechanics' Union of Trade Associations (MUTA) formed, but did not get off the ground until the carpenters' strike. This was the world's first true labor union, which represented at least fifteen trade groups in Philadelphia.[30] Though it was short-lived, with lofty socialistic ideals, it sparked a new trend in the relationship between producers and managers.

By common law, organized labor making demands constituted a "conspiracy" and could result in prosecution. Conversely, the law deemed the masters' monopoly to be fair and desirable. Labor's strong-arm tactics against scabs led to arrests and convictions. Aside from that, they paid minimal fines. In late 1827, a tailors' strike against one particular employer led to a trial and sentencing. It is notable that even when striking as a group, as the house carpenters had, employees negotiated with their individual employer, not as a collective body.[31]

Henry served as secretary for the Mechanics and Work Men group, a sub-chapter of the MUTA.[32] He may have met the Bedford brothers, some of whom were in construction trades, during this labor unrest, or on a construction job. Likely through them, he got to know his sweetheart, Abigail Bedford. Having lost her fiancé to a sudden fever the year before, Abigail probably had diminishing prospects for marriage. She and Henry seemed compatible, though Henry's intense, serious demeanor contrasted with her more lighthearted nature.

Their relationship built in fervor simultaneous with the rise of the union and the carpenters' strike. As Henry fought for his rights, Abigail found herself with child and out of favor with the Society of Friends. Not only was Philadelphia's industrial sector undergoing upheaval, but the Friends were barreling toward a long-term schism. A progressive faction of Quakers wanted to bend the society toward a more Protestant-like worship. The traditionalists shied away from this trend and worshiped with Elias Hicks, who felt his views on the God within were more in line with founder George Fox's vision. His followers became known as Hicksites and were disowned from the Philadelphia Yearly Meeting, which became known as the Orthodox branch. This division lasted well into the twentieth century.

The Bedfords chose the conservative route and joined the Hicksites. Henry's mother, Ann, did as well. The Hicksites retained the plain speech and plain dress that many urban Quakers had already abandoned. Thee and thou never left their vocabulary. Even Henry, who never joined the Society, used this manner of speaking and writing.

Henry, not one to shirk responsibility, knew that the swelling new life Abigail carried sealed their fate as a couple. In late October 1827, they procured the services of a justice of the peace and spoke their vows.[33] The newlywed couple, with Henry out of work and receiving just $2 a week from the MUTA, undoubtedly relied on the benevolence of Abigail's parents for a home, where baby Will came into the world on February 13, 1828, the day before Abigail turned twenty-seven.[34] She was soon pregnant again, and a baby girl named Jane, for Abigail's mother, came along the following year.

By 1830, the Bedfords and Jenkinses had decided the time had come to quit the city. The ruptures in their work and religious life made a change of scene almost a necessity. Adding to their pain and suffering, baby Jane Jenkins went to an early grave. The loss of her left a hole in their hearts. Henry and Abigail needed a fresh start. Development in southwestern Ohio drew those with an entrepreneurial spirit. Quakers from the southern states, seeking to distance themselves from slavery, had developed new communities and embraced the disaffected urbanites.

Before he left Philadelphia, Henry joined another new movement: the Independent Order of Odd Fellows. This fraternal lodge derived its membership from all walks of life, not a particular profession, like the Freemasons. Their charitable purpose focused on providing members with burial services at the close of life. Henry kept his membership active for life, and he brought the organization to Ohio.

Henry and Abigail loaded their meager possessions and their toddler son into a wagon, saying goodbye to the place they had called home for nearly three decades. The road was rough, but many had covered this ground before. Members of the Bedford family had earlier relocated to Springboro, north of Cincinnati. Abigail and Henry may have been attuned to city life, but Cincinnati likely suffered labor issues as well. Maybe rural life would finally provide the independence and opportunity that Henry sought. The Jenkinses packed up again and joined the Bedfords in Springboro.

CHAPTER 11

GATHERINGS

The women had no clubs (except those they kept handy to kill snakes and to drive pigs away from the door) but they had their wool pickings and quiltings . . .
—WILLIAM GRIEST, HISTORY OF BALBEC [IND.] AND VICINITY

FALL AND WINTER 1851—INDIANA

In mid-September, Abby, Ann, and the children waited by the door with bundles of food and accouterments such as candles, pots and plates, bedrolls, and bibles. William and Ann Ransom, with little Cordelia, came by in the wagon to take them to a camp meeting. William and Bedford had cleared space for their tents near Albany, a tiny hamlet eleven miles south of Trenton on the banks of the Mississinewa River. The camp would be a family vacation combined with a revival meeting. For the assembled preachers, it was an opportunity to win new converts and fortify the faithful.

Camp meetings took place in wooded areas with fresh water available, which emphasized man's connection to nature, and hence to God, the Creator. In America, they hit their stride with a massive gathering at Cane Creek, Kentucky, in 1801, fueled by the growing Presbyterian and Methodist sects. The camps became notorious for outlandish behavior, both by the devout in the throes of spiritual ecstasy and by the unconverted with their own version of "spiritual" joy. Their popularity garnered

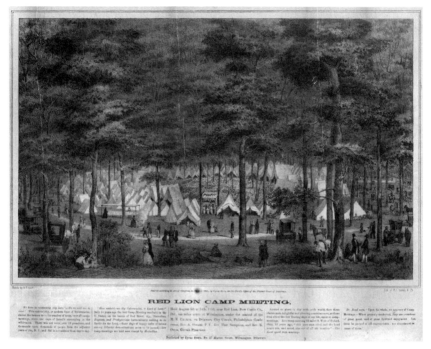

Figure 11.1. Methodist Episcopal camp meeting held in Red Lion, Delaware, in 1853. Credit: Library of Congress.

critical backlash from the newspapers. Journalists also published a bit of camp humor: "A minister at a Camp Meeting said, 'if the lady with the blue hat, red hair, and crossed eyes don't stop talking, she will be pointed out to the congregation.'"[1]

Not that the negative press deterred the faithful. People flocked to the forests to bathe in religious fervor and dip into baptismal pools. The ministers verbally flogged them with visions of hell and damnation for their sins and indiscretions. Brimstone and salvation alternately spewed from their fevered lungs, with equally enthusiastic responses from the crowd. In the early days, they were spectacles to behold but considerably tamed by the 1850s. In Ohio, Indiana, Michigan, and Illinois, the Methodists held sway over a vast territory and sparse populations. People sometimes traveled over a hundred miles to attend. Thus, the need to camp and plan events for several days.

By attending the meetings each fall, Abby's family had a respite from the daily grind: a change of scenery, visits with friends rarely seen. The family sorely missed Henry's presence at camp. Abby understood his desperation for supportive fellowship with his brothers and sisters in Christ. Abby and Henry's mother collected prayers for Henry: for fortification against the evil influences surrounding him, and deliverance from need and greed. The women had faith that these intercessions by his loved ones, dearest friends, and even strangers would cross that unknowable barrier between the earthly realm and the heavenly, back then to earth where needed most. With a continent separating them, it was their only hope of connection (besides the damn slow mail service).

After several days of sermons, prayers, conversions, and enthusiastic singing, the revival came to an end. "Hundreds quickly assembled at the stand, where a short exhortation was given, and a fervent prayer was offered up for a final blessing on that memorable spot. Then the meeting closed, amidst tears, and benedictions, and hearty hand-shakings, and fond embraces, in which feeble nerves and tender bones were in some danger; but none were hurt, and all felt that it was good for them to have been there."[2]

Feeling refreshed in spirit and fellowship but anointed by heavy rains rather than baptismal dunks, the Jenkinses and Ransoms packed up their soggy tents and headed for home.

Camp meetings were not the only gatherings taking place in the region. Eastern Indiana sat at the forefront of several progressive social movements. While Blackford County had proximity and economic ties to Jay County, it had a markedly different political bent. Around Hartford City, there were a fair number of Southern sympathizers.[3] Some people accused the Trenton residents of being among them, but they hailed predominantly from Northern states.[4] However, they were not exactly beating the drums for going to war over the slavery issue. In contrast, Jay County, along with Randolph and Wayne Counties to the south, was clearly under the sway of its Quaker settlers. As early as 1840, Job Carr Jr., Ellis Davis, James Marquis, and others living in the Camden vicinity formed the Jay County Anti-Slavery Society. That same year Job Carr Sr.,

Davis, and Hiram Gregg, all Quakers, established a temperance society determined to keep alcoholic beverage dealers out of Camden.

Back in August, Abby attended a large meeting in Bear Creek Township, east of Camden, to hear James "Jimmy" Marquis, a highly respected Methodist minister in the area. Marquis, a native of Virginia, was a towering figure, reported to be over six and a half feet tall.[5] He was nearly a decade Abby's junior. Davis, on the other hand, was one of the elder members of the community at sixty-five. It seemed the entire township had turned out, but it had been a huge disappointment to her: "2 weeks ago Marquis lectured at the school house. I went to hear him thinking it was on Sabbath day it would be like meeting, but alas it was a political blow and abolition song singing. I was disgusted. Ellis Davis followed Jimmy with some strained anecdotes and called it preaching. They are to try it again in a few weeks."[6] Abby knew Marquis and Davis well, including their activism, but this apparently constituted a desecration of the Sabbath. She had no tolerance for politics. In fact, it could be argued that Abby was apolitical in the extreme.

It is unlikely she disagreed with the abolition movement per se. She came from a family of abolitionists but wanted no involvement herself. Her brother, William S. Bedford, had even gone to jail for helping an enslaved family escape to Canada.[7] Her husband also favored abolition, as demonstrated in his remarks to her from New Orleans. He recorded the address of prominent New York abolitionist Lewis Tappan in one of his memo books. Tappan was well known for his involvement in the Amistad case.[8] Did Henry plan to visit Tappan on his way home, or contribute financial support to the cause once he struck it rich? Either scenario is possible. The proponents of abolition, in many cases, advocated for women's rights as well.

From what had begun in Seneca Falls in 1848, suffragist leaders organized the first National Women's Rights Convention in Worcester, Massachusetts, in 1850. Women thrust into unfamiliar duties by the absence of their gold-seeking husbands fortified the movement. "Out of necessity occupying roles traditionally reserved for men, some women began to ask why they did not have the right to occupy them by choice."[9] This phenomenon grew as new gold rushes materialized out west and with the deaths of hundreds of thousands of men during the coming Civil War. In these early days, the platform focused less on equality than on the reality that women had great responsibilities and were denied representation in the government on matters that had enormous impact on their lives. In 1851, the second annual convention at Worcester acknowledged some progress since the previous year, notably the admission of women into medical schools.

At a women's convention in Akron, Ohio, back in May, former slave Sojourner Truth had electrified the audience. Truth pointed out that "I can't read, but I can hear. I have heard the bible and have learned that Eve caused man to sin. Well if woman upset the world, do give her a chance to set it right side up again." She expounded on how Mary and Martha came to Jesus, asking him to raise their brother, Lazarus, from the dead. He did not turn the women away. Rather, he wept, and Lazarus arose. "And how came Jesus into the world?" Truth continued, "Through God who created him and woman who bore him. Man, where is your part?" She then acknowledged that "man is in a tight place, the poor slave is on him, woman is coming on him, and he is surely between a hawk and a buzzard."[10]

Stemming from a meeting of progressive Quakers in Greensboro, Indiana, a convention on women's rights also took place in Dublin, Wayne County, in October 1851, not terribly far from the Jenkins farm, but still a world away. Abby knew about the convention; some of her acquaintances took part. It is not likely she would have attended, though, even if she could.

The press pointed out that the participants were mostly women of means, at least solidly in the middle class. For the poor, such activism was a luxury. As for women's rights, well, Abby had her own take: "thee knows my sentiments of the fuss that is made about the rights of Woman. I maintain I have a right to my own husband whenever I can get hold of him and keep fast hold if I can."[11] As Henry's absence stretched on, she wearied under her load, "I am sometimes somewhat depressed. The cares of a large family with a mind as weak as mine are heavy—I love female rights—that is a some body to look to in all troubles—to lift the burden off my shoulders and take the lead. It is our prerogative and I hope soon again to gain it."[12] Many women in her position were of a like mind, particularly those who adhered to biblical injunctions circumscribing a woman's place.

One wrote to an Indianapolis paper with her deeply religious perspective on the matter:

> "I have given her as a helpmate," said the voice that cannot err, when it spake unto Adam . . . Since the Creator has assigned different spheres of action for the different sexes, it is to be presumed, from his unerring wisdom, that there is work enough in each department to employment, and that the faithful performance of that work will be for the benefit of both. . . . The true nobility of woman is to keep her own sphere, and to adorn it; not like the comet, daunting and perplexing other systems, but as the pure star, which is the first to light the day and the last to leave it.[13]

She appealed to the "Mothers" in their role of providing love and sanctuary for all, from "cradle to sepulcher." Abby would likely have approved.

As daily routines resumed after the camp meeting, Abby recalled Henry's description of his daily life in the mines before he had his cabin:

> I rise in the morning as soon as light, make a fire, put on water for tea or Coffee, boil some potatoes or fry the cold ones . . . fry a piece of meat. When ready, spread it on a stone in front of my tent, sit down on the ground and take my breakfast with thankfulness. Clear the table and by that time it is time to go to work (if not a chapter of the bible or testament is read), work until 11 ½ Oclock, run to the tent, strike up a fire, boil some potatoes, fry some meat, warm my tea or coffee or Chocolate (I have all three) for I make enough in the morning to last all day, and then take my seat again on the ground. Try to feel thankful and wonder if you at home are fareing as well as I am, sometimes doubting it is not the case. Clear off the things, retire into the tent, read a portion of scripture. If any sewing is needed attend to that. A short

nap (if washing or bakeing does not hinder). We have a bake oven in common about 100 yds from my tent and mostly have light bread. At 2 Oclock return to work, quit at six, then go through about the same routine for supper which takes until quite dark. Sometimes go down to the other tents, six in number . . . mostly turn into my tent and sew if I have any, read a few chapters and retire to my lonely bed mostly sleep soundly until morning.[14]

Well then, Henry's days sounded quite as monotonous as hers, if not more so. At least she had the company of family and friends in the Trenton-Camden surroundings. She wondered if he had made some new friends out there, given the fickle nature of his business partners. Perhaps he had managed to find Willis Wilson or even E.D. Pierce.

The autumn harvest signaled a busy season for farmers. The burden eased somewhat for Abby by having her sons and son-in-law to help with the reaping and butchering. As the young men worked, California plans entered the conversation. Next year would be tough for Abby if Henry did not return. Henry had sent tiny amounts of gold in his more recent letters, but it was not enough to put a dent in the family debt. As Christmas approached, she received Henry's letter bearing the news of his near demise from milk sickness. What a heart-stopping moment. What if he had perished? She would never have a respite from the daunting workload. Certainly, she had the strength, if the need arose. All around her were real widows (not just the gold-rush variety) coping with such a situation. But it was too disturbing to contemplate for long.

Henry's admission to drinking was another matter altogether. It troubled Abby and Ann both.

Though delighted by Henry's gifts—a pressed flower and smattering of gold—his mother had deep concerns about his surroundings. Ann wrote him, "It is greavous to think of thy comfortless situation amongst such profane society but take courage and put thy trust [in] him who is able to save from every danger those that ask for his help in truth and sincerity of heart," urging him to refrain from alcohol. "Dear Henry shun the intoxicating bowl, taste not touch not [handle] not the accursed thing, pardon me for this caution I hope it unnecessary but I am an anxious Mother."[15] Ann had ample experience with alcoholism during her childhood. Her father and brother (both named Jonathan Zane) had been admonished by the Friends for heavy drinking, and both died disturbingly young.

Ann Widdifield Zane witnessed the disintegration of her once-prominent Philadelphia Quaker family. She was born in 1770 to Jonathan Jr. and Mary (Jenkins) Zane. Ann's mother died a few years into the Revolutionary War, when Ann was not quite eight. Her father ran a hardware establishment. Her grandfather, also named Jonathan Zane, had formed Philadelphia's first fire insurance company with none other than Benjamin Franklin. The extended Zane family even had a street named in their honor (now called Filbert St.). The Revolution turned these Quaker merchants' world upside down. Their pacifist doctrine did not go over well with the Revolutionaries. If you were not with them, you were against them—as the thinking went. Jonathan Sr. probably sided with the merchants in their protests against unreasonable taxes. His son, despite being descended from many generations of American-born men, had a rebellious streak of his own; it did not go well for him.

In 1778, the Philadelphia Court of Oyers and Terminers (a type of district court) held trials for individuals accused of treason (against the Revolutionaries). Witnesses told the court that Jonathan Jr., who allegedly served as a captain in the city guard, had proclaimed that he " . . . would fight for the King of Britain as long as he had a drop of blood against the Rebels, meaning the American Army."[16] There is no indication he ever took up arms against Americans, however. He was imprisoned for a time and released after the court declared the indictment against him invalid. Not long after, his father passed away.

His actions also earned the ire of the Friends for the opposite reason—they considered his paying a fine to be aiding the Revolution. Jonathan, reviled on all sides, turned to the bottle. The Society condemned this as well, though they did try to reason with him:

> Jonathan Zane . . . has been ensnared into the pernicious practice
> of taking strong Liquors to excess, and into a departure from our

peacable principles, by paying of Fines imposed for the support of War—On these Occasions he has been tenderly labour'd with, but not appearing sufficiently sensible of his condition . . . we hereby declare our disunion with the said Jonathan Zane, until he through Divine favour witnesseth Repentance & is qualified to condemn his evil conduct, which we, desire he may come to.[17]

Though his estrangement continued, his daughters remained part of the Philadelphia congregations, known as meetings. Through 1780 and 1781, the Friends urged him to mend his ways. Then, in 1782, Jonathan, with three children to rear, chose to remarry—to his dead wife's sister, Hannah. Though it was a practical choice, the Friends disapproved, adding her to their list of expelled members along with her new husband. Jonathan and Hannah spoke their vows in the First Baptist Church.

By the close of the Revolutionary War, the Zane name lost some of its luster, no doubt due in part to Jonathan Jr. He died soon after at age forty-four. Ann was just fifteen. Critical damage to her family had been done—there would be no going back to their pre-war status in the City of Brotherly Love. Ann's older brother, Jonathan III, also chose a path contrary to Quaker doctrines. Given his father's actions during the war, he may have had to endure some uncomfortable scrutiny from both the Quakers and his fellow citizens. He fathered a child out of wedlock with a non-Quaker woman whom he married, got in fistfights, and drank to excess. After suffering the dispiriting deaths of his wife and young daughter, Jonathan III died in 1804 at thirty-nine.

Ann Zane, relying on her aunt/stepmother and probably extended family, grew to womanhood despising the alcohol abuse that had no doubt shortened her father's life and later her brother's. She married David Jenkins (no relation to her mother, Mary Jenkins) in 1790, in the same Baptist church her father and Hannah married in eight years earlier. Jenkins, not being Quaker, earned Ann an expulsion from her congregation. She did not rejoin the Friends until becoming a widow decades later.

The cold that Ann Jenkins had caught in summer seemed to be a permanent affliction. She explained the situation to Henry: "Bedford brought

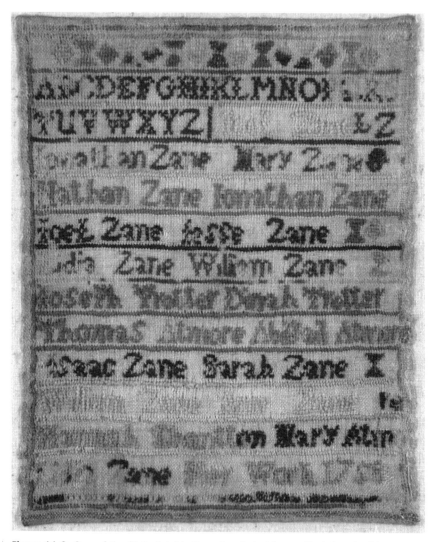

Figure 11.2. One of the Philadelphia Zane family heirlooms that Ann Jenkins passed to her granddaughter, Emma, was this 1758 sampler. It was embroidered by Ann's aunt, Deb Zane, whose death date is unknown, but she is believed to have died before reaching adulthood. Credit: Courtesy of Mark Riederer.

me home in Dr. Beals buggy and it began to rain when we got to the bridge and fell down in torrents all the way home and there was not a dry thread in my cloths, I still feel the effects of it and camp meeting in a muslin tent in rain did not help it." On Christmas Day, she felt well enough to venture from home again. "Mary Spencer & her brother James came with a sled for me to go to their house to dine. I felt pretty well th[at] day but was taken very sick the next day [and] was very bad all day and next night. They do[ne] everything they could for me and would have had me to stay but they brought me home and I was several weeks very bad."[18] She worried that she would never see her son again and about his sobriety.

Abby also attempted to shore up her husband's faltering resolve regarding the sin of intemperance. "My dear Henry . . . a spirit of lone-lyness sometimes comes over me and <u>sometimes</u> a fear that thy long absence from all good examples may have a tendency to darken thy previous light, truly thee has my constant sympathy and prayers that thy feet slip not. I feel quite too small to turn mentor but thee knows me and can excuse. Oh look up continually there is always help at hand."[19] As the cold, dark winter descended, Abby hoped that Henry would have a successful winter and spring. And that summer would bring her dearest helpmate home to her, where he belonged.

In their sturdy brick residence in Chesterfield, Allen Makepeace and his wife celebrated the Christmas holiday accompanied by a "bundle of joy"—their newborn son, Allen Quincy Makepeace. Allen had married Nancy Shimer in 1825, and they had no surviving children until Alvira Jane was born in 1848, when Nancy was forty years old. Allen Q.'s birth was a true miracle for the little family. Makepeace finally had an heir to his growing fortune. He had another reason to celebrate. His hometown of Chesterfield won the railroad lottery—a stop on the Indianapolis and Bellefontaine line.[20] It may not have been luck, given that he was both a stockholder and director. Unlike his neighbors to the northeast in Black-ford and Jay Counties, the people of Madison County were rewarded for their investment in the future of transportation.

Women's rights or no, Nancy Makepeace was undoubtedly part of a strong business partnership with her husband and their extended family. In addition to their mercantile establishment, Allen and Nancy bought and sold real estate, not just in Madison but also in the surrounding counties. When anyone defaulted on a Makepeace loan, they could expect a swift foreclosure action and sheriff's sale. Sometimes that entailed the seizure of personal property as well as land. In November 1851, they acquired a 200-acre parcel from attorney James Swaar for $500. Possibly Swaar had to deed the land to Makepeace in order to repay his loan and avoid legal action. In just a couple months, the California notes from the Blackford Company would be coming due. Perhaps Makepeace had gotten wind of the troubles they were having in California. He evaluated how he should handle the situation. He could foreclose on the properties pledged as security, or he could let the interest accumulate and hope the gold would eventually pay off. One of the men on the note was dead. He had no way of knowing if the others would survive to come home. At least they had families to return to, giving them an incentive to come back, some day. It was an unusually large sum he had lent to those fortune hunters; that had to be on his mind as the new year rolled around. He knew he would get his money, one way or another. It was just a matter of procedure.

William Ransom had waited long enough. He had not gone to California with E.D. Pierce in 1849. He had been left out of his cousin Sam's gold company. Now, it was his turn for a chance at the mines. About twenty men, most from Blackford County, planned a mid-winter departure, following Henry's advice about traveling through the tropics. Another thing they had learned from the earlier adventurers: travel together but do not form a company. Rather than executing large notes like the Blackford Company, each would arrange his own financing for the trip. If the others had done it for $300, they could do it for that—or even less, they figured. William's brother, Robert, and brother-in-law, Will Jenkins, decided to join him. They had been working and saving for several years, but it would be a thin purse each carried.

Early 1852 seemed a good time to get away. Deaths from fevers continued their run. It was not only children and the elderly who perished. Even men in their teens and twenties succumbed. California had a reputation for being a healthy place, assuming you did not die getting there. But perversely, they would leave their wives and children to possibly suffer the fate they might avoid themselves. Unlike some others, William Ransom hoped to make California his home, eventually bringing his wife to join him. He wanted to put some distance between his mercurial father and himself to avoid conflicts. California ought to be far enough away from the old man. If gold did not bring the income he hoped for, agricultural opportunities gave him an additional reason to head west.

This new coterie included the Ransoms' close neighbors Hazelett Lanning, plus Henry and Jackson Cortright; Frank Taughinbaugh, son of the Blackford County recorder; and John Jackson Twibell, from a venerable local family. Most were in their twenties. Like the 1851 group, some of them had wives and small children, including William Ransom and Will Jenkins.

All the young men worked on farms prior to leaving Indiana, except Taughinbaugh, who worked as a saddler. William Ransom dealt in livestock in addition to his farming duties. No doubt some were in the process of learning other skilled trades: cooper, gunsmith, wheelwright, miller, harness-maker, and so on. Unlike their fathers' generation, these pioneers were not bound by indentured apprenticeships. They were merely bound by their own imaginations. They could even conceivably be doctors and lawyers, as many requirements, such as medical licenses, had lapsed by mid-century in most states. William's friend Pierce had no special skills other than natural wit when he became a law student in Hartford City. He could not even properly read and write.

William and friends planned to follow the same route as his father-in-law: New Orleans to Panama to San Francisco. They anticipated a February departure. That day could not come soon enough for William. His one regret would be leaving Ann behind. Female companionship always factored into his pleasure in life.

CHAPTER 12
ON THE MOVE

"The independence and liberality here and the excitement attending the rapid march of this country make one feel insignificant and sad at the prospect of returning to the old beaten path at home."—Charles Plummer, letter from California

1851 AND 1852—CALIFORNIA TO INDIANA

After half-hearted attempts in October and November, the heavens wrung out the clouds just before Christmas—a holiday gift for the Southern Mines. At last, Teach and Henry washed their accumulated dirt. The *Calaveras Chronicle*, published in Mokelumne Hill, reported that many mining companies were profiting from the nearly non-stop deluge. Feeling flush, the gold dust flew from their pokes about as fast as they filled them. Merchants would get their share of the wealth by providing the grungy masses with some holiday cheer beyond the usual fare.

At least two fandangos (a Spanish dance, but generally referring to a dance hall) planned balls for "the Hill." And just below, an arena took shape to stage a bear-and-bull fight featuring the famed grizzly General Scott, named for the victor of the Mexican War, Winfield Scott.[1] But Christmas came and went without the grisly display; the weather impeded construction. The balls were well-attended; one even had a surprising number of females. Not surprisingly, the gathered crowds of various cultures, combined with alcohol, produced a number of violent crimes that night, including one murder and the attempted murder of a constable making an arrest.[2]

For the scattered men of the Blackford company, the weather was a mixed blessing. They had water to work their dry claims, but it made their planned meeting in Stockton on New Year's Day difficult and inconvenient. Henry should have been celebrating his savior's birth in the company of family and friends. Reading Abby's letter about her experiences at the camp meeting emphasized the distance between him and his spiritual rituals. He now attended services in Mokelumne Hill when he could borrow a mule to get there in time. Just after Christmas, though, gale force winds ripped through town, destroying many makeshift shelters. The poorly constructed Methodist Church building splintered to bits as the storm howled through town.[3] It gave any religious man pause about the presence of God in these heathen mining camps.

On New Year's Day 1852, nine men, weary and possibly a little wiser, straggled into Stockton, an aptly named locale for a group about to take stock of their situation. Henry summarized: "Jan 1st Setled up my accounts paid off all demand and find myself in posession of two shares in a quartz Company which I value at fifty dollars each = 100.00 and cash in hand 7.00 makeing in all $107.00. If on disposeing of the above mentioned claims if more should be realised without any additional expense I hold myself bound to settle with H Andersons estate in accordance therewith."[4] It was a slim contribution. If they pooled any amount at all, it certainly did not cover Humphrey's debt. Henry had so little to his name that he had no thought of attempting the trip back to Indiana as planned.

Not all the men had his poor luck. Nineteen-year-old Pete Liestenfeltz demonstrated better sense than many of his California peers. According to Pete, "I sent 600.00 at one time in 1852 home at Cinnanita [Cincinnati]. That was the clocest place that we could get it. Father sent Anty Pitman . . . [the Camden merchant] after our money and brought it home to father. Father took it to Muncie and walked and put it on interest at 8%. He lent it to the Pennsylvania railway. There was no railroad there when we went, only the track was cleared up."[5] Pete refers to the Indianapolis⊠Bellefontaine line—the very railroad in which Allen

Makepeace was a director—later acquired by the Pennsylvania Railroad. The track had been laid since his departure. For some reason, Pete did not pay the $450 he owed to Makepeace. Pete earned money by investing his gold, along with a partner, in a store at McKinneys Creek. Like most in his situation, he probably kept a mining claim going in addition to his mercantile business.

The previous fall, the men had sent remittances home to their families, small amounts such as $25 or $50. They used Adams Express Co., which had an office in Murphys. Abby received one from Henry. These smaller amounts, unlike Pete's $600, could probably be used in Indiana like cash. Merchants such as Pitman would redeem them in Cincinnati or Dayton when they went to purchase supplies.

Aside from the Humphrey Anderson business, the company discussed their original agreement. The Articles stated that they would pool their earnings, and when they first split into smaller groups, they reiterated that provision. However, some of them were clearly doing better than others and were loath to share the profits they acquired with great effort. They voted to dissolve the partnership instead. Henry did not report this to Abby, as he probably disagreed with the decision, but she heard about it—other men had passed the news along. Once it became general knowledge, Allen Makepeace certainly caught a whiff.

While in Stockton, Henry sat for a portrait at a daguerreotype studio. His brush with death in October underscored his mortality. His family should have a picture of him at least. He did not want his youngest children, Mary and Barton, to forget his face. The Jenkinses received it later that spring. His mother remarked, "Thy present of thy likeness came safe to hand, we all think it is a pretty good likeness but would much rather see the original with or without gold."[6] Both Ann and Abby knew that for all his optimistic talk, Henry was having little success at mining or carpentry.

Ann told him, "I feel very sorry to hear that thee has been so unsuccessful in thy persuit after gold and after all what is it but yellow dirt. I sincerely wish that thee had never left thy quiet home for it and hope thee will return as soon as thee possibly can."[7] She did not know that Henry, like most of the others, had decided to remain in California another year.

Abby wrote frankly, "It seems that thy ill luck has followed thee to California—thee has been so long and from what I can gather thee is not any better off than thee would have been if thee had stayed at home and we would have had the pleasure of thy company. Don't keep putting off thy return for fear of not having enough—there is always a way and thy intention was good. There will be a way provided." Abby then undermined her argument, saying, "We hear great accounts of rich mines in the south of Cala . . ."[8]

Miners assumed all would find riches and return home wealthy. Newspapers fueled expectations at home. It pressured the husbands to succeed, or at least save face by not returning home before making even a small profit. Men thought their piles were just around the corner. As with any form of gambling, just a small nugget once in a while kept them going. Failing in their appointed task—bringing home the gold—forced them to make a tough decision. Henry decided he could not leave. He had so much at stake, had taken on massive debt, had made promises his ego would not allow him to renege on. If Henry left before striking a rich vein, he could not live with himself.

Besides, he was a seasoned veteran now. His hesitant early days—learning mining techniques and struggling with his partners—had faded. As the state absorbed ever more immigrants, new opportunities arose. There would always be work for the industrious, he knew. He just needed more time. And, like many others, he appreciated the beauty of the place, the mild climate, the absence of epidemics. Best of all, he had found the congregation in Mokelumne Hill. He felt certain the year ahead held great promise. He would make enough to break even and then some.

Of the Blackford nine, only Harvey Hunt and Dennis Lowry decided to call it quits that spring. They did not travel home together, however. Their long-time partners, Pres Gibson and John Anderson, formed a new partnership after their departure. Harvey would return to his family, even without his pile. He swallowed his pride and made good on his promise to be gone for just a year. Had Susan Hunt made a convincing case for Harvey to come home? Or was it possible that California had broken his spirit? He usually worked with Pres Gibson in the mines. In November 1851, Harvey and Pres sent remittances to their families "and as they have neither of them received any inteligence or letters from home are verry anxious," per Henry.[9] Harvey may have eventually received some communication from his wife, or Susan ignored him completely, compelling him to satisfy his curiosity.

Around the end of May 1852, Harvey headed to San Francisco. He boarded the steamship *Independence* on June 2, among 150 passengers.[10] After crossing the isthmus at Nicaragua—a twelve-mile trek, a boat ride across Lake Nicaragua, then down the San Juan River to the Caribbean side—he boarded the *Northern Light*. On July 2, the ship landed in New York with 300 passengers and $188,000 of gold dust aboard.[11] Harvey Hunt carried very little, if any. He may have had to visit his relatives in the Adirondacks to beg money for the train trip to Indiana.

Upon his return home in early July 1852, he and Susan ran up accounts at the Camden mercantile, Pitman and Chandlee, as well as acquiring goods from Dr. Benjamin Jones.[12] The amount of cloth among the Hunts' purchases suggests a desperate need for new clothing for the family. From the doctor, they received cordwood. Harvey should have been able to procure wood from his own land. It is telling that they did not pay cash. He was on the hook for his fifth of the $2,800 Makepeace note. He had nothing to contribute. By the end of the year, it would no longer be his problem.

Dennis Lowry mounted his horse and strung along a pack animal, possibly accompanied by a dog for companionship. His saddlebags held a small box of gold dust entrusted to him by Henry Jenkins. Henry took a big risk assuming it would be delivered to Abby intact. It is telling that he chose Dennis, though he knew Harvey would surely make it to Indiana first. Dennis chose to go home overland—the hard way. He could not have avoided tales about the Oregon-California trail and, having already gone the sea route, wanted to experience the American interior. He bucked the tide of migrants; few miners took the trail home. Heading westward to California, the trip became hardest toward the end. Traveling east, it would get easier as he went along.

The first part of his journey took him to Hangtown (Placerville), where he turned east to cross the Sierras at Carson Pass. "After crossing the nevada Mts I had A butiful valley to travel in for 80 miles. This is carsons valley. At the East end of this Lay the Desert 40 miles in Length. This Desert Lyes Between the Sink of Carsen River & the Sink of marys or the humbolt River."[13] He reported no traveling companions, but he also failed to mention his associates on the outward passage. It would have been foolhardy to travel solo, but he may have had trouble finding others willing to go that way.

By leaving Calaveras County on Sunday, June 27, he timed his journey well to have the full moon lighting his way across the notorious forty-mile desert, something best done at night. Traveling light on horseback gave him an advantage over the wagon trains that took days to traverse the barren alkali flat. The spring migrants who had wintered in Salt Lake had long since settled in California. The ones who left Missouri in spring would not be arriving for at least another month, so he had a lonely—and creepy—crossing ahead.

He could not lose his way, even if clouds dimmed the lunar beam. Miner Jacob Crum described the scene: "The desert was one of the awfulest places I have ever seen; it was strewed from one end to the other with the carcasses of dead animals, wagons, carriages, harness, chains, clothing, in short every article that you can think of, excepting provisions, that an emigrant would want."[14] In addition to the detritus of the wagon trains, Dennis passed through a forty-mile-long graveyard of migrants. Many had starved or died of dehydration. Others perished from cholera. The desert and Humboldt River portion of the trip humbled, tortured, and killed many migrants. Tramping the trail raised clouds of gray, salty dust that stung the eyes and opened sores. There was no water and no forage. Sometime around July 1, Dennis made this frightful journey in just seven hours.

At the far end of his desert trek, Dennis reached the Humboldt Sink, "where the 300-mile Humboldt (Mary's) River died in a foul-smelling seep. Contemporary guidebooks fittingly described this sink as the place where the river disappeared into the earth. . . . Some of the more imaginative emigrants anticipated that this wondrous sight would be a whirlpool of rushing waters sucked into a gaping hole. Seeing the sluggish Humboldt ooze its final stagnant remains into a soggy slough must have been a great disappointment."[15]

Dennis followed the well-worn path along the river leading to the City of Rocks in present-day Idaho. From there, he took the Salt Lake Cutoff. He saw no settlers between California and Salt Lake City. He wrote that "the Mormons has A Butiful valley all most Surrounded By Mts. I stoped with them 8 days to Rest my Self and creatures. They treated us very kind."[16]

1851 AND 1852—NORTHERN CALIFORNIA

Where E.D. Pierce seems to have had little success in his first two years out, 1851 found things looking up. He formed a business partnership with Paris Pfouts, William S. Good, and James Brown in northern Shasta County, at a place called Scott Bar. They had a store near the river, a stock ranch in the Scott Valley, and mining claims as well. In the spring, Brown had dug up a spectacular nugget, weighing over fifteen pounds, which became a statewide sensation. It was a solid gold oblong lump with only the tiniest speck of quartz. The partners sold it for well over $3,000.[17] When a rich strike near the Shasta River attracted a horde of miners, they relocated their store to the new community of Yreka, which Pierce had a hand in laying out.[18] The four men made fistfuls of money and became well-known throughout the region. Pierce's popularity helped him win a seat as a Shasta County representative to the State Assembly. Of the four candidates, he received the highest vote tally. His friend and fellow Democrat, Samuel Fleming, won the second seat.[19]

As 1851 came to a close, Pierce and Fleming left Yreka and struggled to get over the Scott Mountains to attend the assembly. Early December had been mild, but after Christmas, the snows began in earnest. The two spent a miserable night on the pass, unable to get a fire lit in the heavy, wet, blowing sleet: " . . . lonely and sad were the perilous hours we spent that night . . . I was much more chilled than Mr. Fleming, in fact came near passing the corner and with the most intense agony we watched for the approach of day. The moment it made its appearance we was on the way . . ."[20] They arrived safely in Shasta City and took a stage the next day to Sacramento. From there, they traveled to Vallejo, taking their oaths of office on January 7, 1852. One of their legislative duties was to promote the creation of Siskiyou County from Shasta—a successful outcome of the session. His newfound successes encouraged him to send a letter to his friends in Indiana. He raved about the wonders of the state and vowed to return to Indiana that spring to see his sweetheart, Rebecca, and bring more people back with him. His opinion on the matter would change drastically once the legislative term ended.

1852—INDIANA TO PANAMA

William and Robert Ransom and friends left Blackford County in February. Ann Ransom, with her daughter Cordelia, went to stay with her mother and grandmother, Abby and Ann Jenkins. Will Jenkins's wife and daughter, Jane and Lizzy, were left with her parents, Elizabeth and James Ransom. Elizabeth had a one-month-old infant herself to care for, her last-born child. Robert Ransom said his goodbyes to Emma Jenkins, with a promise to wed upon his return, when she would be old enough by her parents' standards. If things went according to plan, they could then make their home in the land of the setting sun. After the group departed, Henry's letter advising William not to come out to California until Henry had found a paying mine to turn over to him arrived. Reading it, Abby mused, "but if they had [received it] I do not know that it would have stopt them (though they would have believed thee). They think each one must try for themselves to find out all," echoing the sentiments of every parent, ever.[21]

The young men caught a riverboat to New Orleans, riding on the chilly main deck, warmed only by the noisy boilers and cook stove. They were prime candidates to get roped into loading wood all the way downriver. The boat needed to stop about every thirty or forty miles for fuel. Each man hauled six or seven four-foot-long logs on his shoulder per trip, a fine way to warm up on a cold night, but then later, the sweat would chill them to the bone. Though risking a fall into the roiling river, some men relished the opportunity to relieve their idleness and work their muscles. On the Mississippi, the height of the banks and mud created major hazards for the wooders. Sometimes the plank they trod dangled fifteen feet above the shoreline. A muddy boot slipping on the smooth wood could lead to disaster.[22]

Disembarking in New Orleans, the Ransom brothers and Will, along with their companions, looked into purchasing passage on the steamship lines to Panama and on to San Francisco. Ann Jenkins related to Henry that Will and the Ransoms " . . . got as far as Orleans when they found their funds would not hold out and W. Jenkins returned. He had broke up and left Jane and her babe at her fathers and of coarse is quite unstriped—one dime was all he possessed and of course was in a poor way to begin housekeeping. No flour no meat no coffee no sugar no salt no anything but a cow and I think they have one fat hog . . . "[23] Will, Jane, and Lizzy continued to stay on with the Ransoms until they could get back on their feet. If Will felt disappointed about his canceled trip, he did not speak of it.

The Ransoms boarded a steamship in New Orleans that carried them to Havana, where they changed to another ship, arriving from New York, that would take them on to Aspinwall. Located on Navy Bay, Aspinwall replaced Chagres as the arrival and departure point on the north side of the isthmus. There they found a modern port and railway where they could disembark without the need for local boats to ferry them to land. The Panama Railroad, then under construction, still had several years before becoming fully operational. It reached Gatun in November 1851, cutting eight miles off the lower Chagres River portion of the crossing to Panama City. The rest of the trip remained an upriver and cross-country slog.

Transportation to California had become routine, with steamships making scheduled departures, but a backlog of people overflowed the city. By February, all of the Pacific-side steamships were booked solid for two months out.[24] If you did not already have a steamer ticket when you arrived in Panama, one could not be had at any price. Impatience to get to California forced the unprepared to choose from equally bad options. They could not earn money until they got to San Francisco, and staying in Panama for months cost too much for this poor lot.

Stephen Davis, a twenty-year-old traveler on his third trip across the isthmus, noted on February 14, "There are some 4000 persons in this city waiting passage to San Francisco. Hundreds of persons are encamped in the edge of the forest one mile back of the town, where they cook their own food and sleep on the ground. And consequently there is a great deal of sickness, and considerable mortality. Small Pox, Measles, Isthmus Fever and Yellow Fever are the prevailing diseases."[25]

Ships continued to bring more to Aspinwall—the Ransoms were hardly the only ones hungry to get to California that season. By February 24, Davis estimated the transients in Panama at 5,000. The chaos was probably the worst of the entire rush period. These circumstances gave old sailing ships an opportunity to capture part of the market. Agents hawked tickets to the poor and desperate, but they charged exorbitant fares, considering the uncertain nature of the trip's duration and the ships' general decrepitude, sight unseen several miles from shore. A steamship passage cost about the same and would make the journey in roughly twenty days, in much nicer accommodations. A sailing ship, at best, would take twice as long. However, it was a rare sailor that made it to San Francisco in forty days.

One sailing ship waiting offshore was the British barque *Emily*, which had made her way from London to Sydney, Australia, to load coal, and then across the Pacific. *The Panama Star* described the city scene and touted the *Emily* as an alternative to the sold-out steamers.

> We seldom recollect seeing so large a number of passengers in our streets, as we witnessed yesterday afternoon. Main-street was so crowded with emigrants, their mules, and baggage, that it was really difficult to find space to pass by. The passengers by the steamers "City of New York," "Ohio," and "Sierra Nevada," are now in town, and "the cry is, still they come"; and the echo is, how are they to get away? The two steamers now here can carry but a small proportion of the immense number awaiting passage, and we *know* of only one sailing vessel now ready . . . to issue tickets. We mean the fine ship *Emily*, put up by Garrison & Fretz—We presume she will be filled up before noon.[26]

The agency sold tickets for the *Emily* at $150 each. "She was advertised to go through in 35 or 40 day[s]," according to ticket buyer George Blanchard, one of more than 200 men duped by the wily agent.[27] The passengers who had been charged this outrageous sum discovered they had been swindled. "Great excitement concerning the independent tickets. They have attached the agents purs & intend to make a dividend among the passengers having such tickets," related David Gillis, an Ohio man who kept a diary on the voyage of the *Emily*.[28]

The Ransoms also bought tickets for the *Emily*, along with most of their Indiana companions. It would sail on March 7. William wrote a letter to Ann, letting their families and others know the plan. As they prepared to board, they were blissfully unaware that the captain of the *Emily*, J. Harvey, had never been to California and knew nothing about the proper route to take.

SPRING 1852—INDIANA

The anniversary of Henry's departure came and went; the Jenkins family did not celebrate the occasion. About the family, Ann wrote in her March letter to Henry, "They are getting along as well as could be expected . . ." and had settled into a life without him. She acknowledged her eighty-second birthday in her humble way, "How good is our God that has so long spared my useless and unprofitable life even once. Bless and adore his goodness." Responding to Henry's boast about mastering bread baking, she said, "I was much pleased to hear that you took care of yourselves in the eating line but do not think that thee will beat Emma in baking bread for she is a very good baker altho I do not doubt the excellence of thine." As any good mother would, she warned him, "I hope thee will take care of your grissly neighbors and not venture too near them." She told him about the local fascination with the arrival of "the mediems and the wonderful tappings. It is a constant topic of discourse."[29]

Abby chimed in to report that Will's wife, Jane, and her younger sister, Mary Ransom, had gone into Camden "to hear the knockings—there is hardly anything else talked of just now—truly it seems as if the spirit of the air is let loose and it seems as if the last days were approaching."[30] Though eastern newspapers discredited these "Rappers," Jay County had credulous people. Because of rainy weather, they put outdoor work on hold, providing time for amusements. One of Henry and Abby's nearby contemporaries expressed his thoughts on the mediums: "Now Sir this knocking is real . . . I will give an opinion of this as some call it a mystery yet I think it can be explained by some material cause. The medium . . . is a battery slightly charged with these fluids. I judge this from the fact that

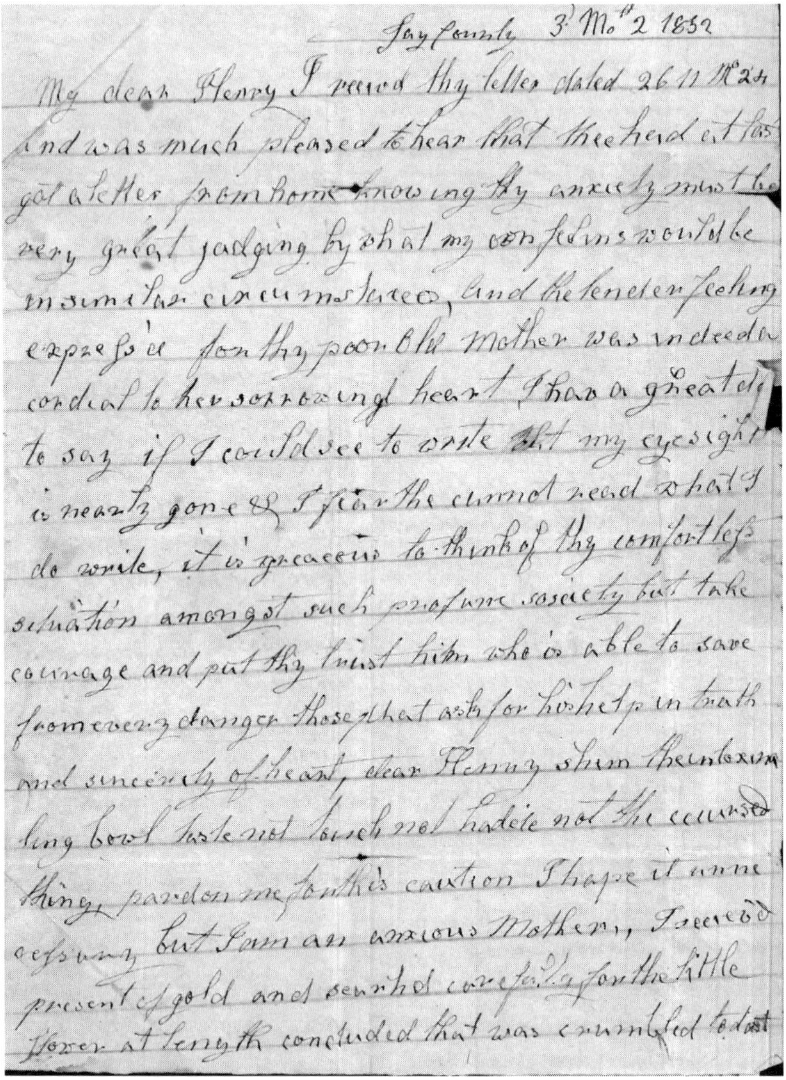

Jay County 3 Mo 2 1852

My dear Henry I recd thy letter dated 26 11 Mo 24
and was much pleased to hear that thee had at last
got a letter from home knowing thy anxiety must be
very great judging by what my own feelings would be
in similar circumstances, and the tender feeling
expressed for thy poor old Mother was indeed a
cordial to her sorrowing heart I have a great deal
to say if I could see to write but my eyesight
is nearly gone & I fear thee cannot read what I
do write, it is grievous to think of thy comfortless
situation amongst such profane society but take
courage and put thy trust him who is able to save
from every danger those that ask for his help in truth
and sincerity of heart, dear Henry shun the intoxicating bowl taste not touch not handle not the cursed
thing, pardon me for this caution I hope it unnecessary but I am an anxious Mother, I received
present of gold and searched carefully for the little
flower at length concluded that was crumbled to dust

Figure 12.1. Letter from Ann W. (Zane) Jenkins to her son, Henry, dated March 2, 1852. Credit: The Huntington Library.

you will see the cold clammy sweat passing from the hands, the hands and arms become very nervous and the mind much affected so much so as to throw the medium into fits . . ."[31]

One professor explained a medium's methods, which he then taught to his students, who proceeded to excel even beyond her abilities.

> Sometimes she made them by pressing her toe against the leather on the inside of her shoe—at other times by the friction of her shoe against the chair post, and at other times she produced detonations by a peculiar action of the respiratory [*sic*] muscles of the chest . . . several of my students . . . can prduce [*sic*] 'mysterious raps' with their toes, knee-joints, ankle-joints and the tendons, all of which are as mysterious as those I detected in the medium of this city.[32]

Abby and Ann did not mention how much the clairvoyant charged her rapt audience. Later though, Abby dialed back on the wonderment, " . . . as to the spiritual knockings thee not be uneasy about our meddleing with it. It did not take with us. It has blown by."[33] Work once again took precedence over dubious distractions.

Abby gratefully welcomed Will back home. The family planned to move to their new property a couple miles east. The land lacked any residential structures, so they would need to build first. Bedford and Will Jenkins enlisted the help of William and Robert's younger brother, Bazel Ransom, to help with preparing the timbers. One day, Bazel cut his foot open, perhaps a slip of the adze as he squared up a log. It put him out of commission but, fortunately, did not result in a deadly infection or amputation. He spent five weeks on crutches, slowing the work.

Everyone in the family put enormous effort into making improvements. The girls collected and burned brush. The boys built fences and prepared logs for the barn and cabin. The neighbors gathered for the "Great raising," as Ann Jenkins called it, in mid-April. One friend brought Ann a gift. He "presented me with a sheet lead box containing ½ a pound of the best gunpowder tea, the best tea I have drank for a long time."[34] At the end of the workday, a rudimentary cabin had been erected, and likely a barn as well. It would be cramped quarters for a time until Bedford, Will, and Bazel could construct additional rooms. The cabin did not have a door, just a hole where a door would go someday. Emma, who had a contract to do some weaving, did not have space to set up her loom. It would all have to wait. Planting took precedence.

March also marked the anniversary of Humphrey Anderson's death. His widow, Harriet, prepared to remarry in early April, though Humphrey's friends were not pleased about it, according to Abby. It seemed a sensible arrangement, though. David Creek's first wife had died in 1849, leaving him a son and daughter to raise on his own. With Harriet Havens Anderson's five children, it would be a houseful, but partnerships eased the effort for single parents. The slow-moving matter of settling Humphrey's estate left Harriet in a financially precarious position. Abby reported Harriet's impending nuptials to Henry. If he had not heard already, John Anderson might be taken aback by the report—a stark reminder that his brother had been gone that long and had not had the chance to see what John and the others had seen. As far as Abby had been able to inquire, the families of the Blackford miners were all doing well.

Though Henry had sent Abby some funds, things had become more desperate than the previous year. She griped to her husband . . .

> We have still some ham and shoulders and flour and are trying to live as well as we can and economical as we know how but my family is large and wants many. The girls are all at home. We have got our flax dressed but a good deal of it was spoiled—we will work up the rest. Mother has just finished a pair of cotton stockings for thee—she says the last she ever expects to knit—she bids me say she does not expect ever to live to see thee again but I think she seems as likely to live as she did a year ago, though this morning she has a bad cold and is somewhat oppressed.[35]

Abby not only had her mother-in-law and children to care for, but she also took responsibility for looking after ill neighbors. She and Ann logically assumed that the Ransom brothers would be in California long before their letters reached Henry. "I suppose W and R Ransom is with thee before this time. I should have like to have seen the meeting. It must have been joyful particularly to thee as thee had been so long without seeing the face of a friend," Ann speculated in her letter on May 3.

Emma and her older sister, Ann, missed the Ransom brothers. It would probably be another month before they got a letter saying they had reached San Francisco. Though she missed her beau, Emma was still young enough to socialize with teens of both sexes, and she did not have any mothering duties. Once her chores were done, Emma could take advantage of her freedom. Her sister, Ann Jenkins Ransom, was approaching her twenty-first birthday. The young man who won her heart, though a little rough in his manner, had natural charm and good looks. Ann, serious, studious, and religious, fell for her suitor in spite of their differences. Watching her mother deal with Henry being gone may not have prepared her for the reality of her own husband leaving. Their daughter, almost eighteen months old now, kept her on her toes and tugged at her heart. The fact that William might be gone for years meant little Cordelia would soon forget her Pap.

Henry's mother arguably had the hardest time dealing with being separated from the man she loved. Though Ann grew increasingly blind and deaf, she wrote long, scrawling letters to her absent son, giving him much-needed spiritual support. But she could not hide her fear. "I still occupy my arm chair in the corner—they are all talking and laughing around me—I hear nothing they say. I don't knit anymore. This 5 past weeks I put my kerchief over my face, put up a petition to my heavenly father for my dear son—shed a shower of tears to ease my full heart, wipe my eyes, hold up my head again and no one knows anything about it but the allseeing God, he drys the widows tears and binds up the broken heart," she confessed to Henry. "In the expectation of my dying before thee returns I have brought myself to that state of resignation that I can say with truth, not my will but thine Gods be done."[36]

Ann did have good days. She may have quit knitting but did whatever small tasks she was capable of doing to help the family, particularly in the vegetable garden. Though occasionally melancholy, she did not lack a sense of humor. She related to Henry that "Emma dreamed this morning that thee had returned with 15 hundred apiece for each of thy children, but dreams, I tell her, mostly turn out contrary. I told her that I thought she was mean not to dream some for old grandmother, too."[37]

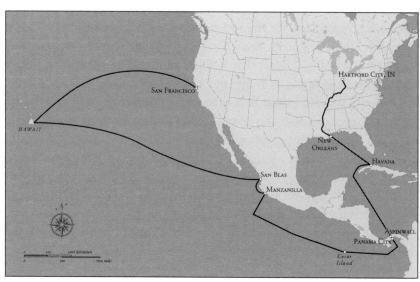

Figure map of California ocean route. Map of the journey the Ransom brothers took to California in 1852.

CHAPTER 13

YAWNS THERE
THE DEEP

After the fracas over inflated ticket prices, the Panama passengers boarded *Emily* on March 7, some brimming with anticipation, others with anxiety. The local launches carried them three miles out to their floating home. There, they discovered that "The Barque was not what she was advertised to be. She was old and had 500 tons of coal on bord."[1] Ships like *Emily*, at a thousand tons burthen, had been built for hauling cargo, not passengers—it just so happened that in 1852, argonauts were a highly lucrative payload.

Emily would have set sail on March 8, but the wind did not cooperate, the first sign of trouble with this unfortunate ship. Roughly 300 passengers and crew filled every vacancy; some already showing signs of serious illness. "About one half of the pasingers were sick soon after we started," said George Blanchard, a passenger from Connecticut. "The principal diseases were the pannama feafor and the Measles all of whitch I escaped."

Some people aboard, including the crew, had made the entire distance from London—the *Emily*'s original embarkation point—or Sydney, itself not an easy feat. At Panama, though, Captain Harvey faced his Waterloo—the northern Pacific. The passengers expected the 3,600-mile trip to San Francisco to take no more than forty days. Unfamiliar with the route, Harvey had sought advice from a local authority. Whether he received incorrect information, or failed to heed it, his poor navigation put everyone in jeopardy. The crew drastically under-supplied her food and water needs for the trip. An experienced sailing captain would go west to Hawaii, then north and east to San Francisco, which worked with the wind and water currents gyrating around the Pacific.[2] Harvey attempted to sail along the coast instead. No one on the ship knew any better.

One of *Emily's* steerage passengers, David T. Gillis, a thirty-two-year-old farmer from eastern Ohio, documented the adventures of his small company of six, as they headed to the mines. They left Ohio about the same time as the Ransoms left Indiana. But the Gillis company took the more common route to Panama by way of New York City. His daily record reflects his view of significant events along *Emily's* journey.

William and Robert Ransom and the other steerage passengers organized into messes. Per Blanchard, "We were divided into messes of ten men each and had 6 pints of water including our tea and coffey and cocking [cooking] and all ½ pound of bread ½ pound of flour whitch we made into what we call a duf. It is made by puting it into a bag and boiling it. One pint of boiled beans peas or rise [rice] one pound of beef or pork per day to the man. This with a little seasning was my living." They had a stove and bread oven to share, usually with a line. The messes were responsible for making their own coffee, tea, bread, and supplemental items. The crew included a cook, but he "was so dirty as you may judge as he one day boiled a piese of his shirt with some rise." Hardly an appetizing "seasning." The hold had provisions for about sixty days, mostly rice, some beans, and a ration of flour and sugar. The crowded conditions and poor quality and quantity of food on board contributed to the spread of disease and even greater distress.

Gillis's friends fell ill even before the ship finally managed to catch enough breeze to breach the harbor at Panama on Saturday, six days after the planned departure. The following day, one of several "deacons" on board gave a sermon in the afternoon and prayers in the evening. The preachers soon had more than Sunday services to keep them busy. At 11 p.m. Monday night, a seventeen-year-old named Julius Bailey, from North Carolina, died of fever complicated by a dose of lobelia, an herbal remedy of dubious benefit, administered by the ship's doctor, probably to induce vomiting. A heavy downpour dampened the already somber mood following Bailey's death.

At dawn the next morning, the captive passengers and crew soberly gathered on deck. Bailey's body lay on a board resting on the railing. Rain and wind lashed the men as a deacon intoned a final blessing over the body. A crewman tipped the board and committed him to the deep, observed by "Old Antiny," the dead man's suddenly unbound slave. The next morning, two Georgians, men in their twenties, followed Bailey's wake into Neptune's watery realm. *Emily*'s death toll had begun. Three men perished the following week from fever: one from Wisconsin, one from New Orleans, and another Georgian.

As the second week aboard came to a close, the passengers appointed a committee to "consult the Capt concerning provision 5 lb flour pr day allowed each mess after."[3] Like the deficient mess kits and food stores for the passengers, deficient winds could not propel the lumbering vessel. After several weeks at sea, they passed Cocos Island, Costa Rica, about 550 miles due west of Panama. A steamship leaving Panama the day of *Emily*'s scheduled departure would be on its final approach to San Francisco.

As the calendar flipped to April, erratic weather continued. Temperatures cracked the hundred-degree mark, stifling breath and blistering skin. Light winds, occasional rain, and periods of calm beset the ship. Lack of progress, heat, and poor diet began straining the passengers' patience; a fight broke out between the slovenly cook and one of the Georgians. The sanitary status of some passengers set off the ire of others. They tallied lice infestations, and the offending parties were given nit combs and told to wash their shirts. One case was so dire that disgusted passengers presented a shirt to the man; presumably the offending garment was pitched overboard. Better the shirt than the man, one would suppose.

Gillis penned a poem about one of his companions receiving a blow to the head by a flying tackle block while trying to assist the crew, receiving a black eye and losing his hat overboard. It conveyed the general ennui among the men, the occasional efforts at helping the sailors, and sporadic moments of levity.

April saw four men expire from various causes, exacerbated by malnutrition. Forward progress remained as sluggish as the passengers; even the healthiest slouched or slept through the day. Many had no idea how far the ship had traveled by then, though they probably realized California was still a long way off.

On a mid-April day, lightning backlit boiling, menacing thunderheads. The wailing wind forced those on deck to holler. A sudden crack of shattering wood startled the men as the mizzen mast snapped, and the main gaff tumbled toward the deck. A ripping noise meant major mutilation of the sail. The crew repaired the damage by nightfall.

On April 26, the last cat went overboard. The rats rejoiced.

Water rationing began. When it rained, the men put out tarps and awnings to fill the barrels. On April 30, an uproar arose over water thefts, but a torrential downpour that night brought relief. On hands and knees, the men washed their shirts in the excess water sloshing around the deck. The next morning, they held their first tribunal—a frequent affair on gold-rush ships. A Mr. Streeter had been "summoned to appear on the fore castle and there tried for making an indecent use of the dishes of another mess." He duly appeared for his trial, "but the evidence of the most important charge being circumstacial the prisoner was acquitted."[4]

Thomas Roberts, age twenty-two, was the first man from Indiana to die, on May 1, with brain inflammation given as the cause. William had some medical texts with him and probably cared for the man, and maybe others as well. Given the number of sick men, the ship's doctor had his hands full. When Blanchard fell ill later that month, he, probably wisely, eschewed the doctor's ministrations. "I had a high feavor and only 3 pints of water and no one to take care of me. You can judge my situation. The docttor told me that I had better take some medison but I would not. I had all my water mad into grewel and drank it hot and covered mself up in my blankets and broke the feavor on me." The incident with Bailey and the lobelia no doubt spooked him.

As the trip stretched into its third month, Captain Harvey consulted the passengers about steering toward the Mexican coast. At first, the passengers deferred to the captain's wishes, believing they had enough provisions aboard. Harvey set course for Mazatlan. By mid-May, though, they insisted he run ashore to the nearest port. Gillis made a chilling observation on May 10: "Passed a timber resembling a mast, while at dinner. Great quantities of sharks and other fish near this place." Deaths continued apace, with six more that month, bringing the total to sixteen. Though Gillis came down with mumps and a cold, mostly confined in the stifling hold, he faithfully maintained his daily log.

Severe rationing began on May 19. "Progress slow. Our rations reduced to ¼ of bread ¼ lb flour all the rice we want—1 pt water" per person. They did not have enough water to cook the rice, so they commandeered all the coffee grinders to reduce it to flour for baking. Some mechanically inclined person set up a condenser to produce fresh water, but others, angered by favoritism in the sharing of it, destroyed the equipment.

Monday, May 24: Gillis confessed to the despair that most passengers must have been feeling for weeks. "Calm most of the time yesterdy and today. Passengers very much discouraged, a great many sick, water selling at from 25 cts to 1.50. It is truly a trying time. It tries the fortitude of every man." The wind picked up the next day, and with a new condenser built, spirits lifted a tad.

All eyes scanned the horizon for a glimpse of the Mexican coast, praying that these people they had recently been at war with would be their salvation. The shoreline came into view on May 27, and the ship put into port at Manzanillo the next day. Once ashore, the passengers complained to the port authorities, who forced Captain Harvey to obtain some supplies before allowing him to sail. He found no flour or bread, only sugar and water. Some people refused to get back on board and went north to San Blas on a Spanish brig. The ship's doctor tried to join them, saying he had never contracted for such a long journey, but the port officials coerced him into reboarding. Morale dropped further when they learned that another distressed ship had pulled into Acapulco and been abandoned by its captain. They feared this would be their fate, too.

A more fortunate traveler, stopping in Acapulco, obtained the following intelligence from the US Consul regarding the stranded gold migrants:

Some of them are sleeping in the streets of Acapulco to-night, having had to-day hardly food enough to sustain life and not knowing where they will get breakfast in the morning. . . . There have been 1476 here in that condition. . . . They came in old vessels, miserable hulks fitted out at Panama, ostensibly for San Francisco, yet with little expectation evidently on the part of owners that they would arrive there. The passengers paid the money and went on board in good faith, but the vessels were not fit for the sea, and had not provisions enough for the voyage, hence they came here, and are abandoned. If sold for the benefit of the passengers, they would not bring enough to pay the costs of the suits and the arrears due the sailors, hence passengers would get nothing.[5]

Stephen Davis—the young man who had reported the crush in Panama City, had managed to obtain passage on the steamship *Fremont*, which left port the same day as *Emily* (and arrived in San Francisco on April 1)—ran into some trouble at Acapulco. The steamer *Pacific* from Nicaragua, with 900 passengers, had crashed and sunk south of Acapulco. No one died, but the passengers lost most of their possessions and had no funds to support themselves. One pitiable man begged Davis to sneak him aboard the *Fremont*, which Davis did and nearly lost his own berth for the infraction. Other stowaways were rousted out of the ship's coal bin.[6] It was an ugly scene all around.

The headwinds along the coast hindered *Emily*'s progress toward San Blas; it took twelve days to cover 154 miles. They arrived in port on June 9, ninety-three days out from Panama, and not even halfway to San Francisco. San Blas is a sandy peninsula bounded by an estuary, a river, and the sea. Nearby cliffs and high mountains form a dramatic backdrop.

The port authority told Captain Harvey he could not claim distress again. He would have to sell his coal to purchase supplies. He refused. He made two trips to the Nayarit state capitol, Tepic, without resolving the matter, but his absence worried passengers that he would not return. *Emily* would not be leaving Mexico any time soon. Harvey persuaded about sixty passengers to charter a French brig sitting in the tiny harbor, offering each a $15 refund. Gillis sold his pistol to help pay the charter fee for *Condor*. The men from Indiana did not have sufficient funds to join them. At least 150 passengers remained with *Emily* in San Blas. As *Condor* prepared to depart on June 22, Gillis stood on deck observing a funeral procession on shore for Paul Stark, of Ohio, *Emily*'s latest victim. He had watched so many of his contemporaries perish on the trip he had just survived, it seems plausible he numbed himself to the horror just to get from day to day.

June 1852—Indiana

Henry wrote to Abby of his intention to stay another year. Stunned by this news, which she received in late June, Abby, in her reply, expressed her disappointment: "My dear Henry, This day week I received thy letter dated April 24th while I was at a quarterly meeting at Portland. Emma brought it from Camden. I received it as usual with joy but when I read that thee did not expect to return till spring my spirits sunk below par. I thought the fall a long way off, but then to hear of passing another dreary winter it seemed too bad," she moaned. "All thy friends eagerly enquired the news and when I said thee did not intend returning till spring they all said well that was right to stay until thee was ready. They do not know how hard it is to be separated from those we love, but I suppose we must submit. I think when we do meet again it will be to part no more until death separates us."[7]

At least her son, Will, was not with the Ransoms, who may have perished at sea. All her children remained in Indiana, but her older daughters faced unprecedented stress. Ann Ransom had not heard from William since his report in early March. Letters from other people traveling to California found their way homeward without incident. Where were hers? He should have reached San Francisco by the end of April. Now in late June, they had received not a word. Emma also worried about her sweetheart, Robert. Abby told Henry that "we feel very anxious to hear from the boys. Ann has kept her spirits up well but she is beginning to fear some disaster has happened to them."

Considering that both her husband and father were now gone, maybe forever, Ann began teaching school at the Ransom farm in May. Her work provided the family with a little income and occupied her attention, allowing her to partially set aside her concerns about her loved ones out west. She left little Cordelia with her mother and Grandma Ann. "Cordelia is with us, a great pet with all," Abby said. Ann spent the weeks in Trenton, and her youngest brother, Barton, transported her back and forth on the weekends by mule.

As for spiritual matters, Abby said, "I was glad to find thee still anxious to go to meeting though at so great a distance. I trust ere this thee has heard the word preached and felt the powerful influence thereof. That is all that in any way reconciles our separation that thee has not forgotten the old land marks that point to the haven of rest." In a not-so-subtle passage regarding Henry's toying with alcohol, she related the sorry tale of a friend. "Poor Brandon has nearly fallen a victim to intemperance; he can not his hand still and looks awful . . . [His wife] is heart broken and dejected. When I looked at her I thanked God from my heart that I had been spared from seeing my companion carried along in that awful course and saved by grace which alone can save." No doubt, Henry got the message.

Her reliable son Bedford had no apparent desire to go west; he had a passionate new love interest, Patience Randall, to occupy his mind. Patience was one of William Place's stepdaughters, which explained the young man's willingness to spend his spare time working for the man. The last thing Abby wanted was to go to California herself. She dreaded the thought. "I think it is the opinion of many that we will all go yet but I have not yet thought so. I am too lazy for the journey." More likely, she had traveled far enough west to suit her, and she did not want to move further from her siblings.

Abby assured Henry that the valuables he sent had arrived. "I recd thy miniature (which I think very like thee) and likewise the draft which I have mentioned in a former letter. If thee sends me any more I will dispose of it as thee advises . . . [Barton] says he does not want anything . . . and as for myself I will be satisfied with nothing short of thyself for a keepsake. I was surprised to see so large pieces of gold as thee sent in thy last. It is a great curiosity."

Henry had been displeased with how she used the funds he had sent previously. Frugal Abby bought as little as possible, but she had to pay for educating their children and settle the debt on their new property. In Henry's absence, the drawbacks of the one-sided ledger system became a burr in Abby's stocking. If anyone owed the Jenkinses, she knew about it. What IOU chits Henry had distributed in the neighborhood, she had no clue about until someone turned up on her doorstep, mumbling something about "a favor." She could hardly blame them. Her husband might never return, and if not, how would they collect their due? They might assume that Henry had sent her great sums of gold that she had stashed away in the modest cabin she called home, or maybe buried under the turnips.

She shared with Henry a brief description of their new place. "I think I have told thee long ago about our cabbin that we built. I am sitting in it writing. It is our parlor furnished in the best style we can and though rough is a great comfort to us." Though pleased with the cabin, she saw poor farming prospects. "There is but few apples in the orchard. The trees look well. Our oats in the meadow and along side the house look pretty well but our corn looks sorry. We have replanted some of it 4 times and still there is but little standing. We are going to sow buckwheat in part of the west field where the corn has failed." After all his effort, "[Bedford] seems much discouraged about it. Our wheat looks middling. I hope that we will at least raise bread enough to last us through, our vegetables, though late look well. We have all from the little run to the orchard planted with truck." It was probably worse than she would ever let on to Henry, knowing he could do nothing to help.

Abby showered Henry with local gossip. Since the company had disbanded, she no longer felt obligated to report on those families. Their dear friend William Place had serious health issues. Death carried off many, and remarriages replaced deceased spouses. "Poor Josiah Vorhas buried his Deborah with a short illness of Typhoid fever. No one thought he would have lasted this long but he is left with a little flock who no doubt will soon be orphans." Several other friends had died or soon would, she supposed.

At least the family remained well, "Mothers health is as good as common . . . we all have good health though [Bedford] is not very stout." And she shared the good news that he could end his futile search for Willis

Wilson. "Joseph Wilson has heard from his son . . . [Willis] is expected home shortly." It would be good for the community to see the return of some wayward young men.

Willis S. Wilson had been just twenty-one when he headed to California in August 1848. Perhaps by 1852, he had found his Mother Lode, or come to the realization that he never would. Perhaps he felt the need to find some female companionship. Family and friends at home would be his treasure instead. What he did not know was that his sister, Deborah Shanks, had died about the time he sent the letter announcing his return. She developed bronchial disease as a result of trying to save her burning home. She did save her baby girl, to be reared by her grieving widower, John P.C. Shanks (an attorney and later a decorated Union War officer and congressman). Willis would return to a family in mourning.

Closing out her newsy letter, Abby said, "I well know that the above is a great medley but I wish to tell thee all I can think of and as I write every week almost I cannot have much news. Write often, it is the greatest comfort I have, with an earnest desire that we may soon meet again, and with an increasing prayer that we may be mutually preserved I remain thy poor, little, faithful wife—A.G. Jenkins."

CHAPTER 14

THE WITHERING

Dont find fault with any thing that you have and I wont beleave that you would after goin throug what I have. Tell all my friends that i have seen hard times but expect to see better. And if thy will take my advise they will stay at home.

—GEORGE B. BLANCHARD

SUMMER 1852—SAN BLAS, MEXICO

William may have learned some Mexican customs and Spanish phrases from Pierce that helped him in San Blas. But he and Robert had no funds. They had no way to send messages to their family at home, or to Henry in California to let them know of their predicament. *Emily* sat at anchor about a mile from shore, surrounded by other vessels. Though the men could sleep aboard ship, they had to get food in the village. The heavy surf made landing a boat onshore challenging. "There is nothing to prevent the sea from rolling directly upon the sand, and it is only in very moderate weather that a boat can land at all."[1] The village consisted of thatched roofs supported by poles tucked in amongst the spreading bows of live oak trees, home to innumerable singing birds. The old stone city of San Blas, built by the Spanish, lay abandoned on a plateau about a mile south. The residents preferred life on the beach, where they collected the natural bounty of fruit.

Because *Emily* could not properly accommodate her passengers, the Ransoms had no choice but to find alternate transportation to San Francisco. "The Captain said that he had not money enough for provisions for only 30 days but the counsel said that his vessel was no sailor and he must put on bord 60 days provisions," per Blanchard. The port authorities refused to let him depart. Harvey gave his miserable, starved passengers a daily allowance for food of just 25 cents. But the famished men needed four times that amount to get the nutrition they craved. Soon the debt to the locals amounted to $2,000.[2]

The citizens of San Blas made money off the travelers but unlikely with much pleasure. Some of the transients probably fought in the recent war, and San Blas—though nowhere near the action—had suffered a terrible blow. The *Batallón de San Blas* had gone to the aid of the small contingent holding Chapultepec Castle on the outskirts of Mexico City. As US general Winfield Scott began his charge to take the city on September 13, 1847, the battalion of roughly 300 men had been annihilated by the American forces. For the small town, the wound of their sacrifice was fresh enough. Salty Americans in their midst poured in painfully.

Seasonal monsoon rains began to inundate the region in late June. The moisture exacerbated the problem of mosquitoes and sand flies. They tormented the argonauts nearly as much as the boredom. Given the dire situation, the marooned men chose two representatives, pooled some funds, and sent them sixty miles to Tepic to visit the US consul there, William Forbes. Forbes was a partner in the British trading house Barron, Forbes & Co. The company dominated foreign business on Mexico's west coast, with headquarters in San Blas. Forbes wisely lived inland, far from the unhealthy coast. He and his partners ran a highly successful enterprise that included smuggling as a matter of course. They primarily exported Mexican silver (illegally). Forbes was rich, though the operation involved a great deal of risk to his wealth.[3]

"Mr Forbes is the great man of Tepic—his house is the point of re-union;—every one drops in to tell the news or to hear it. From morning till night there is a crowd of idlers under the arcade, smoking & prosing," wrote one contemporary. The little committee from the *Emily* had no trouble locating the consul. "His house, like most Mexican a&

Figure 14.1. Watercolor "Plaza at Tepic" by Admiral Edward Gennys Fanshawe, 1850. Credit: Wikimedia Commons.

Spanish houses, is built round a court or patio, into which all the rooms on the ground floor open; a fountain plays in the centre of the patio, and a broad arcade or piazza all round forms a most agreeable lounging place in hot or wet weather."[4] After hearing the passengers' case, Forbes wrote to his superior, the US minister to Mexico, the Honorable R.P. Letcher, who resided in Mexico City, requesting advice.

Robert P. Letcher was the former governor of Kentucky and well connected politically, an intimate of Henry Clay and James Buchanan. After reviewing the request from Forbes, he drafted his response on July 17.

Sir

I regret exceedingly to understand from your note of the 6th inst, which was handed to me yesterday by Mr Barron, that there are two hundred American citizens now in San Blas, left in a destitute condition having been abandoned by the Masters of the English ship "Emily" and the Brig "New Castle" . . .

The passengers hold an undoubted lien upon the vessels for their transportation to the port agreed upon, and it appears to me, you should proceed at once to enforce the lien for the benefit of the passengers . . .

I expect a just Congress representing a liberal and magnanimous people would never consent to allow a Consul who had kindly furnished funds to prevent American citizens from starving in a foreign country to go unrewarded . . .[5]

Letcher's advice arrived back in Tepic too late to be of use to Forbes. But Forbes was shrewd enough to have come to the same conclusion. At least the Minister's letter reassured him that his expenditures would be reimbursed.

When the *Archibald Gracie*, an American barque, arrived in San Blas at the end of June, Captain Peters agreed to take the Americans to San Francisco for $6,000. Harvey refused to make a deal, though. Forbes put on some pressure.

The Counsel told our captain that he must come to terms or he would take his Ship and Cargo and send us on he said that he would Advanse $5500 and pay up the [debt] at San Blass and put a man abord with him and he might go and sell his Coal our Captain told us if we would raise $500 he would Charter the bark we . . . agreed to do it. On July the 17th the Archible Gracia of Boston was Charterd to take us up to San-francisco for $6000, $500 of whitch we paid ourselfes.[6]

Another eleven days passed before the American ship had provisioned to sail. By then, the Ransoms had been languishing for seven long weeks. Two more men were buried in San Blas, including Old Antiny, the former slave.

If they thought things were about to improve, they were grievously mistaken. The *Archibald Gracie* sailed on July 28, heading northwest to San Francisco, via Hawaii. Captain Peters, continuing in the mercenary tradition of his ilk, used little of the charter fee to supply the ship with food and water for his hostage passengers. Once again, the travelers received starvation rations, even worse than they previously lived through. "After we had been out 10 day we wer redused too 3 pints of water and ½ pound of bread . . . On the 28th of Aug we redused to 1 pint of water and no bread at all." Blanchard said. "All that we had to eat was ½ pound of fresh pork and 6 ounses of flower . . . water sold for 200 [2 dollars], per pint." The weather turned much colder as they approached California, an additional discomfort. The harsh voyage lasted forty-four days, and eighteen more men died, as the others wasted to skeletons.

Starvation induces a state of mania in its early stages, but as the body consumes itself in an effort to keep vital organs functioning, lethargy sets in. There was little activity on board the *Archibald Gracie* as she closed in on the California coast. On August 23, the Indiana group suffered the tragic loss of Hazelett Lanning. Just twenty-three years old, he had been a lifelong friend of the Ransom brothers, who could do nothing to save him. Eight others succumbed that week. Two of them, partners from Vermont, breathed their last within five minutes of each other. "They were put on 2 planks and side by side and the shi[p] Hove to and burried both at once I tell you it was a dradful sight."[7]

The long-suffering argonauts from *Emily* arrived in San Francisco on September 10, six months after they boarded in Panama. With the ordeal nearly over, passengers with any strength gazed with relief at the long-awaited destination as they passed through the Golden Gate and approached the pier. What wretched remains of humanity came stumbling down the gangplanks of the *Archibald Gracie*, to the citizens' horror. At least a dozen men were so prostrate from malnutrition that the local police chief arranged to have them carried to the State Marine Hospital for care.[8] (Blanchard put the number at twenty.) Blanchard said, "The People here says that there wan no pasingers ever came in here in so bad a condition." Indeed, the fate of *Emily*'s passengers became notorious.[9] One passenger described his deterioration: "My ordinary weight is 160 pounds, but when I landed in California, I weigh less than ninety pounds, my clothes are all worn out or quite ragged and I have only a $2.50 gold piece in my pocket."[10]

The Ransom brothers made their shaky way off the ship and left the wharf, ready to start a new adventure, once they found some decent food and recuperated from their travels. But first, they needed to send a letter home to let everyone know they were still among the living. Blanchard's sentiments undoubtedly echoed a hundred other letters heading east: "Dearest Parents, It is with pleasure that I have after a passage of seven months and passed through so many troubles and trials at last an opportunity to write to you and let you know that I am alive and well as you know doubt think me dead."

The demand for sea transport to California had been driving a brisk market in unseaworthy ships for years. Even some steamships could not be counted on. In November 1852, *McKim*, a steamer with a screw propeller (not paddlewheels), had so many mechanical and fuel difficulties she had to sail much of the time.[11] Most steamships of that era sported masts as well as motors. It was amazing *McKim* still plied the route at all. She had been in distress even in the early days of the rush in 1849.[12]

The *Emily* tale is just one of many, but it exceeded others by a measurable degree of severity. The California press took note. Many northbound steamships reported her progress when they reached the city. The first seventeen deaths were published in the *Daily Alta California* on August 7, long before any of her passengers reached California. The paper ran a scathing editorial on August 11.

Were the sailing vessels that go to the ports on the Isthmus for passengers, fit for the purpose, and were they well supplied with provisions, and not overcrowded with passengers, they might bring them safely to this place. But the facts of the case are well known to be about thus: An old hulk, on which *nobody* would think of risking merchandise, and which, consequently can get no employment, goes down to Panama, lies off the shore, (while her agent lies on shore,) is "cracked up" as a first rate clipper ship, well provisioned, staunch and sea-worthy, and having very fine accommodations . . . till she has secured as many passengers as she can stow under hatches; and then, with rotten meat, wormy bread, brackish water, and little of either, at that she sets sail . . . So, instead of putting boldly out where a wind would be found, he keeps along the coast, and after being under a broiling tropical sun, and crowded in a filthy old ship, and three-fourths starved on food their dogs would have loathed at home, and famished on a short allowance of water they would never before have used to wash in, for thirty to sixty days, they perhaps arrive at Acapulco, more dead than alive, and less fortunate than the large portion of their comrades they have consigned to the deep before their arrival there.[13]

They proposed to remedy the situation by displaying warning posters in Panama City and San Juan de Sud in Nicaragua, and they implored the eastern newspapers to publicize the problem, encouraging migrants to purchase only "through tickets" (for both the Atlantic and Pacific parts of the voyage) on steam lines, steering clear of sailing ships altogether. By year's end, such tales became a rarity. Men suffering in the mines made headlines instead.

After the emaciated Ransom brothers disembarked in San Francisco, did they look for gold? No. They grew food.

Their Indiana traveling companions headed on their own way. The Ransoms' original plan had been to join Henry in Calaveras County. The state of their health when they got off the *Archibald Gracie* is unknown. Blanchard hinted stouter men had the roughest time of it. The Ransoms were not soft, by any means. They had worked hard on their father's farm and survived all the nasty diseases that swamp-riddled Blackford County could throw at them. Their condition was probably as good as could be expected after such trials. They had no money, however.

It may be that they asked around San Francisco about jobs and someone recruited them to work in Santa Clara. Or maybe they knew about farming opportunities there long before they reached California. William was resourceful and a natural-born charmer—well-liked by people of both sexes. During his seven weeks in San Blas, he almost certainly became acquainted with William and/or Alexander Forbes. Barron, Forbes & Company had business dealings in Santa Clara County in the form of a quicksilver mine. Their business partner in California was James A. Forbes (no known relation), a Scot who had been the British vice-consul at Monterey in 1848. James Forbes, who married a California woman, acquired a land grant from the Mexican governor of California in 1844 known as El Potrero de Santa Clara, containing just under 2,000 acres, situated between the famous Alameda that ran through the town of Santa Clara and the Guadalupe River to the east.

At the conclusion of the Mexican War hostilities, US military personnel in California speculated on land. Commodore Robert F. Stockton, commander of the Navy and other troops during the war, who served briefly as the military governor, purchased El Potrero from Forbes in 1847 for the seemingly ridiculous price of $10,000.[14] Shortly after, he departed for the states. The US takeover of the southwestern territory ushered in an era of unsettled land ownership. Hundreds of land grants, mostly Mexican, but a few back to the Spanish colonial period, were thrown into question. Grantees filed claims with the federal Board of Land Commissioners and went through a protracted process involving surveys, map-making, and presenting documents from earlier governments. In 1861, the Forbes/Stockton claim to El Potrero received a land patent.[15] While the case worked its way through the commission, Stockton proceeded with his plans to subdivide and make money from his speculative investment.[16]

From Alviso, at the south end of San Francisco Bay, Robert and William proceeded to Santa Clara. When they reached the Alameda, they had arrived at their destination, commonly known as the Stockton Ranch. The Alameda was a long thoroughfare built by the Spanish padres to connect the mission with San Jose pueblo to the east. They planted this boulevard with black willow trees on either side and an additional row down the middle. By the 1850s, this exuberant arbor cast the road in refreshing shade any time of day. The young men could easily distinguish the ranch property from the surrounding area; a sturdy iron fence enclosed the entire acreage.

The Ransoms' new employer lived in a two-story home known as the White House. The house featured a wrap-around veranda on the lower floor with another porch above. The roof sported a square cupola topped by a spire. Steps led up to the ground floor. The spacious dwelling accommodated James F. Kennedy, his wife Serena, and their six children. Kennedy served as the Commodore's land agent, arriving in California by way of the isthmus in 1850, along with a shipment of orchard trees.[17] That same year, another large shipment came from Kennedy's hometown of Philadelphia—nineteen prefabricated houses, including the one he lived in. They were designed to be assembled with wooden pegs and were promptly erected on lots in what Kennedy billed the "Alameda Gardens."[18]

Kennedy offered the two farmers a generous wage of $125 a month and probably included room and board.[19] Their services were in demand. California faced a commodity crisis. The state desperately needed home-grown supplies. Santa Clara's landholders had recently constructed a flouring mill; now they needed wheat crops. The brothers could appreciate the stone-free, alluvial loam at their disposal. It virtually ensured a profitable crop. In addition to working for Kennedy, they arranged to lease some Stockton land for their own farming efforts. And naturally, they prospected the area for gold. The brothers rolled up their shirt sleeves and got to work, determined to be successful.

Figure 14.2. "The White House"—a kit home on the Stockton Ranch imported from Philadelphia. Home of ranch manager James F. Kennedy. Credit: Historic American Buildings Survey, Library of Congress.

Fall 1852—Indiana

Well rested after the kindness of the Mormons in Salt Lake City, Dennis Lowry pressed on toward home. He offered no account of his travels from Salt Lake, but he would have followed the established trail over South Pass and along the Sweetwater and Platte Rivers, crossing the plains until reaching the Missouri. From there, he likely took the rivers to either Madison, Indiana, or Cincinnati.

Tarnished with road dust and weary from the saddle, Dennis was a sight for sore eyes when Mary Ann flung wide the puncheon door to welcome home her long-awaited mate in late October. A little over a year and a half had passed between the departure hug and homecoming embrace. "Here was 4 months as hard labor as I Ever Don[e]," he related. "I would all most Dispair Some times and think I never would See the End of the Road." Even the rigors of mining had not worn him down as badly as traveling overland. Happy to be done with the adventure, though grateful for the experience, he settled back into his role at home: father, husband, farmer. "I am Mutch Delited with the trip But it was unprofitable. All I have to grattify my self is what I Saw."[20] Though he had not made a profit, he did have a bit of gold to invest.

The second of the Blackford Company to make it safely home, Dennis made the deliveries entrusted to him, including the box of gold dust for Abby. However, when he surveyed the gold he had mailed home to Mary Ann, one letter came up missing. Abby had picked up the letter from the Camden post office and somehow lost it. Even months later, she was still heartsick over her carelessness. No one could afford to lose even a small amount of the precious metal they had all suffered for. Rather than paying off his debt to Makepeace, Dennis held onto his hard-won gold.

The due date on Blackford notes was six months gone, so it is doubtful the matter had slipped Makepeace's mind. He usually did not initiate legal action without giving his debtors an opportunity to make good on their promissory notes. Plus, the longer he waited, the larger the judgment would be if found in his favor (as it typically was). That autumn, he sued on a note that almost certainly had a connection to the gold rush. As in every other corner of Indiana (and the world at large), groups of men from Delaware County went to the mines in California.

One of those parties left on October 1, 1849.[21] A week earlier, a note for $400 had been made out to James Jordan by three other men: Samuel Peck, Aaron Mote, and Patrick Carmichael—all in their early fifties. These three were connected by marriages amongst their children, and Jordan appears to have been a family friend. The note, immediately upon signing, was assigned to Makepeace for $300 cash, suggesting it was "got up" in the same manner as the Jones notes. It lacked only a provision for interest. Peck joined the company going to California in October. The borrowers refused to make any payments, so Makepeace sued for his $400 plus $200 in penalties, now that it was nearly two years past due.[22] Dennis Lowry may have heard about this suit and others upon his return home but paid the matter no heed.

The Blackford miners' families plied Dennis with questions about when the others would come home. The Jenkins's friend, Joseph Wilson, had eagerly anticipated his son's return long before now, but he waited in vain. Gone since his Mexican War enlistment, the young man had been absent a full five years. He had survived the Army and the rough life of the mines, but Willis Wilson perished on the journey home and was never seen again. Joseph, still mourning his daughter Deborah, joined the swelling ranks of grieving parents who lost their sons to the lust for quick riches.

Word that William and Robert had landed in San Francisco probably did not reach home until early November 1852, nine months after they left. Whichever of the Jenkins family or friends went to Camden to pick up the mail probably screamed, or fainted, at the sight of the letter. They had almost certainly been given up for dead. It was a joyous occasion for the community (except for the Lannings, who learned conclusively about Hazelett's death at sea). There had been little to celebrate so far that season, with a poor harvest and a difficult winter ahead.

William and Robert's cousin, Rebecca Jones, would have been pleased the brothers were alive, but her own hopes to be reunited with her soulmate, E.D. Pierce, had been dashed once again. He had promised her that he would return after serving in the legislature. The term ended in early May, and he anticipated settling up with his business partner in Yreka before making the trip east. In his memoir, he recalled, "I stated I had made a solemn promise, to return to Barnsville Ohio as early as June

1852. Gave them to understand the nature of my business, that I had written to the folks that I would return at that time and that my love and high esteem would not allow me to disappoint the party [Rebecca] and it was my duty to return agreeable to promise."[23]

The partnership had floundered in his absence. William S. Good, who had brought the pack string to the business, wanted out. Pierce and Pfouts agreed to let Good liquidate the livestock to buy out his third of the company (the fourth partner, Brown, having long since departed for home). Pfouts continued running the store in Yreka and managed the boarding ranch they owned. It was too much for one young man to handle. Pfouts took to drinking with the customers—the normal course of business in those days—and soon squandered any profits.[24] Pierce, dismayed at the state of things when he returned, vowed not to head home impoverished. He owed it to his fiancée to have enough money to get them started well in their married life together.

He wrote in September, begging Rebecca's leave to stay another year and get back on track. Seeing no way around it, she responded with encouragement—and her blessing.[25] What could she do? She had little leverage to budge him from the roulette wheel of California fortunes. He would do better on the next round, she surely assured herself, with an empty feeling in the pit of her stomach. In the meantime, she would help her sisters-in-law with their domestic duties, enjoying the company of her nieces and nephews, still the spinster auntie.

Ann Jenkins, like Rebecca, pondered another dreary winter with her son gone in the mines and decided to make a change. She may have sensed that her time was short. Her decade-long experiment with Methodism ended. She wrote a plea to the women of the Camden Society of Friends requesting permission to rejoin their meeting. In January 1853, they welcomed her back into the religion of her youth and middle age. Returning to the bosom of the faith surely soothed her soul.

1852—MINING REGIONS OF CALIFORNIA

The California legislature, during Pierce's term, passed a bill requiring a statewide census. Enumerators began their work in June, catching Dennis Lowry in Calaveras County as he was about to head home. The remaining remnants of the Blackford company had scattered a bit since January. In July, Henry, Teach, and the Liestenfeltz brothers were all in Calaveras County—Jake was closest to Henry, but they worked independently. Teach and Pete still worked together, however. Anderson and Gibson had gone to Mariposa County earlier in the year and still worked there in July, probably remaining until they departed for home. Sam Jones, keeping his distance from his former comrades, chased the latest rumors, moving to the newer mines in the far north part of the state. They tallied him in Shasta County, though there is no way to pinpoint a rambling miner's exact whereabouts.

After sending the box with Dennis in June, Henry continued to pass some of his earnings to his family through the mail. By October, he decided to leave McKinneys and return south to Murphys. He seemed to prefer the residents there over those in the other Calaveras camps, though he had to give up his Sunday mule rides to Mokelumne Hill.

The rains came early that winter, and soon, the roads from Stockton became so deep with mire that few, if any, mule trains would take supplies up to the mines. Any miner who failed to stock his pantry in the fall faced the possibility of starvation. Where food seemed plentiful and cheap the previous year, supplies dried up over the winter, increasing prices. In his early letters, Henry noted the easy availability of fresh beef. As population in the mines grew, this commodity vanished. The same for game meat. Hunting could not make up for the deficit.

Miners in Mariposa began agitating for something to be done about the speculators in San Francisco who bought up all the available flour to drive up the price, and then withheld this vital staple from the desperate men in the rural parts of the state.[26] It foretold a grim holiday season ahead. Henry felt his second Christmas without his family more deeply than miners who reveled in their freedom. He had not come to wallow in the single life, and he knew that his continued sojourn in California caused his wife and mother untold grief. But he shouldered the guilt.

CHAPTER 15
LONG-DISTANCE LONGINGS

EARLY 1853—INDIANA AND CALIFORNIA

By mid-January, Henry had given up on the Murphys claim and returned to McKinneys Creek. He and Abby continued their torturously slow conversation by mail.

Knox Road
1st mo [January] 10th 53
My dear Henry week after week have I sent to the office hoping to get a letter for 6 weeks and still disappointed, until last week I received thine dated October 31st, which thee may needs think was very welcome. I had written twice since I recd some from thee. I recd the book thee sent me before Christmas. I have read it carefully and I think I receive much help from it. I sometimes feel much encouraged to hope all is well with me but again I find the world still has to strong a hold on me . . .

McKinneys Jan 16th 53
Well my dear Abby once more I resume my pen although this is the third time since receiving one from thee. The last one was sent by Anderson and Gibson in which mention was made of my haveing just bought into

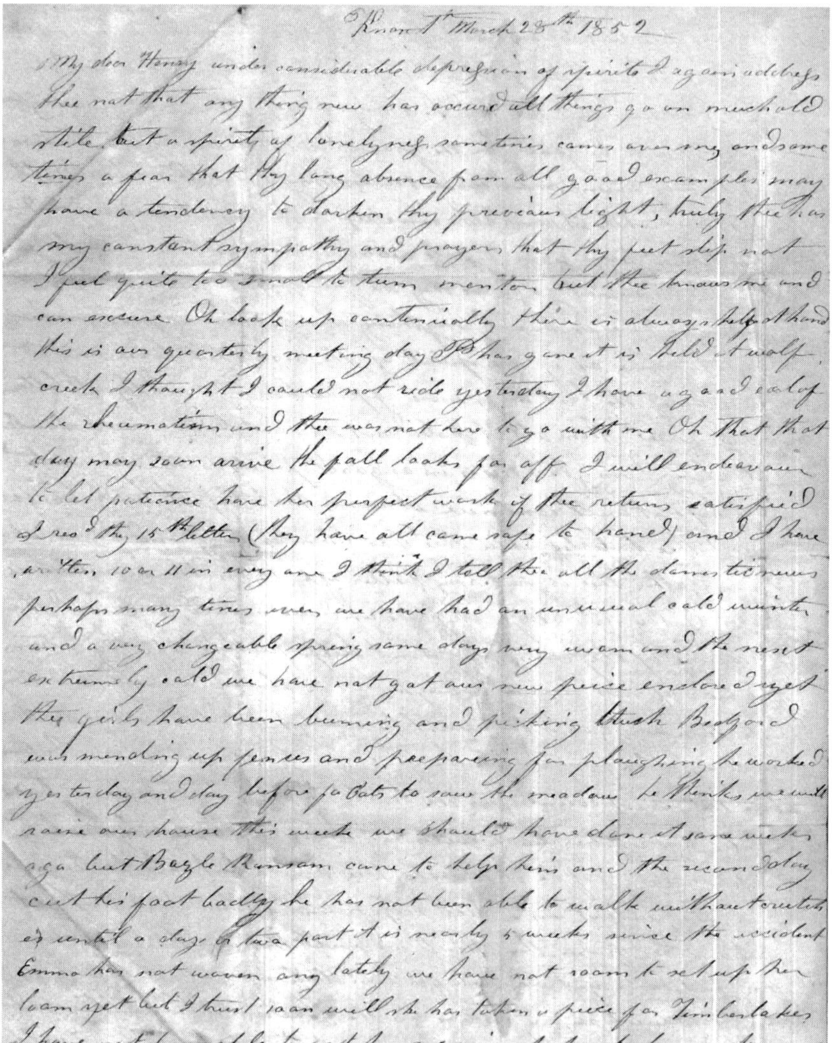

Figure 15.1. Letter from Abigail (Bedford) Jenkins to Henry Z. Jenkins, dated March 28, 1852. Credit: The Huntington Library.

a claim in this place. So far it has paid better than it was represented to do but cant say how it will hold out—the three first days I made 29.96 and last week 10.83 per day or 64.98 in the week. If it only holds out I shall soon pay for it and then begin to lay something [by]. There is plenty of ground to keep the company (5 in number) a full year or more in work and we believe we will have watter sufficient for tomming all summer. We bring it in a ditch over half a mile. We have two ditches both dug previous to my buying in . . .

I have been pretty sorely tried at times to know how to get along. Every way seems hedged up (thee knows all about it). This has been such a failure of corn and potatoes and I having no meat scarcely makes one look about with a family of 9 to provide for. We have wheat but cannot thrash it on account of the wet. (Wm tells me he told thee we had enough.) I think not and think I may as well buy now as any time. B brought home a hog yesterday from Ransom's. He was to have had a fat hog but he sent one that I think 10 bushels of corn will make good. On looking up my sheet I am afraid thee will think I am a croaker. I dont want to be . . .

Provisions are still verry high and scarce but on the decline—we got our last flour at Mokelumne Hill for 70 dollars per hundred—it had been as high as one dollar per lb. Potatoes we paid 25 cts per lb yesterday—they have been as high as 50 and 62½ per lb. We have had good weather for the last week and if it continues another week or two we expect evry thing will come down nearly to their usual rates . . .

I am sorry thee is not pleased with my paying Hattan the 50. I thought it would be best and as to us I feel ashamed to think we cannot maintain ourselves while thee is laboring to pay thy debt, but it seems we cannot. I would have kept school this winter but all were against it and I could not well leave Mother. She cant bear me to go away for a day. She is now very feeble and had a bad cough, often thinks she will not see the spring but I do not think she is much worse than she often is in winter time, only she is still less able to bear it. Her letter is not yet finished nor will it be until we have clear weather which is quite a rarity . . .

I have just seen Teach and the L boys all well but rather think they are not doing much. Jacob talks some of going to Sacramento to work on a ranch with some of his former friends from Springborough by the name of Surydan. Guess it will be the best thing he can do as their claims are about give out and it is verry difficult and uncertain getting others that will pay . . . We live mostly on bread, butter and beans with sometimes a little slice of pork but not often as it is 62½ per lb. Sometimes we get a little venison at from 25 to 37 ½ pr lb and once in a long time a little verry poor beef at 50 cts, but still I feel contented as long as I have a fair prospect of making enough to get home and square up. It has not been long since I had my misgivings of being able to do even that much. In perhaps another year now I have but little doubt of doing rather better . . .

The children all go to school. It has been a hard time to get there. The runs are continually high but they wade along. I sold a calf and bought a ton of hay. Bedford was sick all hay making time and we had none at home. He went to Portland and paid our tax. I borrowed the money of Place to pay it . . . I am truly glad to hear thee is at last in better diggings. I hope thee will not be again disappointed. We know not what is best for us . . . Thee dont say how far from Mokalunny and how is thee getting along. Perhaps this is for a trial of thy faith. Hold on . . .

The only thing that grieves me is my long defer'd return to my beloved family . . . I wrote to Wm Ransom last week by a couple of men formerly of this (our) company who were going right to their neighborhood but have not had a letter from them since last writeing to thee. No especial news in their last only that they were in good health and spirits and verry well pleased with the country, their place and prospects—hope they may continue so and more than realise their most sanguine expectations. Another of my partners expects to sell out in order to return to his family this spring which will be the third that have got their piles out of it within eight months and it makes me feel more confident of my doing something at last than any thing else that has happened to me since being in the mines . . .

Poor [Harvey] Hunt died the day before Christmas, left a helpless family. They say they moved to Camden a short time before his death. I never saw him. I told in one of my letters perhaps more of my great loss of letter and gold sent by Lowry . . . Ann got another letter from Wm and one from Robert. W is still in the same place and expects to stay there. He is going to send for Ann and advises her to leave Cordelia which she will not do. She thinks to go to him in the spring. They represent it as a beautiful place. He says she can make 50 dollars a month by her needle . . . I wish I had never heard of California but perhaps that is not right. I try to submit with patience (R[obert] expects to return next winter) that much I heard from a letter directed to E[mma] J from Cal. The boys have not heard from thee yet. Think thee has come home . . . It takes such a long time to hear from each other. I long to be done with it, I would much rather use tongue than pen. The view of M Hill makes me think worse than ever of the land of gold. It looks dreary, so little wood and so much rough ground . . .

In my last I mentioned my haveing a slight cold from which I have recovered and now enjoy good health not haveing had even the rheumatism for several weeks past for which I feel truly thankful. I hope shortly to be able to make another small remittance but have first to pay for my claim and about thirty dollars at Murphys for provisions got while there. I was compelled to get in debt in that place as I made nothing and paid all I had to buy in. When going there I was so close run as to have to twice borrow postage money—them times are past or I would not name it and I feel confident they will not return, but if they should the same kind of providence will again open a way where there was no way seen. I have always found kind friends when needed (kindest amongst strangers) thee will understand I mean here in this country—of my friends at home I must say nothing. Would that I were in their midst at this present time . . .

14th I had no chance to send my letter to the office in time so I thought I would wait to see if I would get another and I really

did dated Nov 14th which made glad and sorry, glad that thee is well and in better spirits and to hear thee again speak of a time of returning, though it seems far off. Sorry that thee is again removed from the house of God which is a great privation. Where is thy companion thee spoke of at the Hill? How many of you work together? Thee has heard ere this no doubt from the boys. Ann got a letter last post from Wm. He says he just heard from thee and would write that day . . . many of thy friends send thee love but the greatest share receive from Mother, children and wife
A. G. Jenkins

I feel verry uneasy on your account as I know thee must be much harrassed to get along but hope to help thee shortly with a little and intend to remit sufficient to pay Makepeace as soon as possible. In this thee will find a little gold and three currants gathered on the Plains and given to me by a friend. Thee will plant them carefully as I wish to see if they will grow and what they are like. From their appearance they are larger than our common domestic kind. They are black, yellow, and red . . .

Pennville P.O. Camden, Ind.
February 6th 1853
My dearly beloved how much longer must we be separated is a question that often arises with a feeling that none but those similarly situated can feel. It is true time flies, we know not how amid the cares of life, but still it moves slow when feeling lonely. How thee stands it I can hardly tell. I have my children all around me and yet I feel all alone. If it were not for the hope that it will ere long end I should be despondent. I received a letter from thee last week which speaks of one of the partners getting drunk & it made me feel bad to think thee has to be associated with such men. My prayer for thee continually has been that thee might be kept from temptation and guarded from evil. Hold on if thee has greater trials than when here, greater will be thy reward if faithful . . .

Amidst all our hardships and privation we have our bright spots and this day has been one of them as we have treated ourselves to a large gingerbread and four pies all of our own make but verry palatable nevertheless and we have enjoyed [them] and thought while doing so of the many similar feasts we have enjoyed amongst our dear absent friends. We work hard early and late cooking our meals mostly of evenings, takeing our dinners out with us rain or shine . . .

I too have my trials (among my blessings which are many). Wm R is still sending for Ann to come to him if she is not affraid and thee knows how sanguine she is. She thinks she can go alone with her baby, she expects to start in March. The money has not yet arived but I suppose it will soon. Bedford got a letter from Robert R and Wm. Robert told him when his father got home if he wished to come to Cal. they would give him 75 Doll a month until cropping time and then he could realize from 1 to 2 thousand a year and they would send the money to go on. Strong temptation to a boy. He says he thinks he will not go now, I think he never will. I tell him if he ever wishes to go, to go with his sister but he thinks I cannot do without him (it would be hard), but I have got somewhat used to hard things. Hope they will work for my eternal good . . .

I almost evry night dream of seeing some one of you sometimes verry comfortable. At others in much distress and difficulty Mother verry frequently of late. How is she getting along? Tell her I wish much to see her once more and hope she may be spared until we meet again. And now my love I must draw to a close and believe me as ever thy loving and devoted husband
Henry Z Jenkins

I often picture thee in thy lonely tent and hope thee has good books to read when you cannot work. Mother is sitting by me reading. She has been sick for some time past, had a bad cold . . . but I think she is better to day. She dreams as much as ever. She has tried

hard to interpret thy dream. I often think I have lived amid sighs and groans for 20 odd years, but I also think it is for my benefit, for I well know I am inclined to levity, and need a ballast . . . Moses Jenkinson has sold the [Goldsmith Chandlee] farm for 12 thousand dollars 8 thousand in hand . . . I expect when thee comes home all will be hurry, but if we have to sell our place, hard as it may be, there will be a way . . . It is so dark I cannot write until I have a light—evening, I was much pleased with the verses, the deaugeratipe struck me as particularly touching . . . P[hiladelphia] with her usual wildness snatched up a piece of paper with Ill write to pap and Emma coming said, so will I. They wrote a few lines which I enclose. They have been sleighing a great [d]eal and are full of life. There is now a heavy fall of snow and will soon be, girls will you take a ride . . . With as much love as wife can bear to a husband, I am thine.
A G Jenkins[1]

Abby was at a loss about how to make ends meet. Bedford's poor health forced her to buy hay to get their livestock through the winter. She even had to borrow money to pay their taxes. It did not help that their in-laws, the Ransoms, had sent them a scrawny, rather than fattened, pig. The Ransoms could have spared a more suitable animal. Given that the Jenkins family lived on Hatten's land, it seems reasonable that Abby would make a payment on it. But this mild bit of whining did not sit well with Henry. In a later letter, Abby apologized in her typical, self-deprecating manner: "I am sorry if I said anything to hurt thy feelings in the least. I am sure it was far from my intention. No one could feel more keenly than I do for thy privations and difficulties and never yet had a hard thought of thy leaving, well knowing the motive. If I erred it was through ignorance."[x]

The fate of his former partner, Harvey Hunt, may have come as a shock to Henry, or perhaps he already knew about the man's health issues. Harvey's family buried him in the Camden cemetery. Susan Hunt, the mourning widow, had to undertake the duties of dealing with a messy probate case. Harvey's assets came nowhere near to covering his usual domestic bills. There was nothing to contribute to the Makepeace debt. Of the five original note signers who left for California, only three remained to pay the big note: Sam Jones, Dennis Lowry, and John Anderson. Henry Jenkins had his own large sum to cover and the Liestenfeltzes and Teach their separate note. All were coming up on a year past due. Henry's mention of sending Abby a letter with Anderson and Gibson indicates the two had visited with Henry before they shipped home, probably sometime between Christmas and New Year's.

In letters to Ann from William, he pressured her to come out west—without their daughter. William had caught on quickly that it was not the miners getting rich in California. His and Robert's farming efforts on the Stockton Ranch paid well, and they wanted additional help. It remained to be seen if they would get it. Will Jenkins seemed unlikely to leave Indiana; he had borrowed a little money here and there to make a final payment on his own property. Bedford did not seem inclined to take up the offer, either because of his health or his relationship with Patience Randall.

For Henry, daily life remained much the same. Devout Christians with a strong work ethic, like Henry, found much to dislike among their fellow men. Partnerships coalesced and dissolved in rapid succession, as slackers took advantage of the diligent. Henry moved through the Calaveras camps like musical chairs, first to Mokelumne Hill from McKinneys Creek then back to Murphys, and finally to McKinneys again, buying and selling various claims as he went. Having a claim that paid pennies to the pound of dirt could not appease a man hearing tales of dollars. Henry's claims, like most in Calaveras County, were all dry diggings, which is why the upcoming dry season (beginning in April) also tended to be the most difficult time of year for men to make ends meet. Henry thought his latest company's ditches would continue running after the rains stopped, an optimistic claim.

Henry worked some construction jobs in 1853, including a quartz mill, and a house and fencing for one of the Dutch De Fremery brothers. He probably served as foreman on some of the projects, in charge of making payments for labor, supplies, and livestock rentals. It had to be a relief to break away from mining at last, even if it meant working for wages. In mid-February, he sent Abby a draft for $100. It appears to be the last money he ever sent.[3]

PART III
A POUND OF FLESH

CHAPTER 16

A HELPING HAND

Every man is grasping for dollars & every day men become more des-
perate in their methods of getting them. The mines this year have not
yielded so bountifully the precious dust & many impatient at the slow
income take other men's gains & often their lives to get them.
—OLIVER WOODSON NIXON, LETTER TO HIS FATHER

1853—CALIFORNIA
A wave of brutal robberies and murders began in Calaveras County in
January. These were not crimes of the liquor-fueled, bar-brawl variety,
nor the typical outrages that resulted in a job for Judge Lynch, after
which things returned to status quo. For years, certain white Americans
did everything they could to make life difficult for "foreigners" in the
mines (this included the Hispanic Californios, who were also American
citizens). Some people believed that Joaquin Murrieta and his band
of outlaws sought revenge for abuses against his family at the hands
of whites, and for being driven off his mining claim, both assertions
probably fictional. Rather, his targets were most frequently the already
much-victimized Chinese. But his murderous tirade was largely indis-
criminate. He killed French miners, white Americans, and anyone who
resisted being robbed. The man and his cohort relished violence and
bloodshed, and the lawmen were ineffective at putting a stop to it.[1]

The string of crimes started in Yaqui Camp, between San Andreas and McKinneys Creek. One Chinese miner died. A few days later, four more miners were killed in another incident. From there, the brigands headed to a quartz mill on O'Neil Creek, just over the ridge south of McKinneys (perhaps the one Henry helped build), murdering two men guarding the mill. Murrieta and his men evaded capture, due to having excellent horses. (Most miners did not have horses, and the lawmen had trouble finding posse members with good mounts.) Vigilantes pursued the gang and killed several of them, though they may have targeted Mexicans who were not involved in the killings. Many Mexican families fled the area in fear for their lives. Murrieta went north across the Mokelumne River. They held up two hundred Chinese miners in Rich Gulch; they killed two, plus an American, stealing thousands in gold. The next day, they crossed over the hill to another Chinese camp and repeated their atrocities, murdering several more miners. They slipped away from the posse once again. They rode further south, to Mariposa County, and continued their spree of killings and stealing horses. Eventually, the gang headed for the coastal counties and things settled down in the mines.

The outrage remained. First, the American miners convinced the governor to issue a reward for Murrieta's capture. That effort was seen as too little, too late. In May, the state legislature signed a bill authorizing a group of California Rangers, led by Harry Love, to pursue the outlaws. With the help of Murrieta's brother-in-law, Jesus Feliz, the band was finally brought to heel in the San Joaquin Valley, where the Rangers killed Murrieta and a man known as Three-Fingered Jack (Benedicto Garcia), a known murderer, but not necessarily complicit in the Calaveras crimes. In order to prove their success at exterminating these two, Love severed Murrieta's head and Jack's hand.

Events in early 1853 remained indelible in Pete Liestenfeltz's mind for life. He recalled in his memoir:

There was high way robers up in the mountains. The leaders were 5 [Three] fingers Jack . . . Waken [Joaquin] was a Mexican and 5 fingers Jack was an American. They had killed many. They roved the country over. These robers shot gold bullets. There was a big reward Paid for 5 fingers Jacks hand and Wakenes head and there was a Scotchman and two others. There was three Passes, Suthern Pass, Northern Pass, and Middle Pass. They told that they were going to take the Middle Pass and Southern pass but they found it out and took the northern pass and came over a raise in the morning and there they were eating their breakfast and they shot them. Took their head and hand to San Frisco and got their reward and Preserve them in whiskey.[2]

Clearly, Pete took many details from inaccurate rumors and news accounts. He may or may not have had personal encounters with Murrieta while the Mexican roamed Calaveras County, but there were undoubtedly times when Pete and the other Blackford men had reason to fear for their lives while working in the mines.

SUMMER 1853—INDIANA
Roads Knox

June 11th 1853

My dear Henry, I was much gratified last post at receiving 2 letters from thee, one dated April 1st the other 10th. They come almost always 2 together and then such a crowding around me to hear Paps letters. Mother close by that she may hear every word and children all round. It is a feast of fat things. The thoughts of thy working every day in water caused much uneasiness. Surprised thee has good health. I can truly say I feel thankful for it beyond expression. The pot pie was much admired at. Emma wondered if Pap would not cook sometimes when he comes home just to let us see how handy he is. Dont trouble thyself about a gold dollar, I have some curious specimens of gold thee sent me, though I have had to part with many of the pieces. Thee did not tell me to pay E White. I had forgotten thee owed him, wondered what made him so particular to get thy directions. Expected he had some sinister view, knew not what. Oh human nature. I paid T. Johnson and many little debts we had contracted. I am ashamed at the manner we use up thy hard earnings, while trying to be economical we think, as possible. B[edford] is at Williams [Jenkins] ploughing for corn very late but there has been so much rain it could not be helped. Hardly anybody is done planting. Our corn is up and the orchard has been ploughed once but we have not yet planted our late potatoes, expect to this week. Our wheat looks well. Hope this year at least to raise enough to keep us . . . we often wish we had thy clothes here to wash. I am sorry you have to spend the sabbath so contrary to what we believe to be right. I know it must be very unpleasant to thee. I got out to meeting last first day again. Mother is getting quite smart. She can walk with a cane in the house, out of doors she has to use a crutch. I planted those currants thee sent me in a [spot] of good earth and paid good attention to them but there has not one come up. Afraid they will not . . . Emma and Jane have peeled slippery Elm Bark last week at least 6 dollars worth. They think they have done large business. Ann got a letter from Wm. He still, I think, would like her to come to him though it may be on account of his just getting her letter that mentioned her willingness to come. I think she has written since rather differently. He says if she does not come he will start home in march. He wrote his Father [James Ransom] a severe letter, I think enough for the old man. We will let him rest . . . Mother is actually writing, says she will send it when this goes . . . Emma wrote to thee a short time ago. Write to them, it will be very acceptable and profitable . . . Ann took Cordelia to Blackford with her this week. We feel lonely without her. She is a little pratler . . . with much love from all the family and a greater share from thy lonely little wife.

A.G. Jenkins

Abby resigned herself to the fact that Henry had not started for home in the spring as promised. She shared all the local gossip she could glean, knowing he relished every word, reading it over and over until the next arrived. The news about his mother would be a balm on Henry's troubled heart.

Back around mid-March, John Anderson and Pres Gibson returned home—likely to much rejoicing in Trenton. In his later years, Anderson claimed to have walked to California and back.[3] Either this was more of the lying that Henry had complained about, or he had dementia that caused him to swap out others' stories for his own. He reunited with his buddy, Dennis Lowry. They took their earnings and used it to help finance a railroad project, much as Pete Liestenfeltz had done. Railroads seemed the best bet for profiting from the march of progress. Lowry and Anderson's investment took the form of a $965 promissory note from the board of directors of the Fort Wayne and Southern Railroad. The director who signed the note was the company treasurer (and attorney), J. S. Buckles. Makepeace's debt continued to go unpaid.

Summer 1853—California

Henry pressed on, working at mining claims or other work he could get for wages. Sometimes he allowed men to put off paying him for his labor—something he had become habituated to back east in the ledger economy. He still considered people to be trustworthy in general, though the trust may have been misplaced at times.

He heard there might be some carpentry work at the Fifteen Mile Ranch (present-day Linden), so he went there in early August. Contrary to rumor, they had no work, so he continued on to Stockton and, on a whim, decided to visit the Ransom brothers. He boarded a steamer to San Francisco, where he bought new clothes, "pants coat shirt and hat for $12.50," and spent the night.[4] The steamer *Guadalupe* ran the route from the city down the bay to Alviso, where Henry took a stage, or possibly walked, to the Stockton Ranch.

The ranch had been a boon for the Ransoms. They earned a regular salary and probably did side jobs for pay as well. The wheat crop looked exceptional. There would be high-quality Santa Clara flour for sale that fall. The brothers saved their earnings. The raucous lifestyle found in the mines was largely absent in the old mission town and pueblo, making it easier to behave. Neither brother really had a wild streak, anyway. They tended toward sober and industrious. Robert, perhaps from Emma's influence, had a religious inclination, as well.

Surprised by Henry's sudden appearance, the brothers greeted him enthusiastically. They toured him around the ranch and introduced him to the Kennedys. Henry approved of the operation. He wrote in his diary:

> William went with me to San Jose on Saturday [August] 6th—a very businesslike place and the surrounding country verry fine indeed. While walking about Wm proposed for me to return home and send Ann and Bedford out, offering to advance me $400.00 and take Bedford into partnership to farm on the shares as they have a good chance. It is a thing quite unlooked for or thought of. I know not what to do but rather think I will close in with the proposition.

He spent the next day in Santa Clara, attending services at both the Catholic and Methodist churches. He mulled over the idea of returning home, thanks to William's largesse, rather than his own success. It was a bitter pill to swallow, but he missed his family. After services, he "returned and after maturely weighing the matter concluded to close in with Wms offer as it seems to me they have a verry good chance." He would stuff his pride and go home. Concluding his visit with "the boys," he returned to San Francisco and spent a full day exploring the city—his first real opportunity to look around.

Henry returned to the mines and looked up his old friend Henry Angell at the cave he had explored two years earlier near McKinneys because "a couple of men have taken it in hand to fit it up for the inspection of the curious and public in general." Angell was one of the men, and his partner was Widdon McGee. To make the enterprise worthwhile, they decided to construct a hotel at Cave City. Henry spent some time working for them preparing the cave for tourism: opening up passages, shoring them up with timbers, and installing torches. A couple years after the hotel was completed, it was put under mechanic's lien by the lumber supplier and burned to the ground in 1858. Angell remained in California for life but never replicated his earlier success in the mines. When he died in 1897, friends had to take up a collection to give him a proper burial.[5]

While Henry labored at the cave, Teach came by and said that he had heard from home that Makepeace would likely get a judgment against the Blackford Company. The news soured Henry's mood about going home with next to nothing to show for all his time in the mines. He worried he might even lose his home. He counted the days until his departure, anyway.

He wrote a letter to Emma and went to Murphys to send it. He spent several weeks picking up other odd jobs and trying to collect money that people owed him, mostly without success. He stayed in Mokelumne Hill for a time, where he could enjoy Sunday services. At the end of August, he returned home to McKinneys. "[G]ot home in the evening and found two letters from home—one containing the sorrowful information of the death of Jane—I sympathise with Wm. truly and would write to him but expect to start for home [and] arrive as soon as a letter would arrive therefore it would be needless." The news of his daughter-in-law's passing, the only one in the family since he left home, and his inability to console his son, weighed on his spirit. His granddaughter Lizzy was now motherless, but she would be well cared for by the Jenkins and Ransom families, as well as her father, Will.

After doing a little more work in the cave and building a stable, Henry prepared to depart by making the rounds and saying goodbye to his friends. Then the time came to return to the Ransoms to finalize his preparations for leaving California. Henry spent a night in Santa Clara, the first time he slept on a real bed, between sheets, since he left Cincinnati two and a half years earlier. He tried to find some work in Alviso, but failing in that, he spent the week at the ranch observing operations, pleased with what he saw. Confident and encouraged that the Ransoms' success would preserve the dream of the families settling out west and making a good living, he set aside worries about his precarious situation.

It was time to leave; Henry pocketed $700 from William and Robert. Then he . . .

> parted with the boys this morning directly after breakfast and went out to the road, the Alameda or public walk, and got to

Santa Clara just in time for the stage to Alviso at which place got on board the steamer Gaudaloupe and arrive in San Francisco about 3 in the afternoon and put up at the Nickaragua Exchange, a new house and apparently a verry good one. Met with Mr. Harvy Brown who like myself is bout leaving for home—much pleased to find someone that I had known before.

As coincidentally as they had met in Panama on the way to California, the two acquaintances bumped into each other again. This time, they arranged to travel together, at least as far as New York. They paid $70 for through passage on the *Cortez* (Pacific side) and *Star of the West* (Atlantic side), riding in first steerage. The ship was crowded, but the people were well behaved, a tangible relief to Henry.

On the first morning at sea, Henry rose an hour before dawn to watch the scenery and sunrise; the full moon was simultaneously setting in the west. On Sunday, he expressed disappointment at the lack of services—"suppose there are no preachers amongst us." Six days into the trip, they passed Cabo San Lucas, and three days later, the weather turned grim.

[September] 24th—Saturday—commenced raining and blowing about three in the morning and by breakfast time blew quite a gale and still increasing till ten o'clock. Few of us thought the ship could stand it out much longer. I felt a calmness and resignation of mind that was truly surprising, almost any wave and fresh gust of wind I expected to be the last and in the most trying moments such passages as (fear not for I am with thee, be not dismayed for I am thy God or trust in the Lord forever for in the Lord Jehovah there is everlasting strength) and a sweet peace of mind that nothing but an entire trust and confidence in God could give—Praise be his holy name—well the storm kept increasing in violence until about five in the evening when it began to abate so that we got some supper, dinner we had none, and I then laid down in my wet clothes and slept and groaned verry much—and on 25th Sunday—rose much refreshed in body and mind.

The *Cortez* arrived at San Juan del Sud, Nicaragua, on September 29. The travelers were provided with horses and mules to make the twelve-mile trek to Lake Nicaragua. Harvy Brown had his luggage and boarded the first of two steamers waiting at the lake, but Henry waited until midnight for his bags to arrive and took the second boat. Henry described the lake: "A verry high peak rises in the midst of the lake right opposite the City of Pineda (the place where we embark) and everything goes to impress the beholder with the belief that the peak is the centre of a verry large crater, the Lake filling the cavity caused by the sinking of the surrounding country." Even as they boarded, he could see one volcano in the distance "emitting quite a volume of smoke."

The "noisy mirth and carousing" that night seemed to be the worst he had experienced. He huddled miserably on the deck amid the baggage, getting no sleep aside from a brief nap near daybreak. Upon waking, he learned a man had fallen overboard in the night and was never found. Like so many casualties of these trips, no one seemed much to care, until some expected traveler, like Willis Wilson, never arrived at home.

Once they crossed the lake, the passengers were herded onto a series of boats of decreasing size needed to get down the rapids to the Caribbean coast. On the smallest, they were packed like standing sardines. Henry had a thought that his daughter, Ann, might be heading upstream on a different boat, "but as I could not see have to trust she may be still at home." On the Caribbean coast, the *Star of the West* awaited, and they set off for New York. Though Henry and Harvy had paid for upper steerage, they found themselves in a berth below and griped about it being too warm to sleep. They stayed on deck as much as possible, but when the weather turned cold, they had to retreat to their undesirable bunks. As they steamed up the Atlantic coast, sailing ships and steamships became a frequent sight. "It would seem as though we were coming near some much frequented part of the world," Henry wrote. He admired the magnificent view as they steamed into the harbor. "The entrance to N York is the most beautiful part of the world that it has ever been my privilege to see, the various islands covered over with county seats and villages."

Henry and Harvy disembarked at about 4:00 p.m. on Sunday, October 9. They found rooms at French's Hotel, a lodging establishment for men near the southern tip of Manhattan, for 50 cents per night. It sat on Frankfort Street across from City Hall Park, and north of the Tammany Hotel, then the headquarters of the Democratic Party. The street level of the seven-story hotel had a bar, dining room, and reading room. Henry noted the two nearby churches, but the city drew his attention more. "N York is truly a great city and it is wonderful to stand and contemplate the vast crowds continually passing along and the busy hum of hundreds of different kinds of vehickles of every discription is almost stunning and bewildering." Henry did not remark on whether Harvy stayed in the city for long or headed straight for Indiana, where he could pass on the news of Henry's imminent arrival back home. Henry had his own agenda that included a detour to his home city.

Figure 16.1. City Hall Park. French's Hotel, with street sign for City Hall Square on its wall, Tammany Hotel, *Sunday Times*, *Tribune*, and Currier on the left. St. Paul's in the background. Credit: The Miriam and Ira D. Wallach Division of Art, Prints and Photographs: Print Collection, The New York Public Library. New York Public Library Digital Collections.

The next morning, Henry boarded the trolley line, known as the Harlem Rail Road, that ran along the park going north. He exited the car near 42nd Street. He called his destination the World's Fair, but the official title was the Exhibition of the Industry of All Nations ("all nations" consisting of sixteen countries and three British colonies).[6] Adjacent to Croton Reservoir rose the Crystal Palace, which housed the exhibits. President Franklin Pierce had dedicated the building in July. It was modeled after the 1851 Crystal Palace of London, constructed of iron and glass in the shape of a Greek Cross, and crowned by a 100-foot-diameter dome. Henry remarked that "the building did not meet my expectations but the display of Arts and curiosities rather exceeded them." The exhibits were divided into thirty-one classes, from raw materials to manufactured goods, and food to arts and crafts.[7] The ethnic mix was as exotic as any he saw in California, but the opulent apparel and presence of women added color to the scene. Next to the Palace stood the tallest spire in the city, the Latting Observatory. Dubbed "the first skyscraper," the wooden structure reputedly inspired Eiffel's tower and gave fairgoers a panoramic view from 315 feet above the street. The fair kept Henry occupied for the entire day.

Just after sunrise the next morning, Henry rode a ferry across the Hudson River. In New Jersey, he boarded a car similar to the trolley in New York. His first train ride. He stepped on the portable block and then up the metal stairs and turned into the compartment. The chill of the fall day crept in his wake. After hoisting his valise into an overhead rack, he took his seat, listening to the clamor of people milling on the platform and in the train, and the hiss of steam from the locomotive's boiler. A bell rang, signaling departure for Philadelphia. A steam whistle screamed and the squeal of metal wheels on metal rails rent the air as the chuffing engine eased forward. Sulfurous smoke seeped through cracked-open windows.

Along the way, he passed "through several towns and vilages and some verry beautiful country—quite a hard white frost—the corn generally cut and shocked. Arrived in Phila about ten." He knocked on the door of his brother-in-law's downtown home. Isaac T. Bedford's family were "well and seemed much pleased to see me." That same afternoon, he traveled to the Fairmount district and located a house on Spring Garden Street that he had built for his father-in-law, Thomas Bedford. It now belonged to Thomas's nephew and former business partner, also named Isaac Bedford.[8] Isaac was about eight years Henry's senior.

They chatted about family and old times in Philadelphia then Henry returned to Isaac T.'s home, where he spent the night. In the morning, Henry, Isaac, and Isaac's fifteen-year-old son, William, visited the Philadelphia Mint and other attractions. He decided to visit his mother's Widdifield relatives the following day. Hannah and her daughters had a confectionary shop on South 9th Street. Henry could not hide his irritation that his cousins could not meet with him even a moment, "the girls too busily engaged at their business to be seen—I shall call again in the evening alth[ough] I think they might have spared a few minutes at least from their business to see a relative after so long an absence." Well, he would just continue on to Indiana, where he could count on a much warmer welcome. He boarded a train to Pittsburgh the next day.

CHAPTER 17

TURNING TO THE LAW

1853—INDIANA

Long before the Jones brothers hatched their scheme to borrow money, Allen Makepeace had made "loans" to others wishing to join the rush, particularly in Delaware County. For the notes paid per agreement, there is no record. One, created in October 1849, became contested shortly after the James Jordan note that had gone to court in September 1852.

Andrew Collins requested a loan from Makepeace, but the merchant had no intention of lending money for such crazy schemes. Instead, he informed Collins that he was in the business of buying notes made by "good men." By that, he meant men with collateral he could collect (land being preferred). One of Andrew Collins's good men happened to be a woman. Playing along with Makepeace's game, he recruited his brother, Elijah Collins, and a young widow named Rhoda (Wharton) Barrett. The Wharton and Collins families had ties stretching back to Belmont and Guernsey Counties in Ohio, much like the Blackford group. Conceivably they were all well acquainted.

Andrew Collins worded his note like the Blackford ones. Elijah Collins and Rhoda Barrett promised to pay Andrew Collins $400 in one year's time with 6 percent interest. Andrew gave them nothing of value for the note. The major difference from the Blackford notes was that Andrew kept the proceeds, rather than giving them to the signers as Dr. Jones had done. Collins received $300 cash from Makepeace, which he used to go to California. Makepeace's crosshairs zeroed in on Rhoda and

Elijah, officially the debtors on the note. When Rhoda married Noah Lyon, he became jointly responsible for the debt. Allen Makepeace sued Elijah Collins and the Lyons for payment in January 1853. The defendants counter-sued, alleging fraud, saying that Makepeace knowingly violated the usury laws to obtain much more than the legally allowed interest. They hired Walter March as their attorney. March, son of a Muncie hotelier from New York, had been elected judge in the Court of Common Pleas in Delaware County the previous year. He had curly hair with a high forehead and thick brow. He was already well regarded as an erudite public speaker (a good thing because his handwriting was atrocious), a trait that would further his political career for years to come.

On March 25, the Lyons and Elijah Collins made a good-faith effort to settle with Makepeace. They agreed on the sum of $523, including interest and court costs. The three defendants gave Makepeace a combination of cash and Indianapolis-Bellefontaine Railroad stock to pay off $356, releasing the Lyons from the debt. Collins added a new promissory note, due August 20, for the balance of $167. It would seem the matter had been settled satisfactorily, but Makepeace continued his action against the defendants as if nothing had changed.[1]

In all likelihood, Sam Jones and his former partners learned about the Collins/Lyons case. (Sam returned home about the same time as Anderson and Gibson but probably did not travel with them.) Sam refused to make any payment to Makepeace on the $2,800 note and apparently persuaded John Anderson and Dennis Lowry to default, too. Makepeace had surely been putting pressure on Dr. Benjamin Jones and the families of the miners for over a year to come up with the money. The doctor, frustrated at his brother's refusal to make good on the note, made his way to Trenton in late August. Sam already had Makepeace and his attorney, James Swaar, there to deal with. Dr. Jones, losing his temper, yelled, "this note . . . was an honest note and dam them they aught to pay it!"[2] Sam was unmoved. The doctor fumed. He had given his word the note would be paid, even claiming personal responsibility for it, though not in writing.

Makepeace's patience ran out. It seemed the note signers were scattering to the four winds, and he had yet to collect a dime. Two of the debtors had died. Sam decided to move back to Barnesville, Ohio, putting his Trenton farm up for sale. Dennis intended to follow his in-laws to Iowa. Per his habit, Makepeace filed suit on the Jones note. His attorneys, Swaar, Sample & Kilgore, recorded the complaint in the Delaware Circuit Court on September 2, claiming: "The plaintiff says that the defendants nor either of them have paid to him one farthing of said sum although he has often demanded the same, but to pay the same and any part thereof have heretofore wholly failed, and refused and still do refuse, wherefore he prays judgment for that sum and the interest being four thousand Dollars for which plaintiff prays judgement."[3] The suit named all the signers, including those who had not gone to California.

Being the second signer on the note, John Anderson spoke for the defendants in Sam's absence. Adopting the same strategy as the Lyons and Collins, John hired their attorney, Walter March, and J. S. Buckles (the attorney to whom Anderson and Lowry had loaned the railroad money). They drafted a rambling, four-page response to the Makepeace complaint. Anderson admitted to the debt that they received in cash (including the $200 note): $1,867. They balked at the balance of $933 and the 6 percent interest on the full $2,800. They countered that Makepeace knew the actual interest on the debt far exceeded that allowed by law. The effective rate was 50 percent on the cash, plus an additional 6 percent on the face value. This rate was unlawful and usurious, Anderson asserted.[4]

The problem with this defense was that the borrowers knew full well how much they would pay for the cash they needed; they agreed to it anyway. A usury defense was rather audacious and only possible because they had signed the note in their own names, not in the name of the mining company. Indiana had already outlawed a usury defense by corporations. Businessmen in the 1850s laid siege against usury laws around the country. Many states had repealed theirs already. The opponents of such statutes argued that borrowers and lenders should be allowed to agree on a mutually satisfactory interest rate. The market should be the only determinant as to what a borrower would pay and what a lender could earn.

In the cases of *Makepeace v. Collins et al.* and *Makepeace v. Jones et al.*, buying notes at a discount was not illegal. At issue was whether the notes were valid or created under false pretenses. If the latter, then who was scamming whom? Upon receiving the defendant's response in the

Figure 17.1. David Kilgore, c. 1850, attorney for plaintiff Allen Makepeace in the *Makepeace v. Samuel Jones et al.* trial. Credit: Library of Congress, Prints & Photographs Online Catalog.

Jones case on September 17, Judge Joseph Anthony, president judge of the Delaware Circuit Court, docketed the case for the March 1854 term.

Henry Jenkins found himself once again in Knox Township. He evaded shipwrecks and tropical diseases. Avoided gamblers and grizzlies, villains and vigilantes. Averted accidents of all manner. We can only imagine the scene of his homecoming, as he stopped writing in his memo book after boarding a train for Dayton, Ohio.

Henry strolled down the Knox Road dressed in his new city clothes, not the homespun attire he had left in more than two and half years before. His hands, roughened beyond usual from the harsh mining life, gripped his battered valise. Colorful foliage waved in welcome, but he barely noticed. The ripe smells of the autumn harvest whet his appetite for fresh-pressed cider to cleanse the dust from his throat, but a rising lump would make swallowing it impossible. His emotions crescendoed as he passed familiar sights, his legs willing to break into a run if it had been dignified to do so. He reached the Hatten property to find the cabin that had been built by his sons and friends in his absence. The letter he mailed to Emma not long before leaving Calaveras County had only just preceded him.

All had been cleaned and tidied in anticipation of his arrival, but he only had eyes for his family. Abby, a flood of joy spilling from her eyes, did run to greet him with unalloyed relief, not knowing until that very moment that he had survived the perilous journey. She grasped him, not too gently, in her arms, lest he be a chimera. And she would never let him leave her again. The children—Emma, Philadelphia, Bedford, Barton, and Mary—all rushed to welcome the prodigal father, brimming with enthusiasm. Ann Ransom, with her daughter, Cordelia, and Will with Lizzy, took their turn at embracing him. Henry lifted up his little granddaughters each in turn to kiss their wee faces—the girls cringing from this bearded stranger. Was Ann Jenkins there to clasp her son to her bosom once more? We will never know for sure. Since she had been well four months earlier, it seems probable. Bedtime came very late that night.

Word about Henry's return spread rapidly. Soon, friends such as Alec White came calling, not just to hear stories but also to clear the books. Henry made his final payment to Hatten and received a deed to the land on October 27. Then there was the matter of the $800 plus accumulated interest that he owed Makepeace. Henry, made aware of the pending lawsuit against Sam Jones, would not pay the full amount due, in hopes that the usury countercharge just might work. But Makepeace did not sue Henry Jenkins as he had the Jones group. Why not? Most likely because Henry made at least a partial payment on the debt.

Makepeace also did not file suit on the Liestenfeltz note. For one thing, Jake and Pete were still in California, along with John Teach, the third man the note benefited. In addition, Makepeace, as a director of the Indianapolis-Bellefontaine Railroad, knew that the Liestenfeltzes had money invested with the railroad, so there were assets he could attach, if the miners did not pay up. It would not cover the full debt, but it would be a good start. After that, he could go after Conrad Liestenfeltz's land. Makepeace would get his money one way or another.

In November, Dennis Lowry filed an affidavit in the Harvey Hunt probate case. He stated that Hunt's estate was liable for a fifth of the company's debt to Makepeace, plus one-ninth of Humphrey Anderson's share. What the total would be, he did not know. If Makepeace won the suit, it would be based on the full face value plus interest. If their usury counterclaim succeeded, it would be for the amount of money they received from Dr. Jones—roughly $1,900.[5]

CHRISTMASTIME 1853

The holiday was bittersweet at the Jenkins farm. In November, as Henry re-established his relationships with his two oldest children, Will and Ann, and marveled at his two granddaughters, he had to bid three of them goodbye. He and Abby had known that Ann and Cordelia would eventually follow William Ransom to California, and William had sent money with Henry expressly for that purpose. William had also requested that Bedford come out west, but Bed was much too engaged with farming at home—and in the delightful company of Patience Randall. Will Jenkins, on the other hand, was mourning his wife, Jane. She had perished over the summer, possibly from consumption (tuberculosis), one of the nineteenth century's most prolific killers of young adults. Her parents, Elizabeth and James Ransom, buried Jane in the family plot in

Trenton, next to her baby brother, Samuel. Will needed a change of scenery. Escorting his sister and niece to San Francisco seemed a good idea. He wanted to see what William and Robert were up to that was proving so rewarding. Will arranged to leave Lizzy with Abby until his return. She and Cordy had never really been apart; the separation may have been a bit traumatic for the little girl cousins. The Ransoms also hated to see Ann, Cordelia, and Will depart. William and Robert had been gone nearly two years, and no one could be sure if they would ever return. At least James and Elizabeth could enjoy granddaughter Lizzy's company.

Christmas spirit flagged at the Camden home of Dr. Benjamin H. Jones, too. In just a few months, he would be called into court as the principal witness in the case of *Makepeace v. Samuel Jones et al.* He and his brother had been close for all their lives, but now, he felt betrayed. The Blackford miners had left him hanging in the wind by their refusal to pay their debt. Dr. Jones had no legal obligation to pay anything, but he had staked his reputation on that note; he had assured Makepeace it was good and would be paid. He would get through this somehow. Benjamin Jones was no quitter. When he was twelve years old, he had survived the deadly scarlet fever epidemic that had robbed the Jones family of three sons. He was strong-willed, without a doubt. Still, he may have combated the stress with one too many shots of whiskey.[6]

On Christmas Day, or shortly after, Dr. Jones began loading his gun. Guns were common in rural households. Many families supplemented their diets with game birds and mammals, though by the 1850s, finding game in eastern Indiana had become difficult. Settlers also used guns to deal with nuisances, such as raccoons and foxes raiding henhouses, or squirrels in the corn patch. Most were not modern pieces of the time. A surprising number of relics from the War of 1812 lurked in these rustic cabins. Dr. Jones's gun, whether handgun or long-arm, was a muzzle-loader. Carelessly holding the barrel as he rammed the ball and wadding, it suddenly fired. The gun sent hot lead at a speed approaching 1,500 feet-per-second—too fast for the blink of a soon-to-be-vanished eye—directly into Dr. Benjamin Jones's face.

Makepeace and his attorneys received notice that Dr. Jones would be giving a deposition at his home on the morning of December 30. That day, attorneys for the parties in the case of *Makepeace v. Jones et al.* converged on the Jones home in Camden. A justice of the peace arrived to take the deposition. Rebecca Jones sat near her gravely injured brother, prepared to assist in the process. The attorneys put their questions to the doctor in writing, as his hearing was still impaired from the sudden blast of his gun and the stunning impact. His injuries made it difficult for him to see, hear, and speak. Rebecca leaned in close to make out his garbled responses to the queries, his upper palate having sustained serious damage.[7] Then she wrote the responses on the JP's form.

Thomas J. Sample represented Makepeace. A devout Methodist, he was known for quoting from his Bible in courtroom appearances.[8] His partner, James H. Swaar, a witness in this particular case, would likely have been absent. Sample was assisted by David Kilgore. Judge Walter March and his partner, Joseph S. Buckles, represented the defendants. Thirty-four-year-old Buckles had thinning hair, a patrician nose, and a full complement of facial hair, kept neatly trimmed.

Figure 17.2. Joseph S. Buckles and Walter March, attorneys for the defendants in the trial of *Makepeace v. Jones et al.* Credit: Public domain.

The somber assemblage crowded into the doctor's chamber to begin the deposition. The JP began by administering the oath to Dr. Jones to tell the truth, the whole truth, and nothing but. Sample showed Jones the plaintiff's Exhibit A—a copy of a $2,800 promissory note—and asked him to tell anything he knew about the making of the note and its purpose. The laborious answer, which took Rebecca considerable time to decipher and put into writing:

The note was made for those boys to go to California. I went to him (Allen Makepeace) for the money. [I asked him] what per cent he would have for the money. He intimated that he would take twenty five percent. He wanted to see what kind of a note I had. I showed him the note and he said it would not do. And he said he would give me a copy of one and did so; I took it and went home. We set a time and I went [for] the money and I went down and J. Swaar went with me and wanted me to let him get the money for me and I told him that I had the promise of the money. I went on down and saw Mr. Makepeace and he told me he could not let his money go that way for he could make more. I asked Makepeace then and he said two for [three]. [I said the] Boys would not like that and I did not believe that they would take the money . . . I took the money then I went home. They were all mad. I told them they could take it back but they said . . . they would take it.[9]

They completed the deposition the following day. In it, Dr. Jones related how he had come to sell the $2,800 promissory note to Allen Makepeace, described the activities leading up to the sale, and the amount he received. He had not recalled meeting Allen's brother, George Makepeace, at the store in Chesterfield, who would testify as a key witness for the plaintiff.

The deposition concluded:

Q: State whether or not you are laboring under a severe wound from a gunshot through the face and suffering much and very fully in body & much in mind during the whole of this examination and is it not possible from the length of time elapsed, on the condition of the sale of the $2,800 note by you on Samuel Jones and others to Allen Makepeace on the 24th day of February 1851, that your mind may not have served you in any particular as well as it would have done otherwise.

A: It is not worthwhile to answer it. My body is weak but my mind is clear. I have a severe gunshot wound in the face and am afflicted with the hip disease.

Q: State whether or not you are a brother to Samuel Jones, one of the defendants in a suit on the $2,800 note now in controversy in the Delaware Circuit Court in which your deposition is intended to be used by defendant.

A: I am.

Q: State whether or not you are related to any of the other defendants save Samuel Jones in the suit now pending in the Delaware Circuit Court on a twenty eight hundred dollar note sold by you to Allen Makepeace or the lady who interpreted in the taking these depositions.

A: Are you . . . otherwise, the lady who writes this deposition is my sister. I am related to none of the defendants except S. Jones.

Q: In your answers to the first questions in this deposition you use the expression "the boys." What persons do you refer to by that expression?

A: The persons who signed the $2,800 dollar note.

Q: State what county you reside in and your occupation.

A: Jay County and a practicing physician.[10]

ANOTHER TRIP TO CALIFORNIA

Like the two earlier groups, Will, Ann, and Cordelia set out for Panama. They disembarked in Navy Bay. The new town built in the swamp there was officially called Colón (for Christopher Columbus), but Americans knew it as Aspinwall, named after the owner of the steamship company. The railroad now took steamship passengers as far as Barbacoa, about twenty-three miles. They still had to cover part of the distance to Gorgona by boat, then take the mule trains into the city. From Panama, the trio would not make the mistake of taking any sailing ships. They arrived safely by steamer in San Francisco in January 1854.

Anticipating the arrival of his wife, daughter, and brother-in-law, William Ransom traveled to San Francisco. It seems likely that Robert went with him—it had been many months since either had seen family, and that had just been Henry. It had to be a joyous meeting, all these young adults reuniting in a fantastic new setting: a vibrant, burgeoning city. William had not seen his daughter, though, in nearly two years; they were virtual strangers. The three-year-old may have shyly hidden in her mother's skirts. Her Jenkins and Ransom uncles were more like fathers to her than her own. The reunited family probably did not spend more than a day in San Francisco, that den of vice and iniquity. Santa Clara was a much healthier venue.

The ferry ride back to Alviso provided the newcomers with an overview of San Francisco and the surrounding hills, though it would have been a chilly ride in the damp breeze. The party, buoyant from seeing one another again after so long, probably did not even notice the jolting of the stage over the last eight miles to Santa Clara and the ranch.

The Ransom brothers quickly put Will to work farming, the physical routine welcome after two months of leisure. The sea journey had given him too much time to dwell on Jane's death, for which he could not help but feel in some measure responsible. Their brief marriage had been rocky, possibly due to his taciturn nature or their financial struggles. Will could sense his poverty in relation to his in-laws. And, too, leaving Lizzy behind weighed heavily. But maybe he could better provide for her future in this ideal agricultural climate. Ann, for her part, settled back into the duties of being William's wife—and was almost immediately pregnant with her second child. As William had promised in his letters, she soon had plenty of work to keep her busy and adding to the young family's coffers.

CHAPTER 18

A CLAIM OF USURY

The "crowds" at that day thought the holding of a court a great affair. The people came hundreds of miles to see the judges, and hear the lawyers "plead," as they called it. On one occasion there came on to be tried before the jury an indictment for an assault and battery against a man for pulling the nose of another who had insulted him. The court-room was filled to suffocation.

—O.H. SMITH, *EARLY INDIANA TRIALS*

MARCH 1854—INDIANA

The March term of the 7th Circuit Court in Muncie commenced. The circuit covered Henry, Wayne, Randolph, Delaware, Jay, Blackford, and Grant Counties. Joseph Anthony had been elected to the position of president judge of the circuit for a six-year term in October 1852, around the time he completed a four-year term as county auditor. He presided over the courts in all the counties in his district, much to some lawyers' dismay. Judge Anthony was admitted to the Blackford County bar in 1839. He had also been admitted to the Delaware County bar in the late 1830s. Law was not his principal profession in the 1840s and 1850s, however. After moving to Muncie, he became a tavern keeper at a business called the Eastern Hotel, because it was east of the town square. His constituents knew him to be a man of sound common sense and good judgment. He was a fair-minded man, and his even-handed rulings from the bench were usually reasonable compromises. Consequently, neither side derived the satisfaction of winning.

Anthony had an older brother in Ohio who was a respected attorney and legislator. Another older brother, Dr. Samuel P. Anthony, lived in Delaware County and had financial successes rivaling Allen Makepeace's. But the brothers came from a Quaker family and were generous as well as industrious. The Indianapolis press smeared Joseph Anthony as illiterate and incompetent. In truth, he was neither. Not only was Joseph Anthony a capable and competent jurist (with excellent handwriting), but he was also a man of compassion who sought true justice for the citizens in his jurisdiction. Because many lawyers hoped he would step down before his term ended, they continued their cases from session to session. They waited in vain. Judge Anthony had every intention of fulfilling his obligation to the voters.[1]

The case of *Makepeace v. Samuel Jones et al.* began on March 30. Anthony well knew Allen Makepeace and his debt-collection methods. As an attorney in the early 1840s, he filed a case on behalf of one Archibald Parker. Parker had borrowed funds from Makepeace to purchase two forty-acre parcels. In 1841, Makepeace obtained a judgment for non-payment. He forced the execution of the judgment by selling the more valuable south forty acres of land. He purchased it for the $200 owed. The land had been worth at least $600. None of the other seven or eight men at the auction placed a bid.

The appraisers, who valued the land at $350, said Makepeace had not influenced them, but they did not visit the property prior to filing their report. Parker argued that his personal property and the less valuable north forty would have satisfied the debt. He felt Makepeace's seizure of the developed portion, including his home, had been unnecessarily cruel. Anthony pleaded with the associate judges to remedy the situation, to no avail.[2] Despite that history, Judge Anthony would listen to all the evidence presented and render impartial judgment to the best of his ability.

On the morning of the *Makepeace v. Jones* trial, Judge Anthony left his home at the tavern on Main Street; his wife would take care of business and the children. He conveyed himself to the courthouse, less than two blocks away, using a sturdy pair of well-worn crutches. His paralyzed and withered legs served merely as one-third of a moving tripod.[3] The Delaware County courthouse, on the public square in Muncie, was of modest size. The forty-five-foot-square brick building was built in a Flemish bond pattern, unusually ornate for the time and place.[4] There were no front steps; one entered the two-story building from the walkway

Figure 18.1. Delaware County Courthouse 1837–1884. Credit: Minnetrista Heritage Collection.

through double doors. While a great convenience to the judge, it had not been built with his condition in mind.

The attorneys, their clients, and spectators filed into the courtroom. Even civil trials were considered entertainment. The bailiff called the assemblage to rise as Judge Anthony seated himself at the bench and called the court into session. The clerk made no attempt to create a verbatim transcript of the proceedings. Only summaries of evidence and responses given by witnesses were taken down. He generally did not retain the attorneys' questions, remarks from the bench, or closing arguments for posterity. No jury heard the case. Judge Anthony would render the verdict for the court.

The trial began with the plaintiff's evidence.[5] The attorneys submitted copies of the $2,800 note in question, the $200 note from 1850, and two other notes pertaining to the men who had gone to California: $800 signed by Henry Z. Jenkins, Thomas B. Jenkins [Bedford], and Joseph Wilson; $1,350 signed by Jacob, Conrad, and Daniel Liestenfeltz, James Walker, and two others. All the notes had been assigned to Allen Makepeace. This was the extent of the plaintiff's case. In his original complaint and in his answer to the defendants' response, Allen Makepeace stated that he did not know the circumstances behind the note, but bought it like he did any other. He denied the countercharge of usury. The defense read into the record Dr. Jones's deposition, taken three months earlier. Then defense attorneys March and Buckles called their principal witness to the stand: Dr. Benjamin H. Jones.

As the now-disfigured physician, wearing his best clothes, carefully made his way to the witness stand, audible gasps and murmurs rippled through the gallery. A decade in the future, such sights would be commonplace, but were currently rare. Rumors of his ruined face had no doubt reached Muncie, but his visage evoked curiosity and horror, even if masked in some manner. Dr. Jones spoke in a slow, distorted voice as he answered the questions put to him.

"The defendents wished to go to California and wanted me to get some money for them. I had previously sold to Mr. Swaar a $200 note and assigned it to him and the defendents supposed it was so that they might get it too." When he met Makepeace the first time, he "showed him a note, did not seemed disposed to let the money go but said in a few days he would write and let me know about it and perhaps let [me] have it. Swaar had let [me have it] 3$ for 4$." Dr. Jones wanted the same deal from Makepeace, but "he also objected to my note—wanted a percussion [note] and one drawing interest from date and furnished me a copy of such note as required. I told him defts had California fever & wanted to go and got me to get the money for them & were willing to give almost any amount of interest. He called this an accommodation note which would evade the law limiting interest to 6 per cent which [no one would] off[er] to loan it for as it would be a long time [be]fore it would be got & he would do better with it."

According to Jones, Makepeace had additional terms: "Mr Makepeace requested me to get Jacob Brugh to reccomend the dfts which I done and also that I learn from the officers of Blackford County how much land each one had & which was marked on note opposite each name." In truth, some of the borrowers had recorded deeds a day or two after receiving funds from Makepeace.

On cross-examination, Dr. Jones said he sold both the $2,800 and $800 notes to Makepeace on February 24, 1851, three years earlier. He received two-thirds of the face value on each. He denied that the men receiving the money had paid him anything for his part in the deal. He received the money in the store, not the tavern in Chesterfield. Others had been in the room, but he did not know any of them. The money changed hands just before dark.

The defense re-examined Dr. Jones and elicited that he "staid all night at tavern where I borrowed money & I & Mr Swaar slept together with this [money] under my head." He lived over forty miles from Chesterfield, and the winter sun set early, so it was plausible. Then he described his accident,

When I testified before the Justice, I was nearly deaf and could scarcely articulate worse than I now am from a gunshot wound in the face, and was hardly able at all to testify, but what I now say, I was just a few days before that shot in the side of my face from loading a gun and was advised against it by the doctor. It destroyed the eye & upper part of my face and the taking of the deposition was pressed, as I suppose, for fear I would die. My palate was effected & the bone of my left nostril [illegible] and right mind has ever since remained well.[6]

He also clarified that he had told Mr. Hunter—who first took him to Chesterfield to find Makepeace—and others that he was not a partner in the mining company, but had agreed to doctor the miners' families while they were gone. They would compensate him when they returned. He mentioned that he made an earlier version of the $2,800 note (without interest), but the signers on it were different than on the note sold to Makepeace.

Seven additional witnesses testified; they were all from Muncie or Chesterfield, and most were either related to Makepeace or had business dealings with him. The first called was James H. Swaar.

Swaar contradicted Jones on several issues: He said that Makepeace agreed to pay three-fourths if it included the $200 note, and he stated that Dr. Jones had received the money at George Makepeace's store at around 2 p.m. He also insisted that the doctor told him he was an equal partner in the mining company.

The question was put to Jones again: "Did you not tell James Swarr on the road to Chesterfield on the day you sold the note now in controversy to plaintiff that you was to raise the money for the Defendants upon the note and Doctor their families whilst they were gone to California and that for your trouble you were to have an equal share of all the profits of their trip to California?"

Jones replied, "No sir. I did not tell him any such thing."

Swaar did not recall spending the night in Chesterfield, nor did he recall the sale of the $800 note. He stated flatly that Jones received $1,900 in cash, plus the $200 note. Another important admission from Swaar was that he told Makepeace that the note was "gotten up on purpose" to raise money for California. As with Dr. Jones's testimony, this belied Makepeace's plea of ignorance about the note's creation.

The Chesterfield witnesses then testified. Their statements confirmed the amount of money Swaar had stated, a total of $2,100. They also said the exchange happened in mid-afternoon or shortly after the noon mealtime. Neither Allen Makepeace nor any one of the defendants testified. What never came up, probably because it seemed irrelevant, was Dr. Jones's first attempt to sell the larger note to Volney Willson.

After the testimony and a recess, Judge Anthony had the courtroom called to order again on Saturday, April 1, to announce his verdict. The trial had continued over for a second day, with no hearing on Friday, due to other cases. The out-of-town participants were anxious to get home after spending an extra night in Muncie. As the gallery came to a hush, the judge gave a brief summary of the evidence, then announced his finding for the defendants on the countercharge of usury. He did not find Makepeace's feigned ignorance about the note's provenance believable. The penalty for usury was forfeiture of all interest. He also did not believe Dr. Jones's assertion that he had received only two-thirds of the note value. Had the poor country doctor pocketed the difference between what Makepeace paid out and what he had given Sam's company? If so, Sam had to be complicit. Sam had sold the Liestenfeltz note and also given them two-thirds of the value. The prospect seems out of character for the Jones men, but not impossible. Or had Makepeace's witnesses lied on the stand about the payout?

Anthony decreed that the defendants owed the full amount Makepeace said he paid for the note: $2,100, but no more. He banged the gavel to adjourn court, and a hubbub immediately ensued. The verdict favored the defense, but seemed just. This verdict did not please Makepeace. Upon hearing it, the plaintiff's attorneys requested a new trial. Makepeace had provided good cash money to desperate young men, and they had accepted the terms. Justice had not been served, in his view. This would not be the end of the matter. No sir.

Anderson and Lowry conferred with their attorneys. It seemed they had to come up with a substantial sum between the two of them. If Sam had not been adamantly opposed to paying the note, they might not be in this fix. They had invested their California earnings in a loan to a new railroad company—surely a good bet—and did not expect a quick payback. The note signers who had not gone to California were not inclined to lay their necks on the block; they had realized nothing from the arrangement. Those men knew if Jones, Anderson, and Lowry did not pay, Makepeace would eventually file a lien on their land and foreclose. No one doubted his determination or deep pockets for legal fees. He would get his way.

People filed out of the courthouse, making their way to dinner, discussing the merits of the ruling and other aspects of the case. Dr. Jones mounted his horse for a cool and pensive ride back to Camden.

Dr. Jones had endured this humiliating spectacle for his younger brother. Family. He never signed any legal promise to pay anyone, but now it had been recorded in his deposition and court testimony that he had verbally guaranteed that the note would be paid. Would this millstone hang around his neck for the rest of his life? His trials were not over yet. Nine days later, his youngest child, Mary Adeline, nearly four years old, died of an unknown cause. After his horrific accident, and the agony of the court trial, he suffered the heartbreak of losing his daughter. He and his wife buried their little girl in Camden's Hillside Cemetery. Mariah Jones was bereft. The marriage produced no more children.

Now that it was clear the miners would have to pay at least $2,100 to Allen Makepeace, Dr. Jones probably assumed he would have to cover at least part of Sam's share since Sam had left town for good. He needed every penny he could get his hands on, even from a bankrupt estate. He filed a claim against the Harvey Hunt estate for goods provided in 1852.

Sam did not entirely neglect his duty as Blackford Mining Company president, however. Sometime between January and October 1854, Asa Anderson, executor of Humphrey's estate, received from "the President of the California Mining Company from Blackford County" a payment of $350.[7] It was short of one-fifth of the judgment, but at least the men had done something to honor their agreement. Eventually, Humphrey's estate, like Harvey's, would need to cover his portion of the debt to Makepeace.

In September 1854, Allen Makepeace filed his formal motion for a new trial against Sam Jones et al. He cited three justifications: 1) the verdict was contrary to law and unsupported by the evidence; 2) the court should have found for the plaintiff the entire note amount plus interest; and 3) new evidence backed his claim that he did not know the note was

unsupported by good consideration.[8] This assertion he based on testimony from Volney Willson, who had seen the first $2,800 note that Dr.
Jones had shopped around. Willson testified to the court:

> . . . sometime in the winter or spring of A.D. 1851 one Benjamin
> H. Jones called upon him and asked him if he ever bought any
> notes . . . to which he replied he sometimes did when he had the
> funds. Jones said he would wanted about twenty-five hundred
> dollars, to which deponent replied that amount was over the
> size of his pile . . . Jones then asked him, said Willson, whether
> Allen Makepeace . . . ever purchased notes to which he, Willson,
> replied that he sometimes did when he could get them upon suit-
> able terms, that he would not lend money . . . unless it was for a
> short time as a favor, and that if he bought a note he would want
> to be certain that it would be paid at maturity and a good note. A
> short time after that day, said Jones again called on him, the said
> Willson, and showed him a note for twenty-eight hundred dol-
> lars, which he believes to be the one upon which said Makepeace
> has brought suit . . . Said Jones also showed some certificates
> from the officers of Blackford County showing the amount of
> property of the men in said notes held & that there was no liens
> imposed thereon, and the notes and certificates he has since seen
> in the possession of said plaintiff, Allen Makepeace.[9]

According to Jones's testimony, the note he showed Willson (and later,
Makepeace) could not have been the note that Makepeace purchased
from the doctor. Nor did Jones show Willson the information about
property from the Blackford clerk—that had been done at Makepeace's
request. Makepeace had told Jones that his original note lacked certain
elements, such as annual interest. Because Makepeace requested a completely new note, soliciting this testimony from Willson smacked of
suborning a witness.

Judge Anthony held a hearing two weeks later when Makepeace
appeared to argue his case for a re-trial. Anthony shrugged off the insults
to his judicial abilities and sat on the matter until the March 1855 term, a

full year after the original trial. The wheels of justice, at least in civil cases, turned slowly then, as now.

1854—CALIFORNIA

Pete and Jake Liestenfeltz were the last of the Blackford Mining Company still in California, with the exception of John Teach. They had made some money in mining, but the claims played out, and they had trouble finding new places to dig. Larger, well-financed companies invested in the equipment needed to do hydraulic mining or hard-rock mining in the quartz veins. They built better stamping mills to extract gold from the ore. Opportunity for the lone prospector dwindled. Pete had spent the past year or two running his store on McKinneys Creek. By April, he had enough gold to pay off his note to Makepeace and buy some farmland back in Indiana. He and Jake had not seen their family in three years. California had been fun and gave them a head start on the future, but it was not the place for that future to transpire, especially given the dearth of marriage prospects. Pete and his older brother started the homeward journey.

The brothers left Calaveras County on April 3, riding a wagon to Stockton. In San Francisco, they decided to explore the city before catching a steamship to Nicaragua. Pete had amassed $1,500 and had the good sense to avoid the ubiquitous gambling halls. But the two ate well and were grateful for it. On April 15, they boarded a steamer and bid farewell to the golden shore.

After crossing at Nicaragua, the Liestenfeltz brothers took passage on the *Star of the West*, the same steamer that had carried Henry Jenkins and Harvy Brown to New York back in October. Pete and Jake spent $90 a piece to get from California to New York. A journey that had taken them two and half months in 1851 took less than a month in 1854. Pete and Jake rode the rails, first to Albany, New York, then Erie, Pennsylvania. From there, they crossed Ohio heading southwest until they reached Union City on the Ohio-Indiana state line. Pete related his homecoming:

> There was no town there then, only a stoping place right in the woods. Then we went into Winchester. We got at Winchester

about dark . . . We stayed all night at Elick White['s]. Then the next morning we started for home. Then we hired a man by the name of Jim Anderson to haul our trunk to [Camden]. We gave him $4.00. The roads were muddy and bad. We got to [Camden] about 2 oclock. Then we took our trunk and packed it on our back. We saw Sealy duffy. This was the first one we seen we knowed. He thought we had our trunk full of gold. When we got home [thirteen-year-old brother] Conard was the first to meet us. What a happy meeting![10]

During his brief stay in New York City, Pete decided to buy a violin—an instrument he probably learned to play in the mines. According to legend, "the family and neighbors gathered at the Listenfelt home to welcome them and hear of their adventures. In the course of the evening the younger of the two boys produced a 'fiddle' and started to play a lively tune. His mother interrupted him saying sternly, 'Put that sinful thing down!' The fiddle was associated with dancing which was frowned on in this household."[11]

Just two months later, Jake married Lucinda Duffy (making him a brother-in-law to John Teach's son, William J. Teach), and it was time for another family celebration—sans dancing and fiddle music!

Spring 1854 had been cold in Blackford County. The delicate orchard blossoms froze; there would be no apple crop that fall. The plowing was off to a late start, just beginning about the time Pete and Jake got home. Pete helped his father on the farm all summer. In September, he walked to Muncie to pay back the note to Makepeace, honoring the obligation with its astronomical interest rate. He did not relate it specifically, but given the lack of legal action, Jake's and John Teach's shares were paid as well. The following month, Pete bought 120 acres from Jake, where he would build his cabin the following spring. He had every reason to be content and satisfied with his California adventure.

Two weeks after Pete and Jake said goodbye to John Teach at McKinneys Creek, Teach visited the nearby cave. Many miners had left their mark near the entrance and for a few hundred feet beyond. Over the course of

Figure 18.2. Jacob Liestenfeltz with his second wife, Nancy Ann Bell, and nine of his twelve children. Credit: Courtesy of Jessica Dunica.

a century, roughly a thousand people carved their graffiti into its stone walls. The corridor was narrow, and he hunched along its length, inhaling the pleasantly cool and musty air. Holding his light in one hand, he passed a couple "H. Z. Jenkins" and one "P. N. Liestenfelt" on his route to an unadorned panel. He took his time with the tool as he sat on the floor, working in a space no more than three feet from, and tilted toward, the floor of the cave. He wanted this to be legible for all time. It may have been one of the last things of consequence he ever wrote. He stopped corresponding with his family and friends in Indiana, and they never learned his fate.

At last, chiseling complete, Teach unfolded himself from his awkward position and exited the cave, leaving his completed autograph for posterity: "John C Teach Blackford County Indiana April 16th 1854."[12] Completely unaware of the fact, four days later Teach became a grandfather.

Figure 18.3. Graffiti by John C. Teach in California Cavern dated April 16, 1854. Credit: Author's photo.

The Ransom brothers' success working at the Stockton Ranch in 1853 had induced Will Jenkins to come out to California in early 1854. He began the year recalling the assurances that he could expect to make one or two thousand dollars for his labor in the fields by partnering with his brothers-in-law. Plowing and planting in the valley had begun with the arrival of rains in November. The agricultural community in Santa Clara County believed enough land had been planted in wheat to supply the entire state with flour in the coming year. Flour was such an important commodity that speculators regularly bought all that was available, artificially elevating the price. Farmers around the state counted on receiving a good sum on their 1854 crops.[13]

Lush fields with waving heads of grain flourished by June. The fertile soils produced amazing results. One Santa Clara farm reported oats growing over nine feet high. Potatoes weighing three to four pounds could be found. Some claimed that their wheat field would be generating a hundred bushels per acre, but the real yields were more like thirty-five. Fruit orchards, particularly pears, did well. James Kennedy, the Stockton Ranch overseer, successfully grew strawberries on the ranch.[14] The sanguine news in the papers trumpeted that California was destined to become an agricultural powerhouse, feeding not only its citizens but also producing exports as well.[15] The variety and volumes of produce justified this optimism. Will Jenkins and the Ransoms would happily cash in.

The wheat crop fell short of expectations that year, some of it spoiled by smut. However, it was still enough to create a glut in the marketplace. The price of flour plummeted. The Santa Clara farmers sent some of their poorest product to market and hoarded the remainder, hoping for a rebound. There would be no big payoff for the farmers from Indiana that year. Even worse, the valley farmers realized that the supply/demand equation was not in their favor. They decided to fallow their fields the following year, knowing that paying hired labor would result in a loss.[16]

On September 18, 1854, Marietta Alice Ransom, William and Ann's second child, came into the world in San Jose. William claimed he sold his land there for $6,000. All three men started making other plans since farming had taken such a turn for the worse. By year's end, Will Jenkins, William, and Ann Ransom decided to move, with the two girls, to the mining region in Amador County, newly formed from Calaveras County north of the Mokelumne River. When he left home, Will Jenkins intended to return for Lizzy. But what he saw out west changed his mind. Will sent his father, Henry, a power-of-attorney and instructed him to sell his land in Indiana.[17] He would stay out west.

Robert kept his promise to go home and claim Emma for his bride. They would then return to California. He may have spent a little time in the mines, making up for the funds he had not realized from the farm in San Jose. In December 1854, he traveled back to San Francisco to catch the packet to Panama. Rather than carry all of his accumulated funds home with him, he put half into a money belt and deposited half with Adams & Co., to claim when he got home.[18] This type of money transfer had become routine in California. Adams & Co. was the first express company in California and had been extremely successful.

Robert, along with many others, would regret trusting them with his money.

CHAPTER 19

A ROCK AND
A HARD PLACE

He tunnels through the rock / his eyes see all its treasures / He searches the sources of the rivers / and brings hidden things to light. / But where can wisdom be found? / Where does understanding dwell? . . . / It cannot be bought with the finest gold, / nor can its price be weighed in silver.

—BOOK OF JOB 28:10–15

1855—INDIANA

Robert arrived in New York on January 10, 1855. He wasted no time getting to an enthusiastic homecoming in Indiana. Emma Jenkins had not seen her sweetheart in three years. First, she put up with months of anguish while Robert and William were subjected to the whims of Pacific winds and sailing captains. Then, the agony of slow correspondence as the Ransoms worked the fields for two seasons. And finally, the Ransoms and Will had gone up to the mines where, everyone knew, crime and murder were rampant. It seemed a miracle that Robert came home unscathed. She would not waste any time taking Robert to the preacher. Her brother Bedford and sister Philadelphia had been married almost a year now: Bedford to Patience Randall; Philadelphia to Jezreel Decatur Barr.

James and Elizabeth Ransom enjoyed having Robert home, too, but all was not well there. Ransom had a problem with intemperance. His namesake grandson recalled:

> I remember grandfather Ransom pretty well. He was rather slender and walked from father's store pretty often to his home about ½ mile distant with his hands folded behind his back and rather slowly. He was not very rugged when I knew him although he had been when younger, so Uncle Will R. told me. He drank liquor to a considerable extent although I never saw him stagger. Most people at that time were liquor drinkers. I refer to the men of course.[1]

Ransom was not necessarily a benign drunk. His relation-neighbor, Robert Lanning, sued him for "trespass on the case of slander" and won a substantial award. He joined the Hartford City Masonic lodge in 1850; they expelled him in 1853.[2] His son, William, had gladly abandoned the family farm for good, at least in part because of their difficulties. Robert intended to return to California after his marriage to Emma. But his mother could not bear for him to go away and leave her to deal with his father without help. Other things conspired against Robert's hopes and dreams.

The Ransom and Jenkins clans had extensive conversations about the entire bunch packing up and moving out west—some by land, some by sea. James Ransom seemed bent on going, but he lacked physical stamina. No one expected he could survive the journey. But everyone put the matter aside temporarily while the March 1 wedding plans proceeded. Emma and Robert had barely a month to prepare. As he had for William Ransom and Ann Jenkins, Dr. Jones offered his cousin Robert and Emma a place to stay after their matrimonial celebration.[3] They accepted and immediately began a family.

Three weeks after the wedding, disturbing news trickled into the neighborhood about problems in San Francisco, relative to banking. Robert had a significant sum with Adams & Co. in California. William Ransom had also put the proceeds from selling property in San Jose on deposit. Were they about to see all their hard work vanish like wisps of San Francisco fog on a sunny day?

Figure 19.1. Robert Ransom and Emma Jenkins in Hartford City, Indiana, 1870. Credit: Courtesy of Stanley Smith.

As with the 1854 wheat crop, the Ransom brothers seemed to be in the wrong place at the wrong time. And it had all been so unnecessary. Rumor and innuendo caused the spectacular crash of a long-trusted California institution. Adams & Co. of California was believed to be a branch of the widespread Adams & Co. found in many other states. But in fact, the California "branch" was a separately owned cooperative partner. In the same way, the banking firm Page & Bacon of St. Louis was separate from Page, Bacon & Co. in California.

When news reached San Francisco on February 18, 1855, that Page & Bacon of St. Louis was on the verge of collapse and rumors spread that a large amount of gold had been transferred from Page, Bacon & Co. of California to St. Louis, it triggered a run on the California bank. Though Page, Bacon & Co. was solvent, they shut their doors, intensifying the panic. The domino effect caused runs on other California banks. Adams & Co. collapsed in the stampede for withdrawals. The *Daily Alta California* attempted to settle the nerves of depositors on February 23, assuring them: "All that is now required for business to go on as before . . . and whatever of excitement and panic has existed will be at once allayed. Our business men are all in a boat together; the boat is safe if they move and act harmoniously, but if each undertakes to tear out a plank and save himself upon it, they may all be swallowed up in the sea of universal bankruptcy."[4]

Unfortunately for the customers of Adams & Co., unlike those of the other banking houses, matters were shakier. Adams & Co. was an early and widespread express service in gold rush times. At its inception, it was owned by partners in New York, but they had re-formed and disconnected from the California company, leaving only Alvin Adams as a special partner with two general partners, Haskell and Wood. The California company retained liabilities that were not general knowledge. Until the run on February 23, the mismanagement had gone undetected; they might have returned to solvency if the panic had not occurred.

If Robert had been in one of the mining camps, he might have had a chance to retrieve his deposit. The Adams agents in Murphys and Grass Valley defied orders from San Francisco and opened their safes to pay out all the gold on hand to depositors until none was left.[5] In Sonora, a mob broke open the company's safe and distributed about $45,000 by committee.[6] One creditor of the company, Frenchman Louis Remme, engaged in a horse race to Portland, Oregon, to retrieve his $12,500 before the news of the company crash reached the branch there by steamship. He succeeded with only minutes to spare, completing his non-stop 665-mile ride in 143 hours.[7] The Ransom brothers had no chance to participate in these distributions. William was likely gnashing his teeth in San Jose or Amador County while Robert was still blissfully unaware of the situation in Indiana.

Makepeace's case against Sam Jones et al. dragged along through 1855. He and his attorneys had plenty of court action to keep them busy. Samuel Clevenger's heirs filed a suit against him, putting him on the defense for a change. Makepeace had seized the Clevenger property to pay a debt owed to his father's estate and locked the heirs out.[8] He also continued his pursuit of Elijah Collins's debt. The previous September, Makepeace denied to the court that Collins and the Lyons had paid anything or that he had released the Lyons from their obligation. He even said he had not given them the original note in exchange. In addition, his attorney, James Swaar, altered the due date on the new Collins note, making it due the same day it was created. Why Makepeace was not called out for perjury is a mystery. Eventually, he conceded that the transaction occurred as the defendants testified.[9] But the Collins note was small potatoes when compared to the combined balance of the Blackford Company notes: $4,950, more than ten times the original Collins note.

Attorneys in Judge Anthony's circuit also made a move. Politics of the day were personal and brutish, lacking civility and subtlety. Unable to remove Judge Anthony from the bench, the lawyers appealed to the legislature for relief from his balanced verdicts—they wanted clear winners and losers, not compromises. In February 1855, a legislative act passed that created a new circuit—the 13th—which stripped the 7th circuit of all but Delaware and Blackford Counties. Anthony retained Delaware because it was his home county and Blackford because "the Rep. from Blackford . . . declared that his constituency were satisfied with the imbecile."[10]

Judge Anthony had spent the winter mulling over the Makepeace and Volney Willson testimony in consideration for a new trial. At the March 1855 term, on the basis of new evidence alone—the testimony by Volney Willson of Muncie—Anthony granted Makepeace a new trial at the plaintiff's expense. The only defendant still living in the area, aside from the eleven men who stood as surety, was John K. Anderson of Trenton. Dennis Lowry was in Iowa farming, and Sam Jones was in Ohio, planning a return to California for more gold.

Anderson and the defense attorneys pondered their course of action regarding a new trial. In a jury trial in Delaware County, Makepeace's intimidating presence would be prejudicial to their case. On June 13, Anderson went to Muncie to request a change of venue to Blackford County. Anthony presided in the Blackford County Circuit Court, but the jury would be pulled from residents in that county—presumably favorable to the defense. Anthony agreed to the change of venue.

The next term of the Delaware court would not be held until September. Farmers had no time to deal with legal wrangling in the summer. On September 18, Makepeace, through his attorney Thomas J. Sample, sent notice to Anderson that he would be filing his own motion for a change of venue.[11] Makepeace declared the Blackford County residents were prejudiced toward him and under the undue influence of the defendants, likely an overstatement, but it may have been true that the citizens had no good things to say about Allen Makepeace.

In November, Makepeace brought his motion to Judge Anthony's tavern in Muncie and argued his case for a change of venue to Randolph County. This would take the matter entirely out of Anthony's jurisdiction and, though it would be a little less convenient for the plaintiff's witnesses, the defendants could get to Randolph as easily as they could Delaware. The judge agreed to the motion.[12] Anderson's gambit to find a favorable jury had been nullified.

1855—CALIFORNIA

Sam Jones left Eliza and their children in Barnesville, Ohio, while he made a return trip to California in spring 1855. His earlier success had been encouraging. This time, though, he would try the mines in Siskiyou County up near Oregon. He reached Marysville in early June and stopped just outside of town at the home of a Mr. Campbell. It may have been a coincidence, but E.D. Pierce, his sister Rebecca's fiancé, was in Marysville and met Sam, for the first time, at the Campbell home. Pierce was pleased to receive word about the Jones family, especially Rebecca.

Pierce was working on the ninety-five-mile-long Yreka Ditch, helping to sell stock in the ditch company and supervising the construction of sawmills to provide planking. Having had his earlier fortune lost to bad business management, he was assured of earning $10,000 for his work on the ditch project. That would be enough to take him home and begin his married life with Rebecca. The two prospective brothers-in-law agreed that they would travel back east together after Sam spent a year in the mines.[13] For Sam, the matter of Makepeace seemed to vanish like a bad dream in the daylight.

While Robert and Emma consummated their marriage in Indiana, William and Ann Ransom and Will Jenkins settled into life in Amador County. After the farming debacle, mining and providing domestic services to the miners would be their next venture. It was rough territory for a woman with two daughters, but miners were extremely respectful of the rare female presence in their midst, and even more so toward children.

In a spare moment, when she had a respite from children and work demands, Ann sat down to respond to a letter from her mother. A flush of mail from Indiana had recently arrived. In addition to Abby's letter, "Pa" (as she now referred to her husband) got one from his brother Robert ("Bob"). Will had two letters, one from Bedford and one from his brother-in-law, J.D. Barr. Before setting pen to paper, she re-read the news from home, happy that her parents had enjoyed the long-anticipated wedding back in February but wistful at the thought she could not be there herself. Though being with her husband, their daughters, and her older brother gave her a measure of contentment, Ann profoundly missed her mother.

The letters overflowed with California chatter. The state had its pluses. But moving all those people would require capital and some daunting logistics. Not that those obstacles had stopped endless thousands so far. Ann began to write, "My dear Mother . . . I think the folks out there have really got a hard spell of California fever. I should like to see them through with it. It seems to me that that country will look rather funny without any Kansans in it, but of all things it surprises me the most to hear that Mother will come out here if all the family does . . ."[14]

By the spring of 1855, Abby realized that the majority of her family itched to go west, much to her chagrin. Beloved Ann Jenkins had been borne along to her grave after a long life and could not intervene. With her husband back at last, Abby reveled in the comforts of home life. She missed her son, daughter, and granddaughter and wondered if she would ever meet little Marietta, but she had Will's daughter, Lizzy, for consolation. Most of her own children were married now and settled nearby. In spite of life's challenges, they had a community of friends for support, and things would improve. She continued reading Ann's letter from California:

Thee wants to know if I had the most of my relations here if I would be willing to stay and make it my permanent home or would I not wish to come back to my native country. Well mother I will try to tell thee the truth about it just as near as I can; if I had mother, father, Bed[ford], Emma, Phila[delphia], Mary, [Barton] Bradbury, Lizzy and her pa all here I should never want to go back. Indeed, I think I should be foolish indeed for you know my health there took half my time . . . and here I have never been down 1 day, although I am not as stout as some women, but I don't think it is in my constitution and then I have never had a frozen toe. The weather is generally so pleasant all the year and it is such an easy place to get a living, but mother without thee was here I would never be satisfied and would go back. That is just exactly the way it stands but I dont wish to say one word that would bring thee here for if thee didn't like it I should never forgive my self for it.[15]

Ann debated whether her folks should come by land or water. If they came by land, Abby would have to work too hard, but they would have the animals and implements they needed to get right into farming. By sea was easier and quicker, but "wagons never blow up, which steamboats sometimes do." She mused for a while about all of them moving to the valley and out of the mines. Anticipating the upcoming dry season, when the creeks and gullies stopped running and the dry digging got put on hold, Ann and William planned to go down to the Mokelumne River to work for the summer. They had arranged to cook and do other work for a mining company. It would not be as comfortable as life in Amador City, but the money would be better than they could make in town.

Baby Marietta began fussing and Ann put the letter aside for several days. By then, she had come down with some respiratory complaint. William practiced his doctoring on her: "Pa is going to get me some medicine to cleanse my liver and I have taken a large dose of pills. I think when I get that I will be better but mother thee knows I never have calculated on a long life here and what does it matter. God has promised to uphold those that look to him with an eye of faith and I dont feel anyways disposed to doubt his word." She added a postscript from William to Bedford and Robert, perhaps as a bit of incentive, "cows are worth from $75 to 100 here and good american horses 150 to 500 according to quality but bob knows all about that."[16]

On Saturday, she finished the letter. Will was in a rush to get it to Jackson and did not add his own postscript to his daughter or parents. He wanted them to all come out to California, but left it to Ann to convince them.

SUMMER 1855—INDIANA

Henry and Abby read that William and Ann were heading from Amador City down to "the river," but they were not clear if Will would be joining them. Henry wrote to Will, inquiring about his plans, anxious about his distant children, just as his mother had been about him. Except for that brief month in the fall of 1853, Henry had been communicating with Will and Ann by mail for more than four years. After all this time, he could not resist his parental meddling. Unable to hire help, he and Abby struggled financially, having to buy provisions rather than raising their own grains and meats. With only five mouths to feed, though, it was easier than when Abby had to feed nine without Henry. The early spring had been dry, but in mid-May the rains poured down, pushing back the planting season. It looked like another dismal crop year in eastern Indiana. The newspapers touted the wonderful agricultural opportunities in the Golden State, no doubt rekindling Henry's recollections of the finer aspects of west-coast life.

California talk around town did not abate. Henry reported to Will that many of his friends and family planned to go west the following spring: Samuel Babb, A. Pitman, G. Schrack, James and Elizabeth Ransom, and Asa Anderson. Will's siblings and their spouses mulled it over as well: Emma and Robert, Philadelphia and J.D. Barr, Bedford and Patience.

"If all the children go we will follow or go along if we can for we would feel verry lonely indeed if all should leave us," Henry confided to Will. "I think one thing is certain and that is Bedford and Decatur will need assistance and I see no other way for all to come than to make use of the proceeds of thy land if I can sell it. Makeing evry effort to dispose of both that and my own and wish thee on receipt of this letter to let me know whether thee be willing for us (any of us) to use the proceeds."[17] Given the financial pressures (e.g., Makepeace's note) and the fact so many people wanted to leave, driving down real estate prices, getting travel cash seemed nigh on impossible.

Henry related that other neighbors were migrating, some heading to Minnesota, others to Iowa.

All seem to be moving westward as far as they can go. It seems as though the tide of emigration is gaining strength and numbers evry year—doubtless it is of the Almighty and for what purpose is not for us short sighted creatures to know—deep in unfathomable Mines, of never failing skill, he treasures up his bright designs, and works his Sovereign will and with all our imaginary independence we are but instruments in his hands.[18]

Henry's faith in the Creator's "bright designs" would be tested yet again.

The summer wore on in the usual fashion. The Jenkinses delighted in their granddaughter, Lizzy. Henry included news of her in his letter to Will.

Little Lizzy is running round with the old cracked bell round her neck playing with the dog as lively and happy as childhood well can be. She says when we get to Calakorny, Cordy will run out to the wagon to meet us with little Maryetta by the hand and seems to enjoy it in prospect verry much. Says she would like to see her Pap William but I think she has no recollection of thee or very little if any. She was too young when thee left to have much recollection of anything. I rather suppose her Pap would be verry much pleased to see her and would run to meet the wagon if he should happen to see it comeing and knew it to be us. No doubt it would be joyful on all hands big and little. We have just been entertained by an Italian Organ player. He had but one hand and as the children wished to hear it he played off his tunes but Lizzy was more scared than pleased at first and commenced crying but her Aunt Mary took her up and afterwards she seemed to enjoy the music. It reminded thy Mother of thyself when an infant getting so scared with the playing of a flute by Sm Shubert in Philade long long ago.[19]

Henry felt old, now that his son was the age he had been on that distant day in Philadelphia. But the cycle of life would go on as it always had. Unfortunately, Will would never see the letter.

For a second time, Henry found a buyer for Will's land, the first having defaulted. The $200 balance would be given to Henry when he handed over a deed. In order to get the deed, he would need to travel to Dayton, Ohio, where the bankers held Will's mortgage. In the latter part of June, Henry and Abby set out. She expected to swing by Springboro to visit her siblings—perhaps the last time she would ever see them in person. Her previous visit had been over a decade earlier, so she eagerly anticipated the trip.

When they returned to Camden, Henry informed Will that the sale was complete. Will had earlier given Henry permission to use the proceeds to pay Makepeace, but for some reason, he did not, possibly preferring to see the outcome of the re-trial. If Anderson's attorneys prevailed, it would save Henry some money. If Anderson lost, then Henry would just have to pay up, including added interest for waiting for so many years. He told Will, "as that was still not in a shape to do anything with I applied it to satisfying other pressing debts as I intended and still intend to sell my place and thought it would make no difference to thee which debt I paid with it."[20]

Robert also struggled to get by after the Adams & Co. failure. The lawsuits against the company and its manager and receivers dragged on into the 1860s. By mid-summer, he had some hope that he would at least receive a partial payment. But in the meantime, he helped his parents as best he could. Robert began to realize that his dream of returning to California looked less and less likely to come true. Emma was well along in her first pregnancy in September. So instead, Robert negotiated with Henry to construct a building at the crossroads in Trenton to serve as both home and store. Henry would build the nineteen-by-forty-foot structure as cheaply as possible. Prior to working on that, though, he needed to finish building a kitchen onto the James Ransom home.[21]

SUMMER 1855—AMADOR COUNTY

While the Ransoms were working down on the river for the summer, Will Jenkins worked in the Amador County quartz mines. At the end of July, news of murder rocked the county. Two miners noticed a swarm of flies near a pile of loose rocks, and upon investigation, they found the butchered body of a large Swede who had been last seen in Rancheria on July 22.[22] Then, on August 6, a group of about a dozen men, most apparently Mexican, but also an American and a black man of unknown origin, began a spree of crimes reminiscent of the Murrieta days. They started by robbing as many Chinese as they could find in the county, from Q Ranch near Drytown to Rancheria. In the latter place, they proceeded to get drunk at the fandango and began shooting indiscriminately, killing six people, including Mrs. Diamond, wife of the hotelkeeper, and an Indian who attempted to intervene at one point. They also robbed Francis's store in town. "Mr. Francis was found some distance from his store, lying prostrate on the ground, wounded by pistol shots in the face and head, and the bone of one of his legs badly shattered. It was afterwards amputated, and in another hour he was no more."[23] Outrage against the Mexicans led to roundups of many innocent people.

In mid-September, two alleged culprits from the Rancheria murders, found hiding far to the south in Mariposa County, were thrown in jail in

Figure 19.2. The hanging of Rafeal [*sic*] Escobar in Jackson, Amador County, California, on August 6, 1856. This occurred a year after the Rancheria murder hanging. Credit: California Historical Society.

Jackson, the Amador County seat. It did not take long for the infuriated citizens of Lower Rancheria to drag them to their town to atone. Lynch law was mobocracy in action. One eyewitness to the scene reported:

> They were questioned seperately and both told different sto-
> ries . . . Dr. Southel of Sutter got up and made a statement of
> what was known concerning them: he Said these two men had
> been pointed out by Gregory the leader of the band who was in
> custody and acted as states evidence—that they had been found
> hid away in the chapperel—that they had denied ever being on
> this side of the Mokelumne river when there were Several men
> in the crowd who could swear that they had seen them not only
> at Jackson but also at Sutter . . . for me had no doubt of their
> guilt. He asked them then what should be done with them from
> this evidence. A cry of—hang them! hang them! was raised from
> the crowd and it being [put] to vote was unanimously carried;

they were taken up on a hill close by—a rope thrown over the limb of a Pine tree. The prisoners were then placed in a waggen the nooses put over their necks and the waggen driven out from under them. They without confessing but declared their innocence too the last—one of them stood it like a man the other cried like a child.[24]

In pursuit of the actual culprits, the Amador County sheriff received a fatal injury. A few of the guilty were killed, but violence against Mexicans continued apace. Many of their homes were deliberately torched, and they were driven from the county. Though the whites did not have a quarrel with the Chileans working near Drytown, they also burned their camp to the ground—an act that many people condemned. Some regretted the hanging of innocent men, but it did little to change behavior toward Mexicans.

For Ann, with her two little girls and expecting another child, the violent deaths so close by—including a woman!—had to have chilled her very soul. How could she have thought this would be a good place for all her family to live? California had still not achieved social respectability. There were good people around, but the rough element held sway, especially in the mines. Indiana may have been undeveloped, but it had more than a veneer of civility. There were laws and accountability. It seemed a good time to leave the mines and head to the valley where the farmers and their families lived. She undoubtedly campaigned to William for a move.

During the first decade of the gold rush, the vast majority of miners worked at the placers, extracting loose gold from riverbeds and dry diggings. In Amador County (and also in Calaveras and Mariposa), a seam of gold-bearing quartz runs north to south from Plymouth to Jackson and continues through Mokelumne Hill to Angels Camp and beyond to Carson Hill. Many miners made a fortune out of Carson Hill in 1852. Some individual miners did work in the quartz, as Henry had done in Murphys in 1851 and 1852, but successful quartz mining required large investments of capital.

The vein, up to a mile wide, runs primarily in Upper Jurassic-era Mariposa Formation slate. Processing the low-grade ores took anywhere from three to seven tons to produce an ounce of gold, though pockets of high-grade ore existed as well. Two large mines operated right in Amador City, where Will and the Ransoms lived in 1855: the Keystone and the Eclipse. The mining companies required large labor forces and paid daily wages. Some worked in the mines and others in the mills that crushed and extracted gold from the ore. Will may have worked for one of these companies, or maybe he followed his father's example and owned his own quartz claim with a partner. Hundreds of such mines of all sizes pock the landscape around Amador County even today. The California landscape is still convalescing from the infestation of miners.

In order to work the lode, the miners first dug a deep shaft to approach the ore from below at an angle, thus using gravity to move the blasted ore into a pile. From there, it would be loaded onto a cart and hauled up through the shaft. Sometimes a tunnel might access the vein from the side of a hill rather than from above. In the 1850s, miners relied on hand drills and black powder (i.e., gunpowder) for blasting. A hand drill requires one to three men, usually one to hold and turn the heavy metal drill rods, and the others to hammer.

Once a series of holes (seven or nine) is completed to sufficient depth, the miners fill each with powder, attach fuses, pack the holes with some powdered clay or drilling debris, and tamp it down with a rod. Of hard rock mining accidents, premature blasts were common and made the news frequently that summer. The unexpected discharges usually came about during the tamping phase, which could create a spark, igniting the powder. Sometimes the men involved suffered some cuts and bruises, but serious burns to the face happened often, as well as broken bones or worse. Black powder is considered a low-order explosive and does not produce a supersonic blast wave—the type that induces traumatic brain injuries and internal pressure injuries. But flash burns can be life-threatening, and flying debris can cause minor to lethal damage.

By mid-July, the temperatures in the Sierra mining region soared above a hundred and continued rising. Some speculated it could be the hottest summer in gold rush memory. Working the mines, in the cooler subterranean tunnels, provided some relief from the sweltering days aboveground. The work, however, was monotonous and grueling. Will Jenkins and his partner entered the mine shaft at the beginning of the work day, walking through timbered tunnels to the scene of the previous day's drilling and blasting. The smoke and noxious fumes had cleared overnight. As a trained carpenter, shoring the tunnels may have been Will's primary job.

Their first task involved tapping the ceiling to listen for dull thuds, indicating loose rock that needed to be pried from the "hanging wall." After clearing and moving the ore released by the explosives and prying, drilling began. Near the end of the day, holes completed, the man in charge of the powder, probably Will's partner, wrapped paper around a wooden dowel, closed off the end of the tube, filled it with powder, and added a fuse of appropriate length (longer for the outer holes; shorter for the center one). Then he used the wooden dowel to shove the charge all the way into the hole and began packing. During this process, he likely struck the unlucky blow that ignited the charge. In that gravid moment before the detonation, Will and his partner attempted to move faster than the burning fuse—a futile leap. In a split second, the two miners heard the explosion, then nothing more.

CHAPTER 20

RESOLUTIONS

The task of reporting Will's accident fell to his dismayed sister, Ann. In early September, her letter arrived in Camden. Henry's first instinct was to rush to his son's aid, but he had no means. Will's family and friends mourned his misfortune. After the initial shock wore off, they could at least express gratitude that he was alive and, aside from his blindness, intact. His less fortunate partner had lost not only his sight but also an arm as well. Everyone waited apprehensively for further news from the coast. Another five weeks passed.

The next two letters from California created additional upheaval in the Jenkins and Ransom households. First, Robert received a letter from William indicating he had changed his mind about staying out west. He wanted to join Robert in his business ventures in Trenton. The situation with Will probably rattled him and soured him to working in the mines. Robert and Emma decided to stay in Indiana for the time being. Once they got James Ransom settled down—he kept saying he wanted to join his son in California, and no one thought that a good idea—then Robert and Emma could go out. Both families had accepted that the entire clan would move west, and now the Ransoms were nixing the plan. Henry told Will, "I cant help believeing myself that if we were all there together we would be better satisfied than in this country." He added that the family could not make a decision until they settled with Makepeace. Abby remarked to Will, "our plans for California are at the present blown by but I calculate it will burn with fresh vigor after awhile. I think I can see it is only smothered for the present."[1]

The second letter brought some hope that Will would recover his eyesight. Abby told him, "We are all rejoiced to hear that thee will again see the light of day . . . I hope that the darkness of optical vision has enabled thee to turn thy mental eye inward and discover the true light which is never withheld from those that art aright."[2] He was under a doctor's care in San Francisco, along with his disabled partner. Will did not make it clear if he intended to remain out west, so no one knew whether they should still plan a move. Henry hounded him for answers—should we stay, or should we go?

By December, Robert and Emma had moved to their new residence at the crossroads in Trenton, where they opened their mercantile. Two days before Christmas, they welcomed their first child into the world, James Henry Ransom, named after his two grandfathers. The young couple had faith that they could emigrate to California the following spring. If the store did well, they could surely find a buyer.

1856—CALIFORNIA

Will remained in San Francisco in 1856, believing the doctors might restore his sight. He had lost his wife and left his daughter behind in Indiana. His sister lived with her family in Amador City, so he was alone except for his unnamed partner, with whom he lived. This new hardship changed him. For some reason, he developed an optimistic, can-do attitude, whereas before, he had been moody and pessimistic. Rather than ask for charity or beg on the streets, he found a job working as a fruit seller. He made enough money to cover his expenses while he lived in the city, pondering his fate.[3] He found a scribe to take dictation so he could send news back to his family, and who would read aloud his letters from home.

Ann and William Ransom were expecting another child in early 1856. They remained in Amador City, hoping that matters in Indiana would soon be resolved and their families could join them out west. The previous summer's violence must have worried them regarding their children's safety, but they evidently compartmentalized their concerns. They did

Figure 20.1. Robert and Emma Ransom's first child, James Henry Ransom, named for his two grandfathers: James Ransom and Henry Z. Jenkins. Credit: Shared by jeri661 on Ancestry.com.

consider relocating for their peace of mind. On March 13, 1856, Ann gave birth to their first son. They named him Sherman Day, after the state senator from Santa Clara County, whom they may have known while they lived in San Jose. Or perhaps he was just a man whom William admired.

1856—INDIANA
In February 1856, both Makepeace and Anderson rescinded their motions to relocate the trial, which threw it back to the Delaware Circuit Court. It was on the docket for the March term, five years after the Blackford Mining Company had left in the rush for gold. Judge Anthony would preside again, but a jury of local men would decide the outcome. John Anderson alone dealt with the case. Sam Jones was back out west, mining again. However, he left his attorney in charge of collecting a debt from the man who had bought his Trenton farm. This case, too, would be heard in spring, but in the Blackford County court.[4]

Attorney Walter March had plenty of work fighting against the aggressive actions of Allen Makepeace, financier. In addition to representing the Jones case and Collins, he had taken on the case of the Clevenger heirs. All three carried on into 1856. Makepeace was tenacious, patient, and wealthy. He and his attorneys would never relent. The case against Collins proceeded on March 18. Walter March argued that Collins's note had been rendered null and void when James Swaar altered the due date without Collins's knowledge or permission. The jury in that case awarded Makepeace the principal value of the note but no interest.[5]

John Anderson and Dennis Lowry also had a lawsuit in the March term of court. The money they had loaned to the Fort Wayne and Southern Railroad had not been repaid. Judge Anthony had to recuse himself from the case, as his brother, Dr. S.P. Anthony, was one of the defendants. If they lost the re-trial on the Makepeace debt, or even if they won, they were going to have to pay Makepeace something. They needed the railroad board of directors to pay up. Being a straightforward case on an unpaid debt, they prevailed. Collecting was another matter. They decided to sell the judgment to an attorney for a discount, allowing him to go through the hassle.[6] No matter what happened next, they would at least be able to do their part towards paying their debt, plus court costs and attorneys' fees.

Dr. Jones would testify again. Memories of the distant events had dimmed, not only in his, but also in the minds of all the witnesses. But he obeyed the summons to Muncie once more. On Tuesday, March 25, a jury of twelve Delaware County men was sworn in. Dr. Jones took the stand. The defense attorney showed him the $2,800 note and asked if he recognized it.[7]

"I do," he stated and proceeded to give his version of the events, to the best of his recollection. He had made several trips to Muncie and Chesterfield, finally making a deal with Makepeace with Swaar's help. He claimed that Makepeace wanted a "percussion" note and that the note needed to be drawn up so he would not be "implicated." For that purpose, he gave the doctor a sample note, which Dr. Jones gave to Sam. Sam then drew up the note to Dr. Jones, copying the terms from the sample. The only consideration (i.e., what Jones gave for the note) was that the miners would repay him for his trouble when they returned from California, and he would doctor their families. Dr. Jones claimed in court, once again, that he had only received two-thirds of the note's face value, including the $200 note, as if it were cash.

The plaintiff's attorneys cross-examined the doctor, then he answered a question from the defense attorney before court adjourned for the day. His testimony resumed on Wednesday morning at 8 a.m. After Dr. Jones reiterated a few details about the note and its assignment to Makepeace, the plaintiff's attorneys began with their rebuttal witnesses; primary among them was James Swaar, the Muncie attorney.

Swaar's testimony largely corroborated Dr. Jones' with one major exception: Swaar asserted that Makepeace had given the doctor $1,900 in cash, plus the $200 note, for a total of $2,100. In other words, Makepeace paid three-fourths, not two-thirds of the face value of the note.

The plaintiff's attorney asked Jones about the Jenkins note for $800.

"The $800 note was a separate deal. It was some time after [selling the $2,800 note] maybe, I'm not certain . . . I can't say the amount I got for the $800 . . . I think I paid all the money over to Jenkins. I am satisfied I got $2 for $3 . . . I told Swaar I sold the note, but think I did not tell the amount I got for it."

After a little bickering between the attorneys, Dr. Jones added some clarification.

"I told Swaar it was a different transaction . . . I don't think I told Swaar I got $600 for the $800 note . . . My belief is I got between $500 and $600. I think I got $2 for $3. I think I stepped out of store and made the trade."

Makepeace's nephew, Alvin Makepeace, who had been working at George Makepeace's store, then gave a rebuttal.

"They was two separate transactions," he testified. "When I came in they were counting money for the $2800 note. Jones & Swaar left. Jones come back and said he had another note that he would sell of $800 and Makepeace said he would give him $600 for the note and counted the money. There was 6 piles of $100 each." Odd that he recalled this when he said he knew nothing about the second note during the 1854 trial.

Henry Jenkins took the stand, testifying about the money he received on his $800 note.

"I drew up this note and signed it & I gave it to Jones. I called on Dr. Jones the day following the one he come home. He paid me $533 on the note of $800."

At the conclusion of testimony, Dr. Jones and Swaar answered questions from the jury. Jones said he declared the note was good and would be paid one way or another. Despite earlier statements by the two men, they both conceded that they had not explicitly told Allen Makepeace that there had been no consideration given by Jones in exchange for receiving the note from the defendants. But they had made it clear that the note was being used to get money to send the men to California.

The jury retired to deliberate, receiving instructions from Judge Anthony, as well as instructions from the attorneys the judge had approved. The deliberations continued into Thursday, when the foreman returned their verdict:

"We the jury find for the plaintiff and assess his damage at $3,654."

The following morning, the attorneys came before the judge, who affirmed the verdict and awarded Makepeace his attorney's fees and court costs. Anderson's response was to request a re-trial at the State Supreme Court. A hearing on the grounds for re-trial was held in April but was dismissed. The verdict would stand.

Like John Anderson and his partners, Henry Jenkins was on the hook for the full amount of his $800 note to Allen Makepeace, plus five years' accumulated interest. Not his failure in the mines, his son's accident, nor his wife's pleas could turn Henry from his desire to return to California. In the end, it came down to the law and money. There would be no going back to California.

LETTER FROM HENRY Z. JENKINS, KNOX TOWNSHIP, TO WILL Z. JENKINS, SAN FRANCISCO

October 7th, 1856

My dear son Wm, Thy verry acceptible letter dated Sept 2d came duly to hand the 20th of this month as also one from thy sister

254

Ann Ransom dated August 28th. We were truly gratified to get them more especially as you both seem to be mending and in good spirits . . . We received thy Daugertype by the hand of Robert Ransom when he returned and thought it was well executed and a correct likeness. It is verry often looked at by others but more frequently by ourselves with much interest. We will preserve it with all care and if in the all [the] dispensations of Providence thee should never return thy dear Lizzy shall have it. Doubtless she will prize it highly. . . . We intend sending Lizzy to school this winter and when the weather will admit of her going. She is a fine large hearty child but we think rather backward at learning but in no ways deficient in capacity but thee knows some children are more than others. She used to frequently speak of her father and still does sometimes but seems to have lost all recollections of thee than by our naming and talking of thee . . .

It was verry cold and frosty for eight or ten days but is now quite warm and we have had two or three rains and the wheat is generally coming up. Bedford is farming for me on the shares. He has sown the orchard in wheat and the field south of it, one that we have cleared since thee left. We are in hopes of selling this fall as there has been several looking at it and all seem to like the place verry well but think the price is rather steep, but if I keep it until next spring I shall try and have several acres more under fence and shall raise another hundred on the price, but hope to sell rather shortly . . .

Thee says thee will not leave San Francisco before getting another letter from me with information as to my comeing out. I had thought to come out this fall but as yet can see no way to raise the needful funds and thy Mother is very loath to part with me again . . . if thee can raise enough to get home with I believe thee need not be told that thy Parents hearts and home is and shall always be open to receive thee and while we have if only a crust it will be gladly shared with thee . . .

I fear if Wm & Ann stay in the mines this winter she will not be able to stand it and it seems almost more than we can bear to think of never seeing her again, but we have only to leave the event with providence and hope for the best. Mother Ransom says they have never received a line from thee yet and had felt somewhat hurt and jealous, but wish to be remembered in kindness to thee as do all thy brothers and sisters. They all express a lively interest in thy welfare. It is past ten o'clock and all are asleep around me, so I will draw this long epistle to a close by commending thee to the protection of that kind creator who cares for and watches over all his creatures, and believe me ever thy affectionate father until death.

HENRY Z. JENKINS[8]

1857

Will Jenkins had been waiting and working in San Francisco for a year and a half. His hopes for regaining his eyesight were dashed, but he had developed a peaceful resignation to the situation. What he wanted now was for his family to make up their minds to come out and join him or tell him to come home. Henry's letters still dithered on the matter. The family seemed rather pessimistic about the prospect of leaving Indiana. Presidential politics had replaced the talk of gold or even farming.[9] Upon reflection, Will realized it made no sense for him to remain alone in the city. His mining days were done. His daughter knew him not. It was time to return to her and resume his duties as a father. In March 1857, he embarked on the sea journey to New York via the isthmus and arrived on the *George Law* in May. The month following his return, he purchased Henry and Abby's farm, though they lived with him and Lizzy for years afterward.

Of the Blackford groups that went west, only John Teach remained in Calaveras County by 1858. William and Ann Ransom had made California their home, though they had yet to settle in one place. For a couple years, they lived in Vacaville, away from the dangerous mining region. E.D. Pierce had made arrangements to return east when Sam Jones left the Scott River mines in July 1856. But he suffered yet another financial setback and made excuses anew. Sam went home without him, disappointing Rebecca once again. The remainder had either gone to their graves or gone home. Most were worse off financially, but richer for the experience of seeing new places, exotic people, and historical events. Many, like Jake Liestenfeltz and the Ransom brothers, lost their resolve to make a pile of gold and turned to traditional means of making a living. So much love and lust for the yellow dust went unrequited.

The communities they left behind, even if temporarily, were permanently altered by their experiences. The argonauts' adventures inspired those who could afford to leave to migrate westward, if only as far as Illinois or Iowa. The ones left behind suffered a diminished economy and depressed property values. They still had decades of labor to turn their swamp lands into viable farms. Some, like Henry Jenkins, continued to be indebted to men like Allen Makepeace, due to the scarcity of legitimate financing options.

The women who persevered in hardship while their men pursued phantom fortunes, like Abby Jenkins, continued their strenuous existence but in partnership with their returned mates. Abby had always been vital to the family's economic success, meager as it was. Goods women produced—homespun, beeswax, honey, butter, eggs—had a ready market. Some women carved out a larger niche for themselves, not content to return to their pre-rush status in the family. The coming privations caused by a continental war would invigorate women's independence for decades, building on what had begun in the gold rush years.

Whether they ultimately returned east for good or continued their adventures in the west, the Indiana participants in the California gold rush played a role in knitting the breadth of the continent into a single nation, though many growing pains would be forthcoming. They also took part in the country's nascent transformation from an agrarian society to an increasingly industrialized, urbanized one: a shift from self-sufficiency to dependence on wages from ever larger companies—especially in the east. There was still room for a pioneering spirit to roam west of the Mississippi in the decades to come. Decades that would forever alter the face of the west through many bloody conflicts, with much loss of life. Other gold rushes would spark and burn out. But the thirst for instant riches would never be quenched.

Henry's prediction—that generations hence would still be finding gold in California—has come to fruition: miners continue to comb the Sierras for gold to this very day.

EPILOGUE

November 1859—Blackford County, Indiana

Ann Teach, now fifty-seven years old, had not heard from her husband—or about him—for the past five years. He had missed the weddings of his two oldest children, the births of three grandchildren, and the coming-of-age of his younger daughter, Mary. Surely no father would have deliberately chosen exile in California over his family—he must have perished in that vicious, immoral land. Ann likely petitioned the court to declare John deceased so she could move on with her life. She had grown close to her son William's father-in-law, Robert Duffy. One little sticking point: Duffy had a wife already, Ruth Lowry (Dennis's sister), mother of his seven children. The Duffys divorced, and Robert and Ann tied the knot on November 23. They resided in Blackford County until the 1870s, when they moved to Kansas to live near Robert's oldest daughter.

May 1860—Calaveras County, California

John C. Teach apparently never faced up to his failure in the mines. After cutting off contact with his family, he worked at a variety of odd jobs, even making shoes.[1] He likely suffered from alcoholism. On May 17, 1860, Teach . . .

> . . . was found dead near McNair's ranch, above Cave City . . . He had been employed in the woods cutting down a tree and was found about half-way between where he had been at work and the Table Mountain ditch, by Mr. McNair, at whose house deceased

was stopping. It is presumed he had gone for a drink and on his return toward the tree dropped down dead. Everything indicated that he died without a struggle, as his hat was still on his head and the soft ground was undisturbed save by his footsteps. This is one account. Another gentleman writes us that "the probable cause of his death was the drinking of poisonous and adulterated liquor, a bottle of which (partly consumed) he had at the time."[2]

The news of his death never reached his family.

1862—BLACKFORD COUNTY

Robert Ransom parlayed his store and a postal contract into a variety of businesses, creating a mini-empire in Trenton. In addition, he embraced the Methodist Episcopal religion of the Jenkins family. He solicited subscriptions to build a church in Trenton, but this dream did not come to fruition. Neither his financial success nor connection to the Lord protected him and Emma from the scourge of epidemics that swept through Blackford County. In one month, February 1862, scarlet fever and measles robbed them of three young daughters, leaving them just their first-born, James Henry. Devastated by the deaths, a full year passed before Emma chanced another pregnancy. But heartache after heartache followed. A set of stillborn twins and two other children died very young. These losses likely led Emma to wall off her feelings toward her later-born children. A coldness permeated the lineage for generations to come.

Robert finally succeeded at founding a church in Millgrove in 1874 and served as a lay preacher. He sold his business interests in Trenton and moved the family to Hartford City. There, he and his brother, Bazel, bought a bank. They borrowed heavily to invest in real estate. The market collapsed and took the bank along with it. Robert, Bazel, and their wives became embroiled in many lawsuits, prompting them to pack up and start over in Independence, Kansas. Some in-laws and many of Robert's siblings relocated to Kansas, as well. Not long after, Robert contracted pneumonia while serving jury duty and died in 1883. Emma later relocated to Moscow, Idaho, with most of her surviving children. She died there from complications of a stroke in 1902.

January 1863—Jacksonville, Oregon

The respiratory problems that plagued Ann Ransom turned out to be tuberculosis. William's efforts to treat her were futile given that antibiotics were far in the future. On Sunday morning, January 4, the procession to Jacksonville Cemetery began at the family home outside of town. Ann's children—three daughters and two sons, the youngest just a year old—could hardly fathom the loss of their mother. Friends of the family joined the solemn march into town as the wagon carrying Ann's coffin came by. The service began once they reached the grave site.[3]

The past few years had been ones of unusual stability for the Ransom family. Sherman Day had died at the age of two in Vacaville, California, and this may have instigated the move to Oregon. William probably tried his hand at practicing medicine from the time he left Indiana, but he had no formal training. Many years later, he claimed that during his family's time in Vacaville he spent two years interning at a private hospital in Sacramento, thirty miles away. No records have come to light to support this claim. He also stated that he served as an aid to a militia doctor at Fort Klamath in southern Oregon and on an Indian reservation in northern California. No records exist for any military service in the war years; moreover, Fort Klamath did not yet exist during the time he said he served there. These are probably the lesser flights of fancy in his biography.[4] Rather, William returned to dealing in livestock and registered his brand in Jackson County. There is no evidence he claimed to be a doctor while living there; he was always referred to as "Mr. Ransom."

Ann had a third daughter while in Vacaville, whom they named Indiana, but she was always called Nannie. Two more sons came along: Lewis Clark and Frank Hoffman. The family settled into community affairs in Jackson County with vigor. A letter Ann wrote to her parents in 1861 survives in transcript.[5]

> Dear Father and Mother I again seat my self to pen a few lines to you—what a poor excuse for conversation and yet I often feel thankful that I can write. I often look back on the Days of my childhood and think of the pains and trouble and privations that my parents underwent to give me the education that I have and

feel that I never have or can repay them for it . . . We have got our school house finished and school commenced last week and we had church last Sunday and there will be next and we expect before long to have it every Sunday as we have the promise of several preachers.

She remarked on her sister Emma's fecundity:

Pa [William] got a letter from Bob last week. I think they are hurrying up their cakes pretty fast. It must keep Emma pretty busy to take care of her little ones and the company that they are bound to have in the business that they are now in. Watch and not let her work herself to death as I have done. Thee are able to keep help and it is easy got there and it cannot be had here for love or money hardly. The batchelors snatch off every girl that comes to the country in double quick time.

William, like his father-in-law, joined the Odd Fellows in Jacksonville and was serving a term as "Royal Grand." Ann was ready for the term to end, as it kept him away from home too much. He had plenty of work to tend to on the ranch, planting corn and wheat. (Clearly, he was not tending to wounded soldiers.) The war naturally crept into her narrative. "Oh what a cruel trade is war at the best. Many a little one is left fatherless." She worried that the conflict in the east would leave the west coast vulnerable to foreign powers. She also had concern for her family in Indiana. "I hope the war will not reach you. It was always my earnest wish that I might never be the witness of the bloody scenes of a battle field nor the misery that is attendent theiron. It must be a heart rending scene indeed. God help us. God help our country."

Upon Ann's passing, the family's steady rock crumbled. Cordelia's two younger brothers did not survive childhood. William relied on friends and neighbors to help him with his three daughters. In 1864, he remarried to a woman from Crescent City, California. His girls felt they were treated as servants in her household. Finally, finding the domestic situation untenable by mid-1865, and likely hearing about his father's death (and the end of the war), William returned to Indiana. He left Cordelia, Marietta, and Nannie in the care of family friends, Mary and James Clarke, who lived then in Douglas County, Oregon. He did not return to Oregon for thirty years. Sensing abandonment, Cordelia married at age fourteen to Mary Clarke's thirty-one-year-old brother, William E. Rackleff, who promised Cordelia he would treat her younger sisters as his own daughters.[6] She bore their first child in September 1866, at age fifteen.

William Ransom eventually attended medical school and became a licensed doctor in Indiana. He committed bigamy at least twice and, in 1894, swindled the people of South Haven, Michigan, and across the country, with a wild plan to sail a research vessel around the world. (Overcoming the horrors of the *Emily* and *Archibald Gracie*, William developed a lifelong love for sailing.) He never served time for any of his wild or illegal behavior. After spending about eight years in Skagway, Alaska, in the 1890s to early 1900s, he returned to southern Oregon and married his fifth wife. He died in Klamath Falls in 1917 at the senescent age of eighty-eight.

MAY 1863—BLACKFORD COUNTY

Peter N. Liestenfeltz and his wife, Eliza Strait, welcomed their first child and named him Henry. Pete had a short-lived first marriage before he and Eliza wed in 1862. They would have a total of three sons, followed by five daughters. Pete spent the remainder of his life farming in Blackford County. Like his older brothers, Jake and Daniel, Pete enjoyed his many grandchildren. He was religiously active and helped construct six churches in the area, donating land for the Olive Branch (Quaker) Church near his home. On his sixty-seventh birthday in June 1899, seventy-five friends and relatives gathered for a big box dinner to celebrate. He lived to age eighty-nine. It was noted in his obituary that he never required glasses to read his favorite Bible verses.[7]

MARCH 1864—BLACKFORD COUNTY

Dr. Benjamin H. Jones remained with his family in Camden. Nothing suggests he ever reconciled with his brother, Sam. His younger siblings

Figure E.1. Peter N. and Eliza (Strait) Liestenfeltz. Credit: Courtesy of Tanya Waters.

moved to the Chicago area during the war years, including his sister, Rebecca. He worked as a physician and registered for service in 1863, though lacking an eye. He did not serve. On March 15, 1864, Dr. Jones was found lying dead north of Trenton.[8] He presumably suffered heart failure at age forty-three. A few months later, his eighteen-year-old daughter, Geneva, died of unknown causes. They were apparently buried side by side next to little Mary in Hillside Cemetery.[9] Aside from Mary, though, the graves are unmarked. Benjamin never did get a chance to meet Rebecca's fiancé, E.D. Pierce.

Rebecca waited nearly twenty-one years for the man who had proposed to her before joining the gold rush. Pierce spent time trading with the Nez Perce in the northwest; made the first ascent of Mt. Shasta; ranched near Walla Walla, Washington—land that later became part of the city; formed a party that discovered gold in Idaho, leading directly to the creation of that state; opened new roads and ferries in the northwest in the 1860s; prospected for gold; and later mined coal for the railroad. He was never financially successful, though he managed to achieve some fame for his exploits. Hearing that Rebecca was being courted by a widower in Camden, Pierce finally made good on his promise. He returned at last and married Rebecca in Camden on November 1, 1869. They soon departed for California, with a stop in Idaho along the way.

After returning from his second trip to California, Sam Jones moved his family to Effingham County, Illinois, where he bought a mill and other real estate. In 1870, he, Eliza, and three of their children moved to California permanently. Their oldest daughter joined them there years later. For a time, Rebecca, along with her new husband, E.D. Pierce, lived close to Sam's family in El Dorado County and had a partnership in a mine on the American River. Their younger brother, William G. Jones, also brought his family out to California in 1870 but elected not to stay. Sam's business acumen served him well. He sold his El Dorado properties and mining claims and purchased oceanfront land from the government along Big Sur. Two of his children bought adjoining or nearby parcels. Like his cousin, Robert Ransom, Sam became a lay preacher with the Methodist Church. Some of Sam and Eliza's descendants and their families became prominent in the Pacific Grove community. Eliza and Sam had long lives, dying sometime between 1900 and 1910. Their resting place is unknown.

Rebecca and E.D. had a son, Beachy Hill Pierce, who died at about six months old in May 1872. Pierce continued his string of unsuccessful ventures in El Dorado County and later in Napa County. Rebecca went home to Camden around 1880, at least temporarily. Her brother, William G. Jones, built a house for her there. Pierce, suffering from a debilitating disease, joined her in Indiana in 1884. He spent his later years fighting for pension funds from the US government for his Mexican War service and trying to coerce the government into paying him for his services in opening the west to settlement, which he considered his true achievement. Rebecca served as his nurse almost around the clock. They both died in 1897 and were buried in Hillside Cemetery in Camden in unmarked graves.[10]

Figure E.2. Rebecca G. Jones and Elias D. Pierce, about 1870, shortly after their marriage. Credit: W. B. Ingersoll, Oakland, California.

July 1871—Eaton Rapids, Michigan

Allen Makepeace stepped down from the train he had taken from Indiana. He suffered from paralysis and general ill health for the past several years, and his doctors could offer nothing to alleviate his misery. Eaton Rapids boasted healing magnetic springs that might provide some benefit, if not an outright cure. It could not hurt to "take the waters." Eaton Rapids became renowned in the mid-nineteenth century, billing itself as the "Saratoga of the West." (Several other communities made the same boast.) Perhaps his time was nigh. It did not really matter. Now sixty-eight, he had accomplished his goals in life, principally to amass as much money as possible. Having arrived at the spa town, he spent a few days trying to recuperate from the journey, but instead, he slipped into that final sleep from which there is no awakening.[11] Allen Makepeace at last went to meet his maker.

No obituary touted any civic involvement, service organizations, or philanthropy. Every biographical piece instead refers to the size of his estate, estimated variously at $250,000 to $460,000—in 1871 dollars. Makepeace may have been respected in certain circles, but it is doubtful he was loving or much-loved. He was probably just fine with that. His true love was money, and he did not take it with him, any more than anyone ever has. An 1880 article offers some insight as to his motivation: "Mr. Makepeace believed in the continuity of life beyond the grave, in the communion of disembodied intelligences with those yet in the form, and that no change is effected in the character of the individual by death, excepting by the eternal law of higher progress, that sooner or later operates on all."[12]

Allen Makepeace's grave near Chesterfield has a massive monument that has only escaped serious vandalism due to its bulk. His descendants have not maintained his resting place, which is choked with vines and largely hidden from view. For the most part, he has simply been forgotten.

JUNE 1874—JAY COUNTY, INDIANA

Henry and Abby Jenkins rejoiced that their eldest child, Will, had found love again at last. He had been a widower far too long. Even his daughter, Lizzy, had married fifteen years earlier, to William S. Hyde, though that marriage had not been blessed with children. Will would never be a grandfather. His bride was Sarah Stults, a good Quaker woman who would be a dear helpmate. Will never regained the ability to see more than dim light and shadows. He spent a year at the Indiana School for the Blind in Indianapolis during the Civil War, where he learned broom-making and willow-work. He followed that line of business for several years and then opened a store in Camden.[13]

Henry and Abby never again owned real estate after selling their farm to Will. Henry probably used the proceeds from the land sale toward his Makepeace debt. He and Abby managed the farm for Will throughout the war years. After the war, during which sons Bedford and Barton served the Union Army, Henry and Abby moved to Camden where they remained for life. Henry worked as the Pennville postmaster (assisted by Abby) and served as magistrate for seventeen years, putting the experiences of his long life to good use. He remained a member of the Odd Fellows and oversaw the establishment of a lodge in Camden/Pennville in 1854. He served for a time as the "Noble Grand." Undoubtedly, Abby and Henry rented a home near Will Jenkins's store and residence on Lagro Street. It was a short walk east up a low hill to Hillside Cemetery

Figure E.3. Allen Makepeace's overgrown and vandalized grave in the Otterbien Cemetery, Chesterfield, Indiana. Credit: Author's photo.

where they visited Ann Jenkins's (currently unmarked) resting place in the family plot near the entrance. In the 1870s, Philadelphia (Jenkins) Barr and Bedford's wife, Patience, joined her there. Will became incapacitated, possibly due to a stroke, during the last six years of his life. Family friend E.D. Pierce reportedly helped out "Blind Billy Jenkins" in his store during that time.[14] Will passed away in 1894.

Tuesday, February 28, 1882—Jay County

Abby Jenkins spent the morning in the post office sorting through mail and chatting with people coming in to pick up or drop off letters and parcels. She felt better than she had for some time. Her eighty-first birthday had passed two weeks earlier. It had been a long life of service, and she had managed to hold onto her dear Henry from the time he returned from California, just as she promised she would. That evening, she complained to Henry of a chill feeling passing through her body, though she was not cold. The following morning, Henry was distressed to find that she had suffered a stroke in the night. She had had one the previous year and, with perseverance, recovered remarkably well.[15] With some assistance, she managed to get up but could not return to bed. It took enormous effort for old Henry to lift her into the bed. Thursday, she managed to sip a little coffee to wash down a bit of bread and butter. That afternoon, she slipped into her final sleep.

Henry sent for their son, Barton, who lived in Dunkirk. Barton arrived in Camden about 1 a.m. Saturday, but his mother never roused to see him. About noon, Henry's hope that her passing might go easily was not realized. "Instead there was two hours of a hard distressing effect for breath, but at last one gentle sigh a slight quivering of the eyelids and the released spirit quit its clay tenement, and doubtless to hear the master say 'well done good and faithful enter now into thy rest.'" Many friends came to pay their respects at her service on Sunday, and she, too, was laid to rest in Hillside. On Monday, Henry, bound up in his grief at losing his faithful companion of nearly fifty-five years, wrote to Emma out in Kansas. "My Dear Daughter, I can hardly command my feelings sufficiently to convey the sad tiding to thee that thy Mother is no longer with us here on earth but has gone to join the blood washed multitudes that John saw." He closed the letter with, "Dear child dont grieve too much after Mother, try to emulate her example and may we all so live as to make sure of a happy reunion at last where death or parting never enters, thy bereaved parent H Z Jenkins."[16]

After Abby's death, Henry moved in with Will and Sarah, where he lived when his time came that December. His funeral was held at the Methodist Episcopal Church, where he had been a member since the 1830s. Sixty-five Odd Fellows attended to the burial by their characteristic rituals. Their obituary for him reads in part:

A Christian and Odd Fellow indeed has passed away. One who having built for himself his own monument; and having placed upon it the crowning cap-sheaf, and inscribed upon its base in never fading letters his own epitaph, passed quietly to his grave. He built a monument not of iron, not of brass, not of granite, but of deeds. Deeds grand and glorious; deeds which now that he has passed away, leave a lasting impression, making the world the better that he had lived therein; deeds which shall live and grow with ever increasing brightness as the ages roll on; deeds which shall survive when time shall have decayed the metal and crumbled to dust the granite.[17]

Henry and Abby outlived all but three of their eight children.

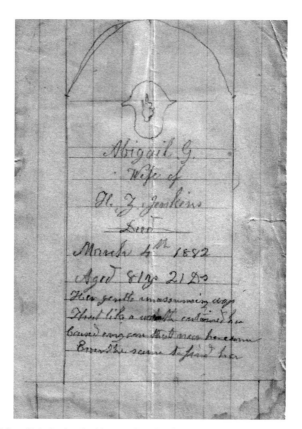

Figure E.4. After Abby's death, Henry sketched the design for her headstone. Credit: Author's collection.

Figure E.5. The author believes, based on some photographic evidence, that this full-plate daguerreotype from the early 1850s is an image of the Blackford Mining Company. Back row: John C. Teach, Jacob Liestenfeltz, John K. Anderson, Dennis Lowry. Front row: Preston M. Gibson, Peter N. Liestenfeltz, Henry Z. Jenkins, Samuel Jones, Asa Harvey Hunt. Credit: Group of Miners, circa 1850, DAG 9G, California Historical Society.

ACKNOWLEDGMENTS

I never knew my great-grandmother, Clara Pearl (Ransom) Davis, but we turn out to have many things in common. Her love of family history came down to me along with a lengthy transcript of the Jenkins family gold rush letters. Clara created the transcript before donating most of the letters, and Henry Jenkins's memo book, to the Huntington Library. As my genealogical research files began bulging, I decided to share stories with my extended family and turned to the gold rush letters for inspiration. The more I dug into their contents, the clearer it became that this was not material for a short tale but something close to epic. However, this collection was just the starting point.

Many people contributed their own family research and photographs to this project. Mary Gill (Ransom and Jenkins families); Sharon Lahti (Jenkins family); Marion Painter (Ransom and Anderson family); Edson Listenfelt and Jessica Dunica (Liestenfeltz family); Jim Baker and Linda Stephens (Lowry family); Jane Anne Hollandsworth and Julie Work Beck (Jones family); Stanley Smith (Ransom family); Jayne Larion (Chandlee family); Michael Sparks (Teach family); and Melody Hull (Makepeace family). Of these, I owe special gratitude to Marion Painter for finding the Delaware County Court records, without which this story would have been woefully incomplete; Mary Gill for pointing me to additional family letters in transcript in the University of Idaho C.J. Brosnan Collection; and Tanya Waters for generously sharing Peter Liestenfeltz's handwritten memoir, a delightful contrast to Henry's version of events.

Heartfelt thanks to the family and friends who agreed to read early drafts and provide critical feedback: Pat Lyon, Kathy Roser, Marion

Painter (two drafts!), Cheri Wisdom, and Barb Hancock. I am very grateful to Dr. Malcolm J. Rohrbough for evaluating the story based on a detailed chapter outline and for offering encouragement and helpful recommendations. Dr. David Vaught graciously agreed to read and evaluate the full manuscript, providing me with suggestions for additional sources, and an excellent critique. Thank you all for your generous donation of time—life's most precious commodity.

Thank you to my editor at TwoDot, Sarah Parke. I appreciate your belief in this project from a first-time author and your kind critique to guide the manuscript to its polished form.

A historical project like *Fortune's Frenzy* relies on the hard work and dedication by the staffs of many libraries, archives, historical and genealogical societies, and museums. I wish I could thank everyone by name, but it simply is not feasible. I am forever grateful for all they do to preserve our common heritage, and to fight censorship and data destruction, a never-ending battle.

I would like to acknowledge some who have responded to multiple requests from me over the years it took to bring this work to fruition. At the Huntington Library, Peter J. Blodgett and Stephanie Arias; at the University of Idaho Special Collections, Darcie Riedner; at the University of the Pacific, Nicole Grady Mountjoy; at the Blackford County Historical Society, Sinuard Castelo; at the Indiana Historical Society, Matt Holdkom; and at the California Historical Society, Frances Kaplan.

A good portion of my research involved traveling to sites referred to in the book. I wish to thank Derek Pierce at California Cavern for arranging a site visit to see the miners' graffiti. Thanks to Judith Marvin, Calaveras County historian, for many insights, resources, and directions. Thank you, Julie Beck, for lodging in Pacific Grove, and road adventures in our search for Sam Jones. Jim Baker for lodging, burgers, and doing lookups at the Family History Library. And I would also like to acknowledge the physically demanding projects undertaken by Annie Hoffmeier to clean and repair headstones in Pennville and Trenton: Henry Z. Jenkins, Abigail G. Jenkins, James Ransom, Elizabeth Ransom, and Sarah (Jellison) Anderson. I had hoped to visit them again in person in 2020, but . . . you know.

ACKNOWLEDGMENTS

Thank you to my mother for always supporting my creative endeavors, from finger painting to bad macramé, and everything else. Thanks to my father for instilling a strong work ethic and encouraging my continuing education and the belief I could do and be anything. Special thanks to my husband, Pat Lyon, for all you do to make it possible for me to research, write, and have fun during my time off.

NOTES

INTRODUCTION

1. Bray Hammond, *Banks and Politics in America: From the Revolution to the Civil War* (Princeton, New Jersey: Princeton University Press, 1991), 329.

2. Hugh McCulloch, *Early Banking in Indiana* (Fort Wayne, Indiana: Public Library of Fort Wayne and Allen Co., 1954), 9–10.

3. Hammond, *Banks and Politics in America*, 29.

CHAPTER 1

1. Cecil Beeson, ed., *Miscellaneous Records of Blackford Co., Indiana: Plus Index* (Fort Wayne, Ind.: Fort Wayne Public Library, 1978), 98.

2. *Biographical and Historical Record of Jay and Blackford Counties, Indiana: Containing . . . Portraits and Biographies of Some of the Prominent Men of the State: Engravings of Prominent Citizens in Jay and Blackford Counties, with Personal Histories of Many of the Leading Families and a Concise History of Jay and Blackford Counties and Their Cities and Villages* (Chicago: Lewis Publishing Company, 1887), 396.

3. Edward E. Chandlee, *Six Quaker Clockmakers* (Philadelphia: The Historical Society of Pennsylvania, 1943), 105.

4. Warren County Clerk. "Indenture from Goldsmith and Phebe Chandlee to Samuel Bedford." (Warren County, Ohio, Deed Book V. 25 p. 127, August 14, 1840), Film #008330935 image 475, Family Search, https://www.familysearch.org/ark:/61903/3:1:3Q9M-CSTC-KQCZ?i=474&cat=303984.

5. M. W. Montgomery, *History of Jay County, Indiana* (Chicago: Printed for the author by Church, Goodman & Cushing, 1864), 149; *Biographical and Historical Record of Jay and Blackford Counties, Indiana*, 254.

6. *Biographical and Historical Record of Jay and Blackford Counties, Indiana*, 254.

7. "Steam Saw and Grist Mill. Advertisement.," *Richmond Weekly Palladium*, March 23, 1839, image copy, p. 3 c. 6, Newspapers.com.

8. *Biographical and Historical Record of Jay and Blackford Counties, Indiana*, 396.

9. Montgomery, *History of Jay County, Indiana*, 110.

10. Jay County Clerk, "Indenture from Henry Z. and Abigail Jenkins to the State of Indiana" (Jay County, Indiana, Deeds, Book B pp. 195–97, December 31, 1840), Jay

County Courthouse (Portland, Indiana); Jay County Clerk, "Indenture from Job and Ruth Carr to Henry Z. Jenkins" (Jay County, Indiana, Deeds, Book B p. 203, December 29, 1840), Jay County Courthouse (Portland, Indiana).

11. Jay County Clerk, "G. Chandlee vs. Henry Z. Jenkins: Debt action." (Court Order Book A p. 197, May 1841), Jay County Courthouse (Portland, Indiana).

12. Jay County Clerk, "Henry Z. Jenkins vs. John G. Chandlee and Benjamin F. Davis, Administrators for the estate of Goldsmith Chandlee: Petition to have judgment cancelled" (Probate Order Book A p. 146, February 21, 1843), Probate Court (Portland, Indiana).

13. Montgomery, *History of Jay County, Indiana*, 208–9.

14. Benjamin G. Shinn, *Biographical Memoirs of Blackford County, Ind.* (Chicago: The Bowen Publishing Company, 1900), 273.

15. Montgomery, *History of Jay County, Indiana*, 39; "Journal of the Senate of the United States of America, Second Session of the Thirtieth Congress," February 19, 1849, 228, ProQuest.

16. "U.S., Army, Register of Enlistments, 1798–1914," > 1847 Jan–1849 Jun> Mexican War enlistments> image 254> Wilson, Willis of Jay County, Indiana, farmer, Ancestry.com, accessed November 14, 2021, https://www.ancestry.com/search/collections/1198 /; "U.S., Returns from Military Posts, 1806–1916,"> Kansas> Leavenworth > 1827 Aug–1850 Dec> image 457, Returns for April 1847, Willis S. Wilson Co. B enlisted March 4, 1847., Ancestry.com, accessed November 14, 2021, https://www.ancestry.com /search/collections/1571/; Tom Ervin, "Willis S. Wilson - Facts," DeVoe/Gault Family Tree, accessed November 14, 2021, https://www.ancestry.com/family-tree/person/tree /17501354/person/19131848129/facts. Attempts to reach Mr. Ervin regarding his source for the letter were unsuccessful.

17. Jane Ann Spencer, *When Grandpa Farmed: A History of Agriculture in Jay County*, vol. 1 (Portland, Indiana: Jay County Historical Society, Inc., 2010), 36.

CHAPTER 2
1. Blackford County Clerk, "Plat for the Town of Trenton, Blackford County, Indiana" (Blackford County, Indiana, Deeds, Book B p. 321, 1847), Blackford County Courthouse (Hartford City, Indiana).

2. Delaware County Clerk, "Allen Makepeace v. Samuel Jones et al." (Delaware County, Indiana, Circuit Court, 1854), Circuit Court> Civil> Jones, Samuel, Defendant, Non-payment of debt, Muncie Public Library-Digital Resource, http://digitalresource .munpl.org. All details in this chapter pertaining to the promissory notes and how the Jones brothers used them to get funds derive from this case file.

3. John L. Forkner and Byron H. Dyson, *Historical Sketches and Reminiscences of Madison County* (Anderson, Indiana: Press of Wilson, Humphreys & co., 1897), 147.

4. Peter N. Liestenfeltz, "Memoir" (Blackford County, Indiana, n.d.), 29, Personal collection of Tanya Waters, Indiana.

5. Delaware County Clerk, "Makepeace v. Jones," 122.

6. Frank D. Haimbaugh, *History of Delaware County, Indiana*, vol. 1 (Indianapolis: Historical Publishing Co., 1924), 192; G. W. H. Kemper, *A Twentieth Century History of*

Delaware County, Indiana, vol. 1 (Chicago: Lewis Publishing Co., 1908), 302; *A Portrait and Biographical Record of Delaware and Randolph Counties, Ind.: Containing Biographical Sketches of Many Prominent and Representative Citizens, Together with Biographies and Portraits of All the Presidents of the United States, and Biographies of the Governors of Indiana.* (Chicago: A.W. Bowen & Co., 1894), 497.

7. Delaware County Clerk, "Makepeace v. Jones," 143.

8. Ibid.

9. Jay County Clerk, "Indenture from Henry Z. Jenkins to Joseph Wilson" (Jay County, Indiana, Mortgages, Book A p. 193, February 28, 1851), Film #008052719 image 128, Family Search, https://www.familysearch.org/search/catalog/1018590.

10. Samuel Harden, *History of Madison County, Indiana, from 1820 to 1874: Giving a General Review of Principal Events, Statistical and Historical Items, Derived from Official Sources* (Markleville, Indiana: S. Harden, 1874), 265.

11. *History of Madison County Indiana, with Illustrations and Biographical Sketches* (Chicago: Kingman Brothers, 1880), 161.

12. "The Makepeace Family" (Computer-generated report, no author, n.d.), 11, Madison County Genealogical Society, accessed April 21, 2017.

13. Hattie Listenfelt, "Sketch of Susan and Conrad Listenfelt," Updated April 17, 2001, Listenfelt Family Reunion, accessed November 14, 2021, https://web.archive.org/web/20200812002808/http://patrushka.tripod.com/.

14. Liestenfeltz, "Memoir," 4.

15. Pete Liestenfeltz stated in his memoir that they all borrowed from Makepeace, but there is no mention of Gibson in any of the trial documentation.

16. Liestenfeltz, "Memoir," 7.

17. Ibid.

18. Blackford County Clerk, "Agreement between Samuel Jones, Dennis Lowry & Others" (Blackford County, Indiana, Deeds, Book C p. 486, March 15, 1851), Blackford County Courthouse (Hartford City, Indiana).

CHAPTER 3

1. Liestenfeltz, "Memoir," 8.

2. Charles Cist, *Sketches and Statistics of Cincinnati in 1851* (Cincinnati, Ohio: Wm. H. Moore & Co., 1851), 49–51.

3. Louis C. Hunter and Beatrice Jones Hunter, *Steamboats on the Western Rivers. An Economic and Technological History* (New York: Octagon Books, 1969), 33.

4. Packets were boats or ships that sailed on a regular schedule; frequently, they carried mail on contract.

5. "The Steamer Indiana," *The Cincinnati Enquirer*, March 12, 1851, image copy, p. 2 c. 5, Newspapers.com; "Steamboat Register: Departures," *The Cincinnati Enquirer*, March 15, 1851, image copy, p. 3 c. 2, Newspapers.com.

6. Henry refers to this letter in his second, but it has not survived.

7. "Henry Zane Jenkins Correspondence 1851–1853" (San Marino, California, n.d.), mssHM 16791–16808, Huntington Library ("Jenkins Letters HL"). Henry Jenkins, March 21, 1851.

8. Celia Pumpelly Ricker Frease, "Celia P. Ricker's Journal, Begun December 4th 1851 at Cincinnati, and Ended March 16th 1852 at New Orleans" (Cincinnati, Ohio, n.d.), 16, PDF scan excerpt of pages 9--3, Cincinnati Historical Society, Cincinnati Museum Center.

9. Hunter and Hunter, *Steamboats on the Western Rivers*, 287. This is probably a conservative estimate and does not include thousands of deaths from collisions, fires, drowning, and snags.

10. Ibid., 436.

11. "The New and Splendid Steamer," *The Cincinnati Enquirer*, December 12, 1850, image copy, p. 2 c. 4, Newspapers.com.

12. Frease, "Celia P. Ricker's Journal," 11.

13. "Notice to Merchants and Shippers," *The Cincinnati Enquirer*, March 13, 1851, image copy, p. 3 c. 4, Newspapers.com.

14. S. L. Kotar and J. E. Gessler, *The Steamboat Era: A History of Fulton's Folly on American Rivers, 1807–1860* (Jefferson, North Carolina, and London: McFarland & Co., Inc., 2009), 77.

15. Hunter and Hunter, *Steamboats on the Western Rivers*, 63.

16. "Jenkins Letters HL." Henry Jenkins, March 21, 1851.

17. "The Great Race of Saturday," *Kentucky Gazette*, October 17, 1839, image copy, p. 2 c. 5, Newspapers.com.

18. "Coonjine in Manhattan," 1939, Library of Congress, Manuscript Division, WPA Federal Writers' Project Collection, https://www.loc.gov/resource/wpalh0.07070413/.

19. Frances Milton Trollope, *Domestic Manners of the Americans* (Paris: Baudry's Foreign Library, 1832), 5.

20. "Coonjine in Manhattan," 2.

21. "Jenkins Letters HL." Henry Jenkins, March 21, 1851.

22. Mrs. W. L. (Effie L. Anderson) Thompson, letter (Topeka, KS) to a cousin, Dorothy, 1932, posted by corcoran32 on January 14, 2013, Ancestry.com. Mrs. Thompson was Humphrey Anderson's great-granddaughter.

23. "1850 U.S. Census, Blackford County, Indiana, Agriculture Schedule," Microfilm Roll #3887 Adams-Cass County, Indiana State Archives, Indianapolis, Indiana.

24. "Jenkins Letters HL." Henry Jenkins, March 21, 1851.

25. Ibid.

26. Ibid.

CHAPTER 4

1. "Jenkins Letters HL." All quotes from Henry in this chapter are from his letter dated March 21, 1851, completed on March 29, 1851.

2. "Arrivals at Principal Hotels, March 23," *Daily Crescent*, March 24, 1851, image copy, p. 2 c. 5, Chronicling America.

3. Porter would go on to become renowned for his service on the Mississippi and western rivers during the Civil War.

4. "For New York. U.S. Mail Steamship Company - For New York, Havana and Chagres," *The Daily Picayune*, March 23, 1851, image copy, p. 1 c. 3, Newspapers.com.

5. Liestenfeltz, "Memoir," 9.

6. A. E. Fossier, *The Charity Hospital in Louisiana*, Reprinted from the New Orleans Medical and Surgical Journal for May to October 1923. (New Orleans, Louisiana: The American Printing Company, Ltd., 1923), 23.

7. *Charity Hospital Report 1852: Report of the Board of Administrators of the Charity Hospital* (New Orleans, Louisiana: Charity Hospital of New Orleans, 1853), 19; Fossier, *The Charity Hospital in Louisiana*, 59.

8. "Passengers - Per Steamer Georgia," *The Daily Picayune*, March 31, 1851, Monday's Evening Edition, image copy, p. 2 c. 6, Newspapers.com.

CHAPTER 5

1. "Jenkins Letters HL," all quotes by Henry from the Caribbean: Henry Jenkins, April 18, 1851.

2. Liestenfeltz, "Memoir," 11.

3. Mary Jane Megquier, *Apron Full of Gold: The Letters of Mary Jane Megquier from San Francisco, 1849–1856* (San Marino, California: Huntington Library, 1949), 19.

4. "Jenkins Letters HL." All Henry's Panama quotes: Henry Jenkins, April 30, 1851.

5. Frank Marryat, *Mountains and Molehills, or, Recollections of a Burnt Journal: The 1855 Edition, Unabridged and with an Introduction by Robin W. Winks* (Philadelphia: Lippincott, 1962), 4–5.

6. John Haskell Kemble, *The Panama Route, 1848–1869* (Berkley and Los Angeles: University of California Press, 1943), 178.

7. Ibid., 170.

8. Hubert Howe Bancroft, *The Works of Hubert Howe Bancroft: California Inter Pocula* (San Francisco: History Co., 1888), 174.

9. Dennis Lowry, letter (Blackford County, Indiana) to "Dear brother & sister" [Rev. Arthur and Nancy (Houser) Badley], February 6, 1854, Private collection of James W. Baker [address for private use] Spring City, Utah, 1984.

10. Marryat, *Mountains and Molehills*, 8.

11. Kemble, *The Panama Route*, 51–56.

12. Ibid., 55–56.

13. Liestenfeltz, "Memoir," 15.

14. Oscar Lewis, *Sea Routes to the Gold Fields: The Migration to California by Water in 1849–1852* (New York: Alfred A. Knopf, 1949), 230.

15. "Jenkins Letters HL." Henry Jenkins, May 24, 1851.

16. Lowry, "Letter."

17. Bancroft, *California Inter Pocula*, 174.

18. One argonaut, sailing on the steamer *Panama* in 1850, kept a diary containing nothing but a list of foods served at each meal. Apparently, nothing else about his trip was noteworthy.

19. Louis J. Rasmussen, *San Francisco Ship Passenger Lists Vol. 1*, digital images (Baltimore, Maryland: Genealogical Publishing Co., 1978), 37–38, https://www.ancestry.com/search/collections/49329/.

20. Ibid.; Liestenfeltz, "Memoir," 17.

CHAPTER 6

1. John Mack Faragher, *Sugar Creek: Life on the Illinois Prairie* (New Haven, Connecticut; London: Yale University Press, 1986), 133–34.

2. "Meterological [*sic*]," *Richmond Weekly Palladium*, April 2, 1851, image copy, p. 2 c. 5, Newspapers.com; "Meteorological," *Richmond Weekly Palladium*, May 7, 1851, image copy, p. 2 c. 4, Newspapers.com. Weather was recorded two miles northeast of Richmond, about fifty-five miles from the Jenkins farm.

3. "Cure for Erysipelas," *The Richmond Palladium*, April 2, 1851, image copy, p. 2 c. 2, Newspapers.com.

4. "Jenkins Letters HL." Henry Jenkins, March 21, 1851.

5. "Cornelius James Brosnan Papers, 1917–1950: Jenkins Letters 1851–1863," Special Collections MG-18, University of Idaho, ("Jenkins Letters UI"). Abigail Jenkins, August 20, 1851.

6. Jay County, Ind. Board of Commissioners and Indiana Historical Records Survey, *Commissioners' Record: Jay County Indiana.*, vol. a 1836–1850 (Indianapolis, Indiana: Indiana Historical Records Survey, 1941), 396.

CHAPTER 7

1. "Jenkins Letters HL." Henry Jenkins, May 24, 1851.

2. Lewis, *Sea Routes to the Gold Fields*, 219.

3. "Great Conflagration-San Francisco in Ashes," *The Indiana Herald*, June 25, 1851, image copy, p. 2 c. 6, Newspapers.com.

4. "Jenkins Letters HL." Henry Jenkins, May 24, 1851.

5. John Doble, *John Doble's Journal and Letters from the Mines: Volcano, Mokelumne Hill, Jackson, and San Francisco, 1851–1865*, ed. Charles Lewis Camp (Volcano, California: Volcano Press, 1999), 31.

6. "Jenkins Letters HL." Henry Jenkins, May 24, 1851.

7. George Henry Tinkham, *A History of Stockton from Its Organization up to the Present Time, Including a Sketch of San Joaquin County; Comprising a History of the Government, Politics, State of Society, Religion, Fire Department, Commerce, Secret Societies, Art, Science, Manufactures, Agriculture . . . within the Past Thirty Years . . .* (San Francisco: W.M. Hinton & Co. printers, 1880), 1–7.

8. "Jenkins Letters HL." All Henry quotes in this section: Henry Jenkins, May 24, 1851.

9. "Jenkins Letters HL." Henry Jenkins, June 11, 1851.

10. "Population of California," *The Indiana Herald* [Quoting the *Sacramento Times*], May 21, 1851, image copy, p. 2 c. 4, Newspapers.com.

11. "Jenkins Letters HL." Henry Jenkins, July 13, 1851.

12. "Jenkins Letters HL." Henry Jenkins, June 11, 1851.

13. Jacob Crum, "Letter from California," *The Indiana Herald*, January 22, 1851, image copy, p. 3 c. 1–2, Newspapers.com.

14. "Jenkins Letters HL." Henry Jenkins, July 13, 1851.

15. A. W. [*sic*; O. W.] Nixon, letter transcript (location of original unknown) (Sacramento City) to "My Dear Father" [Samuel Nixon], October 29, 1850, Manuscript

Collection (gift of Bernhard Knollenberg, 1946), SC 2100, Indiana Historical Society Library.

16. "Jenkins Letters HL." All Henry quotes in remainder of chapter: Henry Jenkins, June 11, 1851.

17. Liestenfeltz, "Memoir," 17–18.

18. Ibid.

CHAPTER 8

1. "Jenkins Letters HL." Henry Jenkins, June 11, 1851.

2. Ralph Pyeatt, "The Story of Murphys," *The Pacific Historian* 19, no. 3 (Fall 1975): 231; Hubert Howe Bancroft, *California Pioneer Register and Index 1542–1848: Including California, 1769–1800 and List of Pioneers*, Extracted from Bancroft, Hubert Howe, *History of California*, p. 258 (Baltimore: Regional Publishing Co., 1964).

3. Calaveras Visitors Bureau, "Unearthing the Mystery of Henry Angell (Link to 15-Page PDF: Henry Pinkney Angell 1826–1897)," GoCalaveras.com, January 29, 2016, https://www.gocalaveras.com/unearthing-the-mystery-of-henry-angell/.

4. "Jenkins Letters HL." Henry Jenkins, March 21, 1851.

5. "Jenkins Letters HL." Henry Jenkins, August 31, 1851.

6. "Jenkins Letters HL." Henry Jenkins, July 13, 1851.

7. Horace Snow, *"Dear Charlie" Letters: Recording the Everyday Life of a Young 1854 Gold Miner . . . As Set Forth by Your Friend, Horace Snow*, 3rd ed. (Fresno, California: Pioneer Publishing Company, 1986), 13.

8. Edward Ely, *The Wanderings of Edward Ely, a Mid-19th Century Seafarer's Diary*, ed. Anthony Sirna and Allison Sirna (New York: Hastings House, 1954), 37.

9. Ibid.

10. "Jenkins Letters HL." Henry Jenkins, August 31, 1851.

11. "Jenkins Letters HL." Henry Jenkins, October 18, 1851.

12. Ibid.

13. Charles D Ferguson, *California Gold Fields*, California Centennial (Oakland, California: Biobooks, 1948), 132.

14. "Jenkins Letters HL." Henry Jenkins, March 21, 1851.

15. Ely, *The Wanderings of Edward Ely*, 87.

16. "Jenkins Letters HL." Henry Jenkins, September 26, 1851.

17. "Jenkins Letters HL." Henry Jenkins, July 13, 1851.

18. "Jenkins Letters HL." Henry Jenkins, August 31, 1851.

19. "Jenkins Letters HL." Henry Jenkins, July 13, 1851.

20. Ibid.

21. "Jenkins Letters HL." Henry Jenkins, September 26, 1851.

CHAPTER 9

1. "Jenkins Letters HL." Henry Jenkins, April 18, 1851.

2. Ibid.

3. "U.S., Quaker Meeting Records, 1681–1935a," March 30, 1826, >Pennsylvania>Philadelphia>Philadelphia Monthly Meeting>Minutes, 1823–1833, Abigail G. Bedford>image 66, Ancestry.com, https://www.ancestry.com/search/collections/2189/; "U.S., Quaker Meeting Records, 1681–1935b," April 27, 1826, > Pennsylvania> Philadelphia> Philadelphia Monthly Meeting> Women´s Minutes, 1823–1833, Abigail G. Bedford> image 53, Ancestry.com, https://www.ancestry.com/search/collections/2189/; "U.S., Quaker Meeting Records, 1681–1935c," March 30, 1826,> Pennsylvania> Philadelphia> Philadelphia Monthly Meeting> Minutes, 1809–1828, Abigail G. Bedford> image 308, Ancestry.com, https://www.ancestry.com/search/collections/2189/.

4. "U.S., Quaker Meeting Records, 1681–1935d," May 9, 1826,> Pennsylvania> Philadelphia> Philadelphia Monthly Meeting> Interments, 1820–1915, Charles Branin> image 75, Ancestry.com, https://www.ancestry.com/search/collections/2189/.

5. Henry mentions receiving these, but neither has survived to the present.

6. "Jenkins Letters HL." Henry Jenkins, July 31, 1851.

7. Ibid.

8. "Jenkins Letters UI." All Abby quotes this chapter: Abigail Jenkins, August 20, 1851.

9. "Jenkins Letters HL." Henry Jenkins, November 19, 1851.

10. "Jenkins Letters HL." Henry Jenkins, July 13, 1851.

11. "Hearts Trumps," *The Owyhee Avalanche*, March 5, 1870, image copy. The article, quoting the Barnesville newspaper, suggests Rebecca left there in 1849; however, she was counted with her parents in the 1850 census. Most likely, she moved to Indiana when Sam took his ward, brother-in-law Jefferson Zinn, back to Belmont County before heading to California.

CHAPTER 10

1. Liestenfeltz, "Memoir," 19.

2. Snow, *"Dear Charlie" Letters*, 19.

3. "Jenkins Letters HL." Henry Jenkins, September 26, 1851.

4. "Jenkins Letters HL." Henry Jenkins, August 31, 1851.

5. "Jenkins Letters HL." Henry Jenkins, September 26, 1851.

6. Ibid.

7. Louise Amelia Clappe and Thomas C. Russell, *The Shirley Letters from California Mines in 1851–52: Being a Series of Twenty-Three Letters from Dame Shirley (Mrs. Louise Amelia Knapp Smith Clappe) to Her Sister in Massachusetts, and Now Reprinted from the Pioneer Magazine of 1854–55; with Synopses of the Letters, a Foreword, and Many Typographical and Other Corrections and Emendations*, 1922, 7.

8. "Jenkins Letters HL." Henry Jenkins, September 26, 1851.

9. Elias D. Pierce, "E.D. Pierce Reminiscences." (n.d.), 40, Special Collections MG 5384, University of Idaho.

10. Walter J. Daly, "The 'Slows': The Torment of Milk Sickness on the Midwest Frontier," *Indiana Magazine of History* 102, no. 1 (2006): 34, http://www.jstor.org/stable /27792690.

11. Eilene Lyon, "A Slow Death," *Myricopia* (blog), March 24, 2019, https://myricopia .com/2019/03/24/a-slow-death/. By the end of the century, fenced pastures and industrial

dairy production, which combined the milk of many cows, thus diluting any toxin present, all but eradicated the affliction. The poisonous compound, tremetol, was not isolated and identified until 1928. The last known human case occurred, somewhat randomly, in 1968.

12. "Cave," *Calaveras Chronicle*, October 25, 1851, East Hampton Library, New York Heritage Digital Collections.

13. "Jenkins Letters HL." Henry Jenkins, November 9, 1851.

14. Liestenfeltz, "Memoir," 20.

15. "Jenkins Letters HL." Henry Jenkins, October 18, 1851.

16. "Cornelius James Brosnan Papers, 1917–1950: Pierce, Elias Davidson" (n.d.), Special Collections MG018, folder 5384, University of Idaho.

17. Ely, *The Wanderings of Edward Ely*, 159.

18. "Jenkins Letters HL." Henry Jenkins, November 9, 1851.

19. Ibid.

20. "Jenkins Letters HL." Henry Jenkins, November 19, 1851.

21. "Jenkins Letters HL." Henry Jenkins, October 18, 1851.

22. Ibid.

23. Ibid.

24. "Jenkins Letters HL." Henry Jenkins, September 26, 1851.

25. "Jenkins Letters HL." Henry Jenkins, October 18, 1851.

26. Ibid.

27. "Jenkins Letters HL." Henry Jenkins, November 9, 1851.

28. "Capital vs. Labor," *Calaveras Chronicle*, December 27, 1851, image copy, p. 2 c. 2, Bancroft Library (UC-Berkeley) Newspapers and Microforms.

29. Leonard Bernstein, "The Working People of Philadelphia from Colonial Times to the General Strike of 1835," *The Pennsylvania Magazine of History and Biography* 74, no. 3 (1950): 331, http://www.jstor.org/stable/20088146.

30. Louis H. Arky, "The Mechanics' Union of Trade Associations and the Formation of the Philadelphia Workingmen's Movement," *The Pennsylvania Magazine of History and Biography* 76, no. 2 (1952): 143, www.jstor.org/stable/20088351.

31. Ibid.

32. "At a Large and Respectable Meeting . . . ," *The United States Gazette*, August 26, 1828, image copy, p. 2 c. 2, Newspapers.com.

33. *Collections of the Genealogical Society of Pennsylvania; Notices of Marriages & Deaths in Poulson's American Daily Advertiser, 1791–1839; 1826–1830*, vol. 79 (Philadelphia: Genealogical Society of Pennsylvania, 1903), 41.

34. Arky, "The Mechanics' Union of Trade Associations and the Formation of the Philadelphia Workingmen's Movement," 155.

Chapter 11

1. "A Minister at a Camp Meeting Said . . . ," *Evansville Daily Journal*, July 16, 1852, image copy, p. 2 c. 3, Newspapers.com.

2. J. C. Smith, *Reminiscences of Early Methodism in Indiana. Including Sketches of Various Prominent Ministers, Together with Narratives of Women Eminent for Piety, Poetry and Song. Also, Descriptions of Remarkable Camp Meetings, Revivals, Incidents and Other Miscellany.*

With an Appendix Containing Essays on Various Theological Subjects of Practical Interest. (Indianapolis: J.M. Olcott, 1879), 90.

3. United States Congress. "The Congressional Globe." Washington: Blair & Rives, 18341873, February 24, 1863, 1257.

4. "Terrible Riot," *Crawfordsville Weekly Review*, October 13, 1866, image copy p. 2 c. 4, Hoosier State Chronicles.

5. Martha C. M. Lynch, *Reminiscences of Adams, Jay and Randolph Counties* (Fort Wayne, Indiana, 1897), 153.

6. "Jenkins Letters UI." Abigail Jenkins, August 20, 1851.

7. Florence Bedford Wright, "A Station on the Underground Railroad," *Ohio History*, Ohio Archaeological and Historical Publications, 14 (1905): 164–69.

8. "United States v. The Amistad," in *Wikipedia*, October 26, 2021, https://en.wikipedia .org/w/index.php?title=United_States_v._The_Amistad&oldid=1052000192. United States v. Schooner Amistad, 40 US (15 Pet.) 518 (1841), was a United States Supreme Court case resulting from the rebellion of Africans on board the Spanish schooner *La Amistad* in 1839. It was an unusual freedom suit that involved international issues and parties as well as United States law. The historian Samuel Eliot Morison described it in 1969 as the most important court case involving slavery before being eclipsed by that of Dred Scott in 1857.

9. Malcolm J. Rohrbough, *Days of Gold: The California Gold Rush and the American Nation* (Berkeley, California: University of California Press, 1998), 231.

10. "Women's Rights Convention-Sojourner Truth," *The Anti-Slavery Bugle*, June 21, 1851, image copy, p. 4 c. 3, Newspapers.com.

11. "Jenkins Letters UI." Abigail Jenkins, June 11, 1853.

12. "Jenkins Letters HL." Abigail Jenkins, February 6, 1853.

13. Mrs. Sigourney, "Woman's Rights," *The Indiana State Sentinel*, November 27, 1851, image copy, p. 4 c. 1, Newspapers.com.

14. "Jenkins Letters HL." Henry Jenkins, August 31, 1851.

15. "Jenkins Letters HL." Ann Jenkins, March 2, 1852.

16. "Pennsylvania, U.S., Oyer and Terminer Court Papers, 1757–1787,"> Philadelphia> 1778, images 17, 89, 91, 124, Ancestry.com, accessed December 23, 2021, https://www .ancestry.com/search/collections/2385/.

17. "U.S., Quaker Meeting Records, 1681–1935,"> Pennsylvania> Philadelphia> Philadelphia Monthly Meeting, Northern District> Index, 1772–1781> image 471, Jonathan Zane, Ancestry.com, accessed December 23, 2021, https://www.ancestry.com/search/ collections/2189/.

18. "Jenkins Letters HL." Ann Jenkins, March 2, 1852.

19. "Jenkins Letters HL." Abigail Jenkins, March 28, 1852.

20. "Bellefontaine Railroad," *The Indiana State Sentinel*, May 1, 1851, Weekly edition, image copy, p. 2 c. 2, Newspapers.com.

CHAPTER 12

1. "Christmas Day," *Calaveras Chronicle*, December 20, 1851, image copy, p. 2 c. 2, Bancroft Library (UC-Berkeley) Newspapers and Microforms.

2. "Another Attempt at Murder," *Calaveras Chronicle*, December 27, 1851, image copy, p. 2 c. 3, Bancroft Library (UC-Berkeley) Newspapers and Microforms.

3. "Blown Down," *Calaveras Chronicle*, January 3, 1852, image copy, p. 2 c. 3, Bancroft Library (UC-Berkeley) Newspapers and Microforms.

4. "Jenkins Letters HL." Henry Jenkins memo book, January 1, 1852.

5. Liestenfeltz, "Memoir," 21–22.

6. "Jenkins Letters HL." Ann Jenkins, May 3, 1852. The daguerreotype apparently has not survived to the present.

7. "Jenkins Letters HL." Ann Jenkins, March 2, 1852.

8. "Jenkins Letters HL." Abigail Jenkins, March 28, 1852.

9. "Jenkins Letters HL." Henry Jenkins, November 19, 1851.

10. Peter E. Carr, *San Francisco Passenger Departure Lists 15 January to 16 June 1852*, vol. IV (San Luis Obispo, California: TCI Genealogical Resources, 1995), 85.

11. "One Day Later from California," *New-York Daily Times*, July 3, 1852, image copy, p. 3 c. 1, Newspapers.com; "Manifest for Steamship Northern Light July 2, 1852,"> New York Passenger Lists, 1820–1891> 115–21 Jun 1852–5 Jul 1852> images 726 & 728 for passenger A H Hunt, age 34, Family Search, accessed July 13, 2017, https://www .familysearch.org/search/catalog/1849782.

12. "Indiana, U.S., Wills and Probate Records, 1798–1999,"> Jay> Probate File, Box 6–8, Isaac Barrick-John Journey, 1851–1853> images 1430–1551 for Harvey Hunt, Ancestry.com, accessed December 23, 2021, https://www.ancestry.com/search/collections /9045/.

13. Lowry, "Letter."

14. Crum, "Letter from California."

15. JoAnn Levy, "Crossing the 40-Mile Desert," *The Californians* V, no. 5 (October 1987): 16–31.

16. Lowry, "Letter."

17. "The Greatest Lumps of Pure Gold . . . ," *Sacramento Daily Union*, June 23, 1851, image copy, p. 2 c. 3, California Digital Newspaper Collection; "The Greatest Lump of Gold Yet Found," *Sacramento Daily Union*, July 21, 1851, image copy, p. 2 c. 2, California Digital Newspaper Collection; "Beautiful Specimen," *Daily Alta California*, July 23, 1851, image copy, p. 2 c. 6, California Digital Newspaper Collection; "Scott's River Bar May 30, 1851," *Daily Alta California*, July 2, 1851, image copy, p. 2 c. 2, California Digital Newspaper Collection.

18. Paris S. Pfouts, *Four Firsts for a Modest Hero: The Autobiography of Paris Swazy Pfouts*, ed. Harold Axford (Portland, Oregon: The Grand Lodge, Ancient Free and Accepted Masons, of Montana, 1968), 69.

19. "Shasta-Official," *Daily Alta California*, September 20, 1851, image copy, p. 2 c. 5, California Digital Newspaper Collection.

20. Pierce, "E.D. Pierce Reminiscences," 83–84.

21. "Jenkins Letters HL." Abigail Jenkins, March 28, 1852.

22. Hunter and Hunter, *Steamboats on the Western Rivers*, 426–27, quoting James Logan.

23. "Jenkins Letters HL." Ann Jenkins, March 2, 1852.

24. F. A. Isbell, *Mining and Hunting in the Far West, 1852–1870* (Stevenson, Connecticut: F.A. Isbell, 1871), 1.

25. Stephen Chapin Davis, *California Gold Rush Merchant; the Journal of Stephen Chapin David*, ed. Benjamin B. Richards (San Marino, California: Huntington Library Publications, 1956), 57, https://www.loc.gov/item/56012476/.

26. "Another Crowd," *The Panama Star*, February 26, 1852, image copy, p. 2 c. 3, Readex-NewsBank.

27. "Letter to His Parents by George B. Blanchard" (San Francisco, September 14, 1852), WA MSS S-676 B592, Yale Beinecke Library (New Haven, Connecticut).

28. "David T. Gillis Diary, 1852–1854," Gillis Family Papers, 1809–1888 mss100 Holt-Atherton Special Collections - University of the Pacific (Stockton, California), accessed November 15, 2017, transcription by the author at: https://scholarlycommons.pacific.edu/grcc/40/.

29. "Jenkins Letters HL." Ann Jenkins, March 2, 1852.

30. "Jenkins Letters HL." Abigail Jenkins, March 28, 1852.

31. Timothy Stratton, "Timothy Stratton Letter," 1852, Rare Books and Manuscripts, S1263, transcribed material in finding aid, Indiana State Library.

32. "Spirit Knocking-Ism Exposed," *The Richmond Palladium*, May 28, 1851, image copy, p. 1 c. 6, Newspapers.com.

33. "Jenkins Letters UI." Abigail Jenkins, June 26, 1852.

34. "Jenkins Letters HL." Ann Jenkins, May 3, 1852.

35. "Jenkins Letters HL." Abigail Jenkins, March 28, 1852.

36. "Jenkins Letters HL." Ann Jenkins, May 3, 1852.

37. Ibid.

CHAPTER 13

1. "Blanchard Letter."

2. A. G. Findley, "Oceanic Currents and Their Connection with the Proposed Central-America Canals," ed. Norton Shaw, *The Journal of the Royal Geographic Society* 23 (1853): 217–41.

3. "Gillis Diary." March 22, 1852.

4. "Gillis Diary." April 30 and May 1, 1852.

5. William M. Thayer, *The Price of Gold: A Sermon Occasioned by the Death of Henry Martyn Allard Who Died at the Gold Mines of California July 10, 1852, Aged Nineteen Years* (Boston: "Published by the friends" Press of J. B. Chisholm, 1852), 9–10.

6. Davis, *California Gold Rush Merchant*, 65.

7. "Jenkins Letters UI." All Abby's quotes in this section: Abigail Jenkins, June 26, 1852.

CHAPTER 14

1. Ely, *The Wanderings of Edward Ely*, 109–10.

2. "Blanchard Letter."

NOTES

3. John Mayo, "English Commercial Houses on Mexico's West Coast, 1821–1867," *Ibero-Amerikanisches Archiv* 22, no. 1/2 (1996): 173–90, http://www.jstor.org/stable /43393097.

4. John Mayo, *Commerce and Contraband on Mexico's West Coast in the Era of Barron, Forbes & Co., 1821–1859* (New York: Peter Lang, 2006), 372, quoting Capt. Henry Byam Martin.

5. "Consular Dispatch from R.P. Letcher, U.S. Minister to Mexico, to U.S. Consul William Forbes of Tepic, Nayarit, Mexico," July 17, 1852, MF 0550.41 Mexico City, MX Consular Dispatches Vol. 10, Arizona Historical Society Library & Archives (Tempe and Tucson).

6. "Blanchard Letter."

7. Ibid.

8. "Sick Passengers," *Daily Alta California*, September 13, 1852, Sec. Supplemental, image copy, p. 1 c. 3, California Digital Newspaper Collection.

9. When a British barque named *Emily* arrived in San Francisco a week after the *Archibald Gracie*, the *Daily Alta California* insinuated (but did not explicitly say, probably to avoid a libel suit) that this was the notorious ship with seventeen deaths that had stranded her passengers in San Blas. It was not that ship. Registered in Hull, this 334-ton ship (tonnage being an estimate of cargo capacity) sailed from Liverpool in September 1851 under the command of Charles Clinch, who died en route and was replaced by Chief Mate Charles Richard Lygo. Her cargo consisted of quicksilver bottles, shot, whiskey, wine, rope, and various other trade goods.

The British barque *Emily* that picked up passengers in Panama in March 1852 was registered in London and left that city in April 1851 on course for Sydney. She was erroneously reported lost in heavy storms off Madras, India, in June. In Sydney, master J. Harvey loaded her hold with coal and sailed to Panama, where Harvey placed an ad in the Panama newspapers to lure passengers. After abandoning those passengers in San Blas, Harvey sailed south to Acapulco, where he could sell his coal to the steamships that stopped there regularly for fuel and food. This *Emily*, a 1,000-ton ship, was reported in that port on August 15 and September 7. It appears that after selling the cargo, Harvey returned to Sydney for another load. He never sailed to San Francisco.

10. Adam Christopher Thompson, ed., *California and Back . . . An 1850s Adventure: A Memoir by Martin Noble Hine*, 2nd ed. (United States: Adam Christopher Thompson, 2020), 29.

11. Doble, *John Doble's Journal and Letters from the Mines*, 21–22.

12. "Californians in Distress," *The Evening Post*, March 5, 1849, image copy, p. 2 c. 5, Newspapers.com.

13. "Immigrant Frauds - Recklessness of Human Life," *Daily Alta California*, August 11, 1852, image copy, p. 2 c. 1, California Digital Newspaper Collection.

14. "Notes of a Trip of the S. F. B. D. Agricultural Visiting Committee," *Daily Alta California*, August 21, 1860, image copy, p. 1 c. 1, California Digital Newspaper Collection.

15. J. P. Munro-Fraser, *History of Santa Clara County, California* (San Francisco: Alley, Bowen & Co., 1881), 210; Paul W. Gates, *Land and Law in California: Essays on Land Policies* (Ames, Iowa: Iowa State University Press, 1991), 133.

16. Clyde Arbuckle and F. Ralph Rambo, *Santa Clara Co. Ranchos* (San Jose, Calif.: Rosicrucian Press, 1968), 15–17; "Alameda Gardens - Valuable Real Estate for Sale or Lease," *Daily Alta California*, December 16, 1850, image copy, p. 1. c. 1, California Digital Newspaper Collection.

17. Eugene T. Sawyer, *History of Santa Clara County California with Biographical Sketches* (Los Angeles: Historic Record Company, 1922), 136, 880; Leigh H. Irvine, ed., *A History of the New California: Its Resources and People*, vol. 2 (New York and Chicago: The Lewis Publishing Co., 1905), 665.

18. Sawyer, *History of Santa Clara County California with Biographical Sketches*, 365, 880; "Marine Intelligence: Port of San Francisco," *Sacramento Transcript*, September 21, 1850, image copy, p. 2 c. 7, California Digital Newspaper Collection; "Alameda Gardens - Valuable Real Estate for Sale or Lease."

19. *Portrait and Biographical Record of Kalamazoo, Allegan and Van Buren Counties, Michigan.* (Chicago: Chapman Bros., 1892), 802–3.

20. Lowry, "Letter."

21. Kemper, *A Twentieth Century History of Delaware County, Indiana*, 1:113.

22. Delaware County Clerk, "Allen Makepeace v. Samüel Peck et al." (Delaware County, Indiana, Circuit Court, 1852), Circuit Court> Civil> Makepeace, Allen, Plaintiff, Non-payment of debt 21-B, Muncie Public Library-Digital Resource, http://digitalresource.munpl.org.

23. Pierce, "E.D. Pierce Reminiscences," 80–81.

24. Pfouts, *Four Firsts for a Modest Hero: The Autobiography of Paris Swazy Pfouts*, 67–70.

25. Pierce, "E.D. Pierce Reminiscences," 85–86.

26. "Meeting of the Miners at Mariposa - The Flour Monopoly," *Daily Alta California*, December 17, 1852, image copy, p. 1. c. 7, California Digital Newspaper Collection.

CHAPTER 15
1. "Jenkins Letters UI." Abigail Jenkins, January 10, 1853; "Jenkins Letters HL." Henry Jenkins, January 16, 1853; Abigail Jenkins February 6, 1853.
2. "Jenkins Letters UI." Abigail Jenkins, June 11, 1853.
3. "Jenkins Letters HL." Henry Jenkins memo book.

CHAPTER 16
1. The version of the Murrieta tale in this section is largely based on John Boessenecker, *Gold Dust and Gunsmoke: Tales of Gold Rush Outlaws, Gunfighters, Lawmen, and Vigilantes* (New York: Wiley, 1999), 73–99, and a variety of other sources.
2. Liestenfeltz, "Memoir."
3. "Newspaper Items from the Hartford City Telegram, Hartford City, Indiana: A - Z" (Typescript of abstracts, Fort Wayne, Indiana, 1972), Blackford County Historical Society, 5.
4. "Jenkins Letters HL." All quotes from Henry in the remainder of this chapter are from his memo book.

5. Calaveras Visitors Bureau, "Unearthing the Mystery of Henry Angell (Link to 15-Page PDF: Henry Pinkney Angell 1826–1897)"; Judith Marvin, Linda Thorpe, and Alice Olmstead, "Cultural Resources Investigations for the Proposed Gendler-Young Lot Line Adjustment near Mountain Ranch, Calaveras County, California - Draft Report," August 2002, 8, Courtesy of Judith Marvin.

6. *Official Catalogue of the New York Exhibition of the Industry of All Nations* (New York: G. P. Putnam & Co., 1853), Table of Contents.

7. *Official Catalogue of the New York Exhibition of the Industry of All Nations*, 19.

8. Clara Bedford, letter (Springboro, Ohio), to "Dear Aunt" [Abigail (Bedford) Jenkins], May 14, 1865, collection of the author.

CHAPTER 17

1. Delaware County Clerk, "Allen Makepeace v. Lyons and Collins" (Delaware County, Indiana, Circuit Court, 1853), Circuit Court> Civil> Makepeace, Allen, Plaintiff, Non-payment of debt, Muncie Public Library-Digital Resource, http://digitalresource.munpl.org; Delaware County Clerk, "Allen Makepeace v. Elijah Collins" (Delaware County, Indiana, Circuit Court, 1855), Circuit Court> Civil> Makepeace, Allen, Plaintiff, Non-payment of debt 34-K, Muncie Public Library-Digital Resource, http://digitalresource.munpl.org.

2. Delaware County Clerk, "Makepeace v. Jones," 113.

3. Ibid., 157.

4. Ibid., 81–84.

5. Hunt probate case, "Indiana, U.S., Wills and Probate Records, 1798–1999."

6. *Biographical and Historical Record of Jay and Blackford Counties, Indiana*, 210.

7. Delaware County Clerk, "Makepeace v. Jones," 146.

8. *A Portrait and Biographical Record of Delaware and Randolph Counties, Ind.*, 426.

9. Delaware County Clerk, "Makepeace v. Jones," 107–27.

10. Ibid.

CHAPTER 18

1. Leander J. Monks, Logan Esarey, and Ernest Vivian Shockley, *Courts and Lawyers of Indiana*, vol. 2 (Indianapolis: Federal Publishing Co., 1916), 650–51; Haimbaugh, *History of Delaware County, Indiana*, 1:254–55.

2. Delaware County Clerk, "Archibald Parker vs. Allen Makepeace" (Delaware County, Indiana, Circuit Court, 1843), Circuit Court> Civil> Archibald Parker, Plaintiff, Non-payment of debt 120-D, Muncie Public Library-Digital Resource, http://digitalresource.munpl.org.

3. Haimbaugh, *History of Delaware County, Indiana*, 1:255.

4. Ibid., 1:162.

5. Delaware County Clerk, "Makepeace v. Jones." All details in this chapter regarding the court case taken from this case file.

6. Delaware County Clerk, "Makepeace v. Jones," 146.

7. Blackford County Clerk, "Report of Asa Anderson, Administer of the Estate of Humphrey Anderson; October Term," 1854,> Blackford> Complete Record, Vol 1, 1852–1857; Vol 1, 1839–1848; Vol C and 2a, 1853–1876> image 156, Ancestry.com, https://www.ancestry.com/search/collections/9045/.

8. Delaware County Clerk, "Makepeace v. Jones," 40–41.

9. Ibid., 28–30.

10. Liestenfeltz, "Memoir," 22–29.

11. Listenfelt, "Sketch of Susan and Conrad Listenfelt."

12. Personal observation by the author at California Cavern, November 2017.

13. "Wheat in Santa Clara County," *Sacramento Daily Union*, April 24, 1854, image copy, p. 3 c. 1, California Digital Newspaper Collection.

14. "Late Strawberries," *Sacramento Daily Union*, October 9, 1854, image copy, p. 2 c. 5, California Digital Newspaper Collection.

15. "Agriculture," *Sacramento Daily Union*, November 23, 1853, image copy, p. 2 c. 5, California Digital Newspaper Collection.

16. "Abandoned," *Sacramento Daily Union*, November 25, 1854, image copy, p. 2 c. 2, California Digital Newspaper Collection.

17. Jay County Clerk, "William Z. Jenkins to Henry Z. Jenkins, Power of Attorney" (Jay County, Indiana, Deeds, Book I p. 54, April 27, 1854), Jay County Courthouse (Portland, Indiana).

18. Clara Pearl Davis, "Robert Ransom" (Moscow, Idaho, n.d.), collection of the author.

CHAPTER 19

1. James H. Ransom (Portland, Oregon), letter to "Dear Sister Clara" [Clara Ransom Davis], February 10, 1921, collection of the author.

2. Blackford County Clerk, "Robert H. Lanning v. James Ransom" (Blackford County, Indiana, Civil Order Book 1 pp. 278–83, May 1845), Family Search> Civil Order books, 1829–1922> images 278–83, https://www.familysearch.org/search/film/008053272?cat =1457692; Wanda Smith, "To: [Email for Personal Use] Re: John W. Ransom. From: Indiana Grand Lodge Office," May 17, 2022.

3. "Jenkins Letters UI." Ann Ransom, April 17, 1855.

4. "The Crisis Past," *Daily Alta California*, February 23, 1855, image copy, p. 2 c. 1, California Digital Newspaper Collection.

5. Leonard W. Noyes, "Dairy [*sic*] of Leonard Withington Noyes" (diary, n.d.), 85, copied with permission by the Calaveras County Historical Society (San Andreas, CA), Essex Institute Library; Hubert Howe Bancroft, *The Works of Hubert Howe Bancroft Vol. XXIII, History of California, Vol. VI 1848–1850* (San Francisco: The History Company Publishers, 1888), 156.

6. "Continuation of the Annals of San Francisco," *California Historical Society Quarterly* 15, no. 3 (1936): 273.

7. "Remme's Great Ride," *American Heritage* 24, no. 1 (December 1972), https://www.americanheritage.com/remmes-great-ride.

8. Delaware County Clerk, "Daniel Clevenger et al. vs. Allen Makepeace" (Delaware County, Indiana, Circuit Court, 1855), Circuit Court> Civil> Daniel Clevenger et al.,

Plaintiff, Non-payment of debt 72-E, Muncie Public Library-Digital Resource, http://digitalresource.munpl.org.

9. Delaware County Clerk, "Makepeace v. Collins."

10. "Judge Anthony," *Indiana American*, March 2, 1855, image copy, p. 2 c. 2, Newspapers.com.

11. Delaware County Clerk, "Makepeace v. Jones," 63–64.

12. Ibid., 99.

13. Pierce, "E.D. Pierce Reminiscences," 122.

14. "Jenkins Letters UI." Ann Ransom, April 17, 1855.

15. Ibid.

16. Ibid.

17. "Jenkins Letters UI." Henry Jenkins, June 17, 1855.

18. Ibid.

19. Ibid.

20. Henry Jenkins and Abigail G. Jenkins, letter, (Knox Township, Jay County, Ind.) to "My dear son Wm" [William Zane Jenkins], October 19, 1855, collection of the author.

21. Ibid.

22. "Amador County Correspondence. Horrid Murder - Business in Volcano," *Sacramento Daily Union*, July 31, 1855, image copy, p. 3 c. 2, California Digital Newspaper Collection.

23. H. Barlow, "The Rancheria Massacre," *Sacramento Daily Union*, August 11, 1855, image copy, p. 3 c. 1, California Digital Newspaper Collection.

24. Ben Bowen, "Ben Bowen Diary and Notebook 1854–1856" (diary, Amador County, California, n.d.), MSS C-F 192, Bancroft Library (UC-Berkeley), accessed April 16, 2019.

CHAPTER 20

1. Jenkins and Jenkins. October 19, 1855.

2. Jenkins and Jenkins.

3. *Biographical and Historical Record of Jay and Blackford Counties, Indiana*, 397.

4. Blackford County Clerk, "Samuel Jones for the Use of Allen Makepeace vs. William Armstrong No. 16 Complaint on Note" (Blackford County, Indiana, Civil Order Book 2 p. 181, Spring Term 1856), Film #008053272 image 568, Family Search, https://www.familysearch.org/search/film/008053272.

5. Delaware County Clerk, "Makepeace v. Collins."

6. Delaware County Clerk, "John Anderson & Dennis Lowery vs. Fort Wayne & Southern Rail Road Co." (Delaware County, Indiana, Circuit Court, 1855), Circuit Court> Civil> John Anderson, Dennis Lowery, Plaintiffs, Non-payment of debt, Muncie Public Library-Digital Resource, http://digitalresource.munpl.org.

7. Delaware County Clerk, "Makepeace v. Jones." All trial details and quotes in this chapter.

8. "Jenkins Letters UI."

9. James Buchanan, the Democratic candidate, handily won by carrying nineteen states, including California and Indiana. Fremont won eleven states. Former president Fillmore, only Maryland. (He had completed Zachary Taylor's term.)

EPILOGUE

1. "U.S., Federal Census Mortality Schedules, 1850–1885," > 1860> California> Calaveras for John C. Teach image 3, Ancestry, accessed January 23, 2022, https://www.ancestry.com/search/collections/8756/.

2. "Died in the Woods," *San Andreas Independent*, May 26, 1860, United States> California> Calaveras> San Andreas Independent, NewspaperAbstracts.com.

3. "Died," *Oregon Semi-Weekly Sentinel*, January 3, 1863, image copy, p. 3 c. 2, Historical Oregon Newspapers.

4. *Portrait and Biographical Record of Kalamazoo, Allegan and Van Buren Counties, Michigan.*, 802–3; O.W. Rowland, *A History of Van Buren County, Michigan: A Narrative Account of Its Historical Progress, Its People, and Its Principal Interests*, vol. 2 (Chicago and New York: The Lewis Publishing Co., 1912), 904–6.

5. "Jenkins Letters UI." All the following quotes from Ann Ransom, May 18, 1861.

6. Mary Gill, telephone interview by Eilene Lyon [Address for personal use], Durango, Colorado, summary notes, February 2, 2016.

7. "Peter Listenfeltz, 90, Dead," *The Star Press*, February 6, 1922, image copy, p. 3 c. 1, Newspapers.com.

8. Van Cleve, "Van Cleve Journals Index 1856–1880" (Hartford City, Indiana, n.d.), Blackford County Historical Society, accessed April 17, 2017.

9. The author hired Ball State University to conduct a ground-penetrating radar survey around the grave of Mary A. Jones, which revealed the presence of several adjacent graves that may be Benjamin H. Jones, Geneva Jones, and a son who died as an infant. Mary's grave is surrounded by much open space lacking headstones, making these graves likely to be her relatives.

10. A Blackford County historian had a veteran's grave marker installed for E.D. Pierce in the 1970s, but he did not know the precise location of the grave. He also confused him with a Blackford County attorney who had a similar name.

11. "Another Pioneer Gone: Death of Allen Makepeace," *The Democratic Standard*, July 13, 1871, Anderson Public Library; "Obituary," *The Democratic Standard* [Quoting the *Eaton Rapids* (Michigan) *Journal*], July 27, 1871, image copy, p. 1 c. 5, Anderson Public Library.

12. *A Biographical History of Eminent and Self-Made Men of the State of Indiana: With Many Portrait-Illustrations on Steel, Engraved Expressly for This Work* (Cincinnati, Ohio: Western Biographical Publishing Co., 1880), 9–19.

13. *Biographical and Historical Record of Jay and Blackford Counties, Indiana*, 397.

14. Ralph Burcham Jr., "Elias Davidson Pierce, Discoverer of Gold in Idaho: A Biographical Study" (Master's thesis, Moscow, Idaho, University of Idaho, 1950), 79, University of Idaho.

15. Henry Zane Jenkins, letter (Camden, Indiana) to "Well Emma" [Emma (Jenkins) Ransom], February 22, 1881, collection of the author.

16. Henry Zane Jenkins, letter (Camden, Indiana) to "My Dear Daughter" [Emma (Jenkins) Ransom], March 6, 1882, collection of the author.

17. "Death of Henry Z. Jenkins, Oldest Odd Fellow in Indiana," [Unattributed, undated clipping from the Collection of Mary Gill (Florence, Oregon)], n.d.

BIBLIOGRAPHY

NEWSPAPERS
Alta California (San Francisco)
Anti-Slavery Bugle (Lisbon, Ohio)
Calaveras Chronicle (Mokelumne Hill, California)
Cincinnati Enquirer (Ohio)
Crawfordsville Review (Indiana)
Crescent (New Orleans, Louisiana)
Democratic Standard (Anderson, Indiana)
Evansville Journal (Indiana)
Evening Post (New York)
Indiana American (Brookville)
Indiana Herald (Huntington)
Indiana State Sentinel (Indianapolis)
Kentucky Gazette (Louisville)
Los Angeles Star (California)
New-York Daily Times
Oregon Sentinel (Jacksonville)
Owyhee Avalanche (Idaho)
Panama Star (Panama)
Picayune (New Orleans, Louisiana)
Richmond Palladium (Indiana)
Sacrament Transcript (California)
Sacramento Union (California)
San Andreas Independent (California)
Star Press (Muncie, Indiana)
State Sentinel (Indianapolis)
United States Gazette (Philadelphia, Pennsylvania)

MANUSCRIPTS/UNPUBLISHED MATERIAL
Alberts, Phil D. "A History of Mountain Ranch El Dorado." 1967. Calaveras County
    Historical Society.

Bedford, Clara. Letter (Springboro, Ohio) to "Dear Aunt" [Abigail (Bedford) Jenkins], May 14, 1865. Collection of the author.

Blackford County Clerk. Deed books, Probate books, and Civil Order books. Hartford City, Indiana. (Also available on Ancestry.com and FamilySearch.org.)

Bowen, Ben. "Ben Bowen Diary and Notebook 1854–1856." Diary. Amador County, California, n.d. MSS C-F 192. Bancroft Library (UC-Berkeley). Accessed April 16, 2019.

Burcham, Ralph Jr. "Elias Davidson Pierce, Discoverer of Gold in Idaho: A Biographical Study." Master's thesis, University of Idaho, 1950. University of Idaho.

"Consular Dispatch from R.P. Letcher, US Minister to Mexico, to US Consul William Forbes of Tepic, Nayarit, Mexico." July 17, 1852. MF 0550.41 Mexico City, MX Consular Dispatches Vol. 10. Arizona Historical Society Library & Archives (Tempe and Tucson).

"Coonjine in Manhattan." 1939. Library of Congress, Manuscript Division, WPA Federal Writers' Project Collection. https://www.loc.gov/resource/wpalh0.07070413/.

"Cornelius James Brosnan Papers, 1917–1950: Jenkins Letters 1851–1863." n.d. Special Collections MG-18. University of Idaho. Accessed January 23, 2022. ("Jenkins Letters UI")

"Cornelius James Brosnan Papers, 1917–1950: Pierce, Elias Davidson." n.d. Special Collections MG018, folder 5384. University of Idaho.

"David T. Gillis Diary, 1852–1854." Gillis Family Papers, 1809–1888 mss100 (transcription by Eilene Lyon). Holt-Atherton Special Collections—University of the Pacific (Stockton, California). Accessed November 15, 2017. https://scholarlycommons.pacific.edu/grcc/40/.

Davis, Clara Pearl. "Robert Ransom." Moscow, Idaho, n.d. Collection of the author.

Davis, Stephen Chapin. *California Gold Rush Merchant; the Journal of Stephen Chapin David.* Edited by Benjamin B. Richards. San Marino, California: Huntington Library Publications, 1956. https://www.loc.gov/item/56012476/.

Delaware County Clerk. http://digitalresource.munpl.org.

Frease, Celia Pumpelly Ricker. "Celia P. Ricker's Journal, Begun December 4th 1851 at Cincinnati, and Ended March 16th 1852 at New Orleans." Cincinnati, Ohio, n.d. PDF scan excerpt of pages 9–53. Cincinnati Historical Society, Cincinnati Museum Center.

Gill, Mary. Telephone interview by Eilene Lyon [Address for personal use], Durango, Colorado. Summary notes, February 2, 2016.

Griest, William. "History of Balbec and Vicinity." 1923. Indiana Historical Society.

"Henry Zane Jenkins Correspondence 1851–1853." San Marino, California, n.d. MssHM 16791–16808. Huntington Library. ("Jenkins Letters HL")

Jay County Clerk. Deed books, Mortgage books, and Court Order books. Portland, Indiana. (Also available on Ancestry.com and FamilySearch.org.)

Jenkins, Henry, and Abigail G. Jenkins. Letter (Knox Township, Jay County, Ind.) to "My dear son Wm" [William Zane Jenkins], October 19, 1855. Collection of the author.

Jenkins, Henry Zane. Letter (Camden, Indiana) to "Well Emma" [Emma (Jenkins) Ransom], February 22, 1881. Collection of the author.

———. Letter (Camden, Indiana) to "My Dear Daughter" [Emma (Jenkins) Ransom], March 6, 1882. Collection of the author.

"Letter to His Parents by George B. Blanchard." San Francisco, September 14, 1852. WA MSS S-676 B592. Yale Beinecke Library (New Haven, Connecticut).

Liestenfeltz, Peter N. "Memoir." Blackford County, Indiana, n.d. Personal collection of Tanya Waters, Indiana.

Lowry, Dennis. Letter (Blackford County, Indiana) to "Dear brother & sister" [Rev. Arthur and Nancy (Houser) Badley], February 6, 1854. Private collection of James W. Baker [address for private use] Salt Lake City, Utah, 1984.

Marvin, Judith, Linda Thorpe, and Alice Olmstead. "Cultural Resources Investigations for the Proposed Gendler-Young Lot Line Adjustment near Mountain Ranch, Calaveras County, California - Draft Report." August 2002. Courtesy of Judith Marvin.

"Newspaper Items from the Hartford City Telegram, Hartford City, Indiana: A—Z." Typescript of abstracts. Fort Wayne, Ind., 1972. Blackford County Historical Society.

Nixon, A. W. [sic; O. W.]. Letter transcript (location of original unknown), (Sacramento City) to "My Dear Father" [Samuel Nixon], October 29, 1850. Manuscript Collection (gift of Bernhard Knollenberg, 1946), SC 2100. Indiana Historical Society Library.

Noyes, Leonard W. "Dairy [sic] of Leonard Withington Noyes." Diary, n.d. Copied with permission by the Calaveras County Historical Society (San Andreas, CA). Essex Institute Library.

Pierce, Elias D. "E.D. Pierce Reminiscences." n.d. Special Collections MG 5384. University of Idaho.

Ransom, James H. (Portland, Oregon) letter to "Dear Sister Clara" [Clara Ransom Davis], February 10, 1921. Collection of the author.

Smith, Wanda. "To: [Email for personal use] Re: John W. Ransom. From: Indiana Grand Lodge Office." May 17, 2022.

Stratton, Timothy. "Timothy Stratton Letter." 1852. Rare Books and Manuscripts, S1263, transcribed material in finding aid. Indiana State Library.

"The Makepeace Family." Computer-generated report, no author, n.d. Madison County Genealogical Society. Accessed April 21, 2017.

Thompson, Mrs. W. L. (Effie L. Anderson). Letter (Topeka, Kansas) to a cousin, Dorothy, 1932. Posted by corcoran32 on January 14,2013. Ancestry.com.

Van Cleve. "Van Cleve Journals Index 1856–1880." Hartford City, Indiana, n.d. Blackford County Historical Society. Accessed April 17, 2017.

PUBLISHED WORKS

A Biographical History of Eminent and Self-Made Men of the State of Indiana: With Many Portrait-Illustrations on Steel, Engraved Expressly for This Work. Cincinnati, Ohio: Western Biographical Publishing Co., 1880.

A Memorial and Biographical History of the Counties of Merced, Stanislaus, Calaveras, Tuolumne and Mariposa, California . . . Chicago: The Lewis Publishing Company, 1892.

A Portrait and Biographical Record of Delaware and Randolph Counties, Ind.: Containing Biographical Sketches of Many Prominent and Representative Citizens . . . Chicago: A.W. Bowen & Co., 1894.

American Life in the 1840s. Carle Bode, editor. New York: New York University Press, 1967.

Arbuckle, Clyde, and F. Ralph Rambo. *Santa Clara Co. Ranchos.* San Jose, California: Rosicrucian Press, 1968.

Arky, Louis H. "The Mechanics' Union of Trade Associations and the Formation of the Philadelphia Workingmen's Movement." *The Pennsylvania Magazine of History and Biography* 76, no. 2 (1952): 142–76. www.jstor.org/stable/20088351.

Aspinwall, Jane L. *Golden Prospects: Daguerreotypes of the California Gold Rush.* New Haven, Connecticut and London: Hall Family Foundation in association with The Nelson-Atkins Museum of Art, distributed by Yale University Press, 2019.

Bancroft, Hubert Howe. *California Pioneer Register and Index 1542–1848: Including California, 1769–1800 and List of Pioneers.* Extracted from Bancroft, Hubert Howe, History of California, p. 258. Baltimore: Regional Publishing Co., 1964.

———. *The Works of Hubert Howe Bancroft: California Inter Pocula.* San Francisco: History Co., 1888.

———. *The Works of Hubert Howe Bancroft Vol. XXIII, History of California, Vol. VI 1848–1850.* San Francisco: The History Company Publishers, 1888.

Beeson, Cecil, ed. *Miscellaneous Records of Blackford Co., Indiana: Plus Index.* Fort Wayne, Indiana: Fort Wayne Public Library, 1978.

Bernstein, Leonard. "The Working People of Philadelphia from Colonial Times to the General Strike of 1835." *The Pennsylvania Magazine of History and Biography* 74, no. 3 (1950): 322–39. http://www.jstor.org/stable/20088146.

Biographical and Historical Record of Jay and Blackford Counties, Indiana: Containing . . . Portraits and Biographies of Some of the Prominent Men of the State: Engravings of Prominent Citizens in Jay and Blackford Counties, with Personal Histories of Many of the Leading Families and a Concise History of Jay and Blackford Counties and Their Cities and Villages. Chicago: Lewis Publishing Company, 1887.

Blake, Anson S., and Charles T. Blake. "Working for Wells Fargo-1860–1863: Letters of Charles T. Blake." *California Historical Society Quarterly* 16, no. 1 (1937): 30–42.

Boessenecker, John. *Gold Dust and Gunsmoke: Tales of Gold Rush Outlaws, Gunfighters, Lawmen, and Vigilantes.* New York: Wiley, 1999.

Borthwick, J.D. *3 Years in California, with eight illustrations by the author.* Index and Foreword by Joseph A. Sullivan. Oakland, California: Oakland Biobooks, 1948.

Brands, H. W. *The Age of Gold: The California Gold Rush and the New American Dream.* New York: Doubleday, 2002.

Brereton, Roslyn. "Mining Techniques in the California Gold Field During the 1850's [*sic*]." *The Pacific Historian* 20 no. 3 (1986): 286–302.

Bruff, J. Goldsborough. *Gold Rush: The Journals, Drawings, and other Papers of J. Goldsborough Bruff; Captain, Washington City and California Mining Association. April 2, 1849–July 20, 1851*. Edited by Georgia Willis Read and Ruth Gaines. New York: Columbia University Press, 1949.

Burrell, O.K. *Gold in the Woodpile: An Informal History of Banking in Oregon*. Eugene, Oregon: University of Oregon Books, 1967.

Calaveras County Illustrated and Described. Oakland, California: W.W. Elliott, 1885.

Calaveras Visitors Bureau. "Unearthing the Mystery of Henry Angell (Link to 15-Page PDF: Henry Pinkney Angell 1826–1897)." GoCalaveras.com, January 29, 2016. https://www.gocalaveras.com/unearthing-the-mystery-of-henry-angell/.

Carr, Peter E. *San Francisco Passenger Departure Lists 15 January to 16 June 1852*. Vol. IV. San Luis Obispo, California: TCI Genealogical Resources, 1995.

Chandlee, Edward E. *Six Quaker Clockmakers*. Philadelphia: The Historical Society of Pennsylvania, 1943.

Charity Hospital Report 1852: Report of the Board of Administrators of the Charity Hospital. New Orleans, Louisiana: Charity Hospital of New Orleans, 1853.

Cist, Charles. *Sketches and Statistics of Cincinnati in 1851*. Cincinnati, Ohio: Wm. H. Moore & Co., 1851.

Clappe, Louise Amelia, and Thomas C. Russell. *The Shirley Letters from California Mines in 1851–52: Being a Series of Twenty-Three Letters from Dame Shirley (Mrs. Louise Amelia Knapp Smith Clappe) to Her Sister in Massachusetts, and Now Reprinted from the Pioneer Magazine of 1854–55 . . .*, 1922.

Collections of the Genealogical Society of Pennsylvania; Notices of Marriages & Deaths in Poulson's American Daily Advertiser, 1791–1839; 1826–1830. Vol. 79. Philadelphia: Genealogical Society of Pennsylvania, 1903.

"Continuation of the Annals of San Francisco." *California Historical Society Quarterly* 15, no. 3 (1936): 266–82.

Cornford, Daniel. "We All Live More Like Brutes Than Humans: Labor and Capital in the Gold Rush." *California History* 77 no. 4 (1998/9): 78–104.

Daly, Walter J. "The 'Slows': The Torment of Milk Sickness on the Midwest Frontier." *Indiana Magazine of History* 102, no. 1 (2006): 29–40. http://www.jstor.org/stable/27792690.

Damrosch, Leo. *Tocqueville's Discovery of America*. New York: Farrar, Straus and Giroux, 2010.

Doble, John. *John Doble's Journal and Letters from the Mines: Volcano, Mokelumne Hill, Jackson, and San Francisco, 1851–1865*. Edited by Charles Lewis Camp. Volcano, California: Volcano Press, 1999.

Ely, Edward. *The Wanderings of Edward Ely, a Mid-19th Century Seafarer's Diary*. Edited by Anthony Sirna and Allison Sirna. New York: Hastings House, 1954.

Faragher, John Mack. *Sugar Creek: Life on the Illinois Prairie*. New Haven, Connecticut; London: Yale University Press, 1986.

Ferguson, Charles D. *California Gold Fields*. California Centennial. Oakland, California: Biobooks, 1948.

Findley, A. G. "Oceanic Currents and Their Connection with the Proposed Central-America Canals." Edited by Norton Shaw. *The Journal of the Royal Geographic Society* 23 (1853): 217–41.

Forkner, John L., and Byron H. Dyson. *Historical Sketches and Reminiscences of Madison County.* Anderson, Indiana, 1897.

Fossier, A. E. *The Charity Hospital in Louisiana.* Reprinted from the New Orleans Medical and Surgical Journal for May to October 1923. New Orleans, Louisiana: The American Printing Company, Ltd., 1923.

Gates, Paul W. *Land and Law in California: Essays on Land Policies.* Ames, Iowa: Iowa State University Press, 1991.

Groh, George W. *Gold Fever: Being a True Account, Both Horrifying and Hilarious, of the Art of Healing (so-called) During the California Gold Rush.* New York: William Morrow & Company, Inc., 1966.

Haimbaugh, Frank D. *History of Delaware County, Indiana.* Vol. 1. Indianapolis, Indiana: Historical Publishing Co., 1924.

Hammond, Bray. *Banks and Politics in America: From the Revolution to the Civil War.* Princeton, New Jersey: Princeton University Press, 1991.

Harden, Samuel. *History of Madison County, Indiana, from 1820 to 1874: Giving a General Review of Principal Events, Statistical and Historical Items, Derived from Official Sources.* Markleville, Indiana: S. Harden, 1874.

History of Amador County, California with Illustrations and Biographical Sketches of its Prominent Men and Pioneers. Oakland, California: Thompson & West, 1881.

History of Madison County Indiana, with Illustrations and Biographical Sketches. Chicago: Kingman Brothers, 1880.

Holliday, J.S. *The World Rushed In: The California Gold Rush Experience.* New York: Simon and Schuster, 1981.

———. "Reverberations of the California Gold Rush." *California History* 77 no. 1 (1998): 4–15.

———. *Rush for Riches: Gold Fever and the Making of California.* Berkeley and Los Angeles: University of California Press, 1999.

Hunter, Louis C., and Beatrice Jones Hunter. *Steamboats on the Western Rivers. An Economic and Technological History.* New York: Octagon Books, 1969.

Irvine, Leigh H., ed. *A History of the New California: Its Resources and People.* Vol. 2. New York and Chicago: The Lewis Publishing Co., 1905.

Isbell, F. A. *Mining and Hunting in the Far West, 1852–1870.* Stevenson, Connecticut: F.A. Isbell, 1871.

Jay County, Ind. Board of Commissioners and Indiana Historical Records Survey. *Commissioners' Record: Jay County Indiana.* Vol. a 1836–1850. Indianapolis, Indiana: Indiana Historical Records Survey, 1941.

Johnson, Susan Lee. *Roaring Camp: The Social World of the California Gold Rush.* New York: W.W. Norton & Co., 2000.

"Journal of the Senate of the United States of America, Second Session of the Thirtieth Congress." February 19, 1849. ProQuest.

Kemble, John Haskell. *The Panama Route, 1848–1869*. Berkley and Los Angeles: University of California Press, 1943.

Kennedy, Martha. "The California Historical Society's Collection of Daguerreotypes." *California History* 60 no. 4 (1981): 370–75.

Kemper, G. W. H. *A Twentieth Century History of Delaware County, Indiana*. Vol. 1. 2 vols. Chicago: Lewis Publishing Co., 1908.

Ketchum, Liza. *The Gold Rush*. Boston: Little, Brown & Co., 1996.

Kotar, S. L., and J. E. Gessler. *The Steamboat Era: A History of Fulton's Folly on American Rivers, 1807–1860*. Jefferson, North Carolina, and London: McFarland & Co., Inc., 2009.

Lacour-Gayet, Robert. *Everyday Life in the United States Before the Civil War 1830–1860*. Translated by Mary Ilford. New York: Frederick Ungar Publishing Co., 1969.

Levy, JoAnn. "Crossing the 40-Mile Desert." *The Californians* V, no. 5 (October 1987): 16–31.

Lewis, Oscar. *Sea Routes to the Gold Fields: The Migration to California by Water in 1849–1852*. New York: Alfred A. Knopf, 1949.

Limbaugh, Ronald H., and Willard P. Fuller, Jr. *Calaveras Gold: The Impact of Mining on a Mother Lode County*. Reno and Las Vegas, Nevada: University of Nevada Press, 2003.

Lippincott, Horace Mather. *Early Philadelphia: Its People, Life and Progress*. Philadelphia and London: J.B. Lippincott Co., 1917.

Listenfelt, Hattie. "Sketch of Susan and Conrad Listenfelt." Updated April 17, 2001. Listenfelt Family Reunion. Accessed November 14, 2021. https://web.archive.org/web/20200812002808/http://patrushka.tripod.com/.

Lynch, Martha C. M. *Reminiscences of Adams, Jay and Randolph Counties*. Fort Wayne, Indiana, 1897.

Lyon, Eilene. "A Slow Death." *Myricopia* (blog), March 24, 2019. https://myricopia.com/2019/03/24/a-slow-death/.

Marryat, Frank. *Mountains and Molehills, or, Recollections of a Burnt Journal: The 1855 Edition, Unabridged and with an Introduction by Robin W. Winks*. Philadelphia: Lippincott, 1962.

Mayo, John. *Commerce and Contraband on Mexico's West Coast in the Era of Barron, Forbes & Co., 1821–1859*. New York: Peter Lang, 2006.

———. "English Commercial Houses on Mexico's West Coast, 1821–1867." *Ibero-Amerikanisches Archiv* 22, no. 1/2 (1996): 173–90. http://www.jstor.org/stable/43393097.

McCulloch, Hugh. *Early Banking in Indiana*. Fort Wayne, Indiana: Public Library of Fort Wayne and Allen Co., 1954.

Megquier, Mary Jane. *Apron Full of Gold: The Letters of Mary Jane Megquier from San Francisco, 1849–1856*. San Marino, California: Huntington Library, 1949.

Monks, Leander J., Logan Esarey, and Ernest Vivian Shockley. *Courts and Lawyers of Indiana*. Vol. 2. Indianapolis, Indiana: Federal Publishing Co., 1916.

Montgomery, M. W. *History of Jay County, Indiana*. Chicago: Printed for the author by Church, Goodman & Cushing, 1864.

Munro-Fraser, J. P. *History of Santa Clara County, California.* San Francisco: Alley, Bowen & Co., 1881.

Official Catalogue of the New York Exhibition of the Industry of All Nations. New York: G. P. Putnam & Co., 1853.

Paul, Rodman. *California Gold: The Beginning of Mining in the Far West.* Lincoln, Nebraska: University of Nebraska Press, 1947.

Peavy, Linda, and Ursula Smith. *The Gold Rush Widows of Little Falls: A Story Drawn From the Letters of Pamelia and James Fergus.* St. Paul, Minnesota: Minnesota Historical Society Press, 1990.

———. *Women In Waiting in the Westward Movement: Life on the Home Frontier.* Norman, Oklahoma, and London: University of Oklahoma Press, 1994.

———. *Pioneer Women: The Lives of Women on the Frontier.* Norman, Oklahoma: University of Oklahoma Press, 1996.

Pfouts, Paris S. *Four Firsts for a Modest Hero: The Autobiography of Paris Swazy Pfouts.* Edited by Harold Axford. Portland, Oregon: The Grand Lodge, Ancient Free and Accepted Masons, of Montana, 1968.

Portrait and Biographical Record of Kalamazoo, Allegan and Van Buren Counties, Michigan. Chicago: Chapman Bros., 1892.

Pyeatt, Ralph. "The Story of Murphys." *The Pacific Historian* 19, no. 3 (Fall 1975): 230–40.

Rasmussen, Louis J. *San Francisco Ship Passenger Lists Vol. 1.* Digital images. Baltimore, Maryland: Genealogical Publishing Co., 1978. https://www.ancestry.com/search/collections/49329/.

"Remme's Great Ride." *American Heritage* 24, no. 1 (December 1972). https://www.americanheritage.com/remmes-great-ride.

Rohrbough, Malcolm J. *Days of Gold: The California Gold Rush and the American Nation.* Berkeley, California: University of California Press, 1998.

Rowland, O.W. *A History of Van Buren County, Michigan: A Narrative Account of Its Historical Progress, Its People, and Its Principal Interests.* Vol. 2. Chicago and New York: The Lewis Publishing Co., 1912.

Royce, Sarah. *A Frontier Lady: Recollections of the Gold Rush and Early California.* Ralph Henry Gabriel, editor. Lincoln, Nebraska, and London: University of Nebraska Press, 1977.

Sawyer, Eugene T. *History of Santa Clara County California with Biographical Sketches.* Los Angeles: Historic Record Company, 1922.

Schweikart, Larry, and Lynne Pierson Doti. "From Hard Money to Branch Banking: California Banking in the Gold-Rush Economy." *California History* 77, no. 4 (1998): 209–32.

Shinn, Benjamin G. *Biographical Memoirs of Blackford County, Ind.* Chicago: The Bowen Publishing Company, 1900.

Smith, J. C. *Reminiscences of Early Methodism in Indiana. Including Sketches of Various Prominent Ministers, Together with Narratives of Women Eminent for Piety, Poetry and Song . . .* Indianapolis, Indiana: J.M. Olcott, 1879.

Snow, Horace. *"Dear Charlie" Letters: Recording the Everyday Life of a Young 1854 Gold Miner . . . As Set Forth by Your Friend, Horace Snow.* 3rd ed. Fresno, California: Pioneer Publishing Company, 1986.

Spencer, Jane Ann. *When Grandpa Farmed: A History of Agriculture in Jay County.* Vol. 1. Portland, Indiana: Jay County Historical Society, Inc., 2010.

Starr, Kevin. "The Gold Rush and the California Dream." *California History* 77 no. 1 (1998): 56–67.

———. *California: A History.* New York: The Modern Library, 2005.

Thayer, William M. *The Price of Gold: A Sermon Occasioned by the Death of Henry Martyn Allard Who Died at the Gold Mines of California July 10, 1852, Aged Nineteen Years.* Boston: "Published by the friends" Press of J. B. Chisholm, 1852.

Thompson, Adam Christopher, ed. *California and Back . . . An 1850s Adventure: A Memoir by Martin Noble Hine.* 2nd ed. United States: Adam Christopher Thompson, 2020.

The Letter of a Young Miner: Covering the Adventures of Jasper S. Hill During the California Goldrush 1849–1852. Edited by Doyce B. Nunis. San Francisco: John Howell—Books, 1964.

Tinkham, George Henry. *A History of Stockton from Its Organization up to the Present Time, Including a Sketch of San Joaquin County; Comprising a History of the Government, Politics, State of Society, Religion, Fire Department, Commerce, Secret Societies, Art, Science, Manufactures, Agriculture . . . within the Past Thirty Years . . .* San Francisco: W.M. Hinton & Co. printers, 1880.

Trollope, Frances Milton. *Domestic Manners of the Americans.* Paris: Baudry's Foreign Library, 1832.

Twain, Mark. *Life on the Mississippi.* New York and London: Harper and Brothers, 1917.

———. *Mark Twain: The Innocents Abroad, Roughing It.* New York: Viking Press, 1984.

United States. Congress. "The Congressional Globe." Washington: Blair & Rives, 18341873, February 24, 1863.

Watkins, T.H. *Gold and Silver in the West: The Illustrated History of an American Dream.* Palo Alto, California: American West Publishing Co., 1971.

Way, Frederick, Jr. *Way's Packet Directory 1848–1994. Passenger Steamboats of the Mississippi River System Since the Advent of Photography in Mid-Continent America.* Athens, Ohio: Ohio University Press, 1983.

White, Richard. "The Gold Rush: Consequences and Contingencies." *California History* 77 no. 1 (1998): 42–55.

Wright, Florence Bedford. "A Station on the Underground Railroad." *Ohio History*, Ohio Archaeological and Historical Publications, 14 (1905): 164–69.

ABOUT THE AUTHOR

Eilene Lyon immersed herself in American history from an early age, when her parents took her to iconic sites such as Williamsburg, Philadelphia, and Gettysburg. She has been putting history into context through studying the lives of her ancestors for over twenty years. Her work has appeared in various history journals and can be found on her blog at Myricopia.com. She speaks on genealogy and family history writing at regional and national conferences. Eilene lives in Durango, Colorado, with her husband and husky-lab Sterling (named for a great-grandfather, naturally).